This is not just another book. This is a manual that will help you navigate one of the most difficult realities you will ever face in life. I have felt the pain and loneliness of living out the principles contained in this book. Dr. Malachi has written a masterpiece on one of the most overlooked yet destructive problems in the body of Christ. Once you pick this book up, you will not want to put it down.

—Greg Locke
Pastor, Global Vision Bible Church

Bold faith demands words and action. Today it confronts a rising tide of deconstructing activism that seeks to erode biblical truth, attacking the church from within and without. This hostility targets families, local ministries, prominent leaders, and entire evangelical movements, often aiming to weaken the gospel's power.

Dr. Malachi O'Brien's book stands as a powerful defense, championing preservation and restoration over deconstruction and demolition. In an era where some revel in tearing down the church, this work boldly upholds the believer, the family, and the body of Christ against a spirit of accusation. Get Dr. Malachi O'Brien's book for your friends—it's a vital call to stand firm and rebuild with unwavering faith.

—Travis Johnson
Lead Pastor, Pathway Church
Member, National Faith Advisory Board

I have met very few people like Malachi O'Brien. It seems from the first time we met that God was entwining our stories together to be brothers in the spiritual battle. Malachi is one of the most passionate Christians I have ever met, and he reminds me of a modern-day Ravenhill or Tozer. For years I have been urging him to write a book and especially on the topics of praying, fasting and revival. He is hungry for God like few I know. He is simply a humble and resilient pastor who is more concerned about the prayer room and actually walking with the Lord than anything else. It is from this burning heart that comes this message for the church. A prophetic call to be careful to not get pulled into the cultural confusion of accusation even while we ask God to purify His church.

—Matt Brown
Evangelist; Founder, Think Eternity
Author, *Truth Plus Love*

You will be shocked, convicted, and inspired to shed the schemes of the enemy and move on toward your eternal purpose after reading my friend Dr. Malachi O'Brien's book, *Time to Rise*.

Not only is this book masterfully written cry to our generation. Quite frankly, I'm ta book had on me. Every page is a powerful tur

Dr. O'Brien articulately confronts one of the devil's most destructive schemes against the body of Christ today. Written to those who are accused, victims, the attackers themselves, onlookers, and anyone who carries the label "Christian," this hard-hitting read doesn't simply rebuke or point out all the wrongs; it goes well beyond that, showing the reader there is a door to liberty and a life-giving way to your God-given destiny.

Bravo, Dr. Malachi O'Brien, for writing this letter to the church. May we all discover it is time to rise!

—JOSEPH Z
AUTHOR, BROADCASTER, PROPHETIC VOICE

When I first met Dr. Malachi O'Brien, it was more than just a meeting—it was a divine connection. We quickly found ourselves talking about the accuser of the brethren, and I was stunned to discover that the Lord had been speaking the same message to him as He had to me: that the body of Christ is entering a season of the accuser of the brethren.

Dr. O'Brien brings incredible spiritual insight into these demonic strategies. The way he boldly confronts the accuser spirit reminds me of how Elijah confronted the Jezebel spirit.

I've personally learned so much from him. His revelation, humility, and love for the church have impacted me deeply, and I know every reader will experience the same.

When I say this book is going to be a divine encounter for you, I mean it. Just as the sons of Issachar understood the times, I believe you'll find God's heart and clarity in these pages for the season we're in.

—LANDON SCHOTT
SENIOR LEAD PASTOR, MERCY CULTURE CHURCH

TIME TO RISE

Malachi O'Brien, DMin

Time to Rise by Malachi O'Brien
Published by Charisma House, an imprint of Charisma Media
1150 Greenwood Blvd., Lake Mary, Florida 32746

Copyright © 2025 by Malachi O'Brien. All rights reserved.

Unless otherwise noted, all Scripture quotations are taken from the New International Version®, NIV®. Copyright © 1973, 1978, 1984, 2011 by Biblica, Inc.® Used by permission of Zondervan. All rights reserved worldwide. www.zondervan.com. The "NIV" and "New International Version" are trademarks registered in the United States Patent and Trademark Office by Biblica, Inc.®

Scripture quotations marked ESV are from The ESV® Bible (The Holy Bible, English Standard Version®), copyright © 2001 by Crossway, a publishing ministry of Good News Publishers. Used by permission. All rights reserved.

Scripture quotations marked MEV are from the Modern English Version. Copyright © 2014 by Military Bible Association. Used by permission. All rights reserved.

Scripture quotations marked NKJV are taken from the New King James Version®. Copyright © 1982 by Thomas Nelson. Used by permission. All rights reserved.

Scripture quotations marked NLT are taken from the Holy Bible, New Living Translation, copyright ©1996, 2004, 2015 by Tyndale House Foundation. Used by permission of Tyndale House Publishers, Carol Stream, Illinois 60188. All rights reserved.

While the author has made every effort to provide accurate, up-to-date source information at the time of publication, statistics and other data are constantly updated. Neither the publisher nor the author assumes any responsibility for errors or for changes that occur after publication. Further, the publisher and author do not have any control over and do not assume any responsibility for third-party websites or their content.

For more resources like this, visit MyCharismaShop.com and the author's website at DrMalachi.org.

Cataloging-in-Publication Data is on file with the Library of Congress.
International Standard Book Number: 978-1-63641-530-7
E-book ISBN: 978-1-63641-531-4

1 2025
Printed in the United States of America

Most Charisma Media products are available at special quantity discounts for bulk purchase for sales promotions, premiums, fund-raising, and educational needs. For details, call us at (407) 333-0600 or visit our website at charismamedia.com.

To my wife, Rachel

Rachel—
Your love and support have been the fuel behind every step of this journey—not just this journey but life and ministry. You have believed when others doubted, have sacrificed when no one saw, and have stood by my side every step of the way.

This book is the product not only of my calling but also of your unwavering strength, your prayers, and your relentless support.

You are my greatest encourager and my fiercest ally. Your passionate love for Jesus and His presence provokes me.

This book is for you, and this book is for our entire family.

TABLE OF CONTENTS

Foreword by: Eric Metaxas ix

Author's Note xi

Preface: Time to Rise xiii

Introduction: One Thing Is Needed xvii

Part I: The Power of Words—Shaping Our Reality

Chapter 1 Prophecy or Poison? 3

Chapter 2 The Power of Perspective 9

Chapter 3 The Industry of Shame 12

Chapter 4 Whispers of the Enemy: How Accusation Fuels Doubt 16

Chapter 5 Slandered and Silenced 19

Chapter 6 The Hidden Agenda Behind Accusation 22

Chapter 7 The Enemy of God's Work 26

Chapter 8 Jesus and the Spirit of Accusation 30

Chapter 9 The Cheap Seats Belong to the Critics 33

Chapter 10 The Power of Words: Principles for Life and Victory 36

Part II: The Gift of Perception—Navigating Truth and Deception

Chapter 11 Life Is Not What Happens to Us 43

Chapter 12 Why People Do What They Do 47

Chapter 13 The Six Human Needs and the Power of Accusation 51

Chapter 14 The Ministry of Exposure: A Demonic Counterfeit 56

Chapter 15 Weapons of Mass Emotion 59

Chapter 16 No Problem Is Permanent 63

Chapter 17 Understanding the Patterns of Accusation 67

Chapter 18 Not Everything That Glitters Is God 70

Chapter 19 The Power of Personality 74

Chapter 20 Monks and Mystics 79

Part III: Identity and Authority—Knowing Who We Are

Chapter 21 You Are Not Your Past: You Are Who God Says You Are 87

Chapter 22 The Hero's Journey: Your Path to Transformation 90

Chapter 23 Knowing Who You Are in a World of Opinions 94

Chapter 24 Attacked at the Core: Why Identity Is Satan's Primary Target 97

Chapter 25 The Spirit of Comparison 100

viii | TIME TO RISE

Chapter 26 Fight, Fight, Fight: The Spirit of Resilience......................103

Chapter 27 From Orphan to Heir: Walking in Your True Identity..........106

Chapter 28 The Roar of the Redeemed 110

Chapter 29 The Silent Killers: Sarcasm, Cynicism, and a Critical Spirit......112

Chapter 30 Ten Principles for Identity and Authority 116

Part IV: The Weight of Choices—Walking in Power

Chapter 31 Living Without Offense.....................................121

Chapter 32 Limiting Beliefs and the Limitless Life 125

Chapter 33 Committed to a Local Church 129

Chapter 34 How to Pursue Unity and Not Destroy Relationships 133

Chapter 35 The Domino Effect: How One Choice Changes Everything......136

Chapter 36 When the Wrong Social Media Post Feels Right................139

Chapter 37 You Are Not a Victim......................................142

Chapter 38 Revival Starts with One Decision—Yours 145

Chapter 39 Internal Identity and the Power of Choice 148

Chapter 40 Ten Principles for Walking in Power 152

Part V: The Right Questions—Unlocking Wisdom and Purpose

Chapter 41 Who Am I Becoming? Asking the Right Questions 157

Chapter 42 Toward Values: The Path to a Life of Passion and Purpose.......161

Chapter 43 Away Values: What You Must Leave to Step into God's Best.....166

Chapter 44 The Question That Controls Your Life 170

Chapter 45 What Is Real Forgiveness?..................................174

Chapter 46 Who Would Jesus Love? 179

Chapter 47 Are You Going to Rise or Keep Making Excuses? 181

Chapter 48 Will I Stop Revival? 184

Chapter 49 Order of the Flame: A Call to Burn..........................186

Chapter 50 Legacy in the Fire: The Final Choice.........................190

Appendix 195

A Personal Invitation from the Author 197

Notes...199

About the Author 203

FOREWORD

WHAT YOU ARE holding is not simply a book. It's more like a bugle blast. Or a war cry. It's a jarring and glorious wake-up call from a dear friend of mine, who just happens to be one of the most passionate voices in the church today: Malachi O'Brien.

In *Time to Rise*, Malachi does what prophets must do: He refuses to let us slumber. He exposes the poisonous undercurrent sweeping through our generation—the spirit of accusation—and names it for what it is: demonic. He diagnoses a crisis that most Christians feel in their bones but haven't had language for: the weaponization of shame, the culture of cynicism masquerading as discernment, and the tragic ease with which the church now devours its own. This book is not polite. It is not tame. It is not meant to be read passively.

Thank God for that.

We are living in a moment where truth is despised, outrage is monetized, and cowardice often disguises itself as compassion. In such a climate, clarity is rare—and costly. But Malachi O'Brien has chosen clarity over comfort. With the fire of a reformer and the heart of a revivalist, he challenges us to stop echoing the accuser and start aligning with the Advocate, Jesus Christ.

I've long known that the next move of God will come not through the sanitized halls of religious respectability but through the radical surrender of those who refuse to bow to cultural idols or religious intimidation. Malachi is one of those voices. He runs marathons for breakfast, yes—but more importantly, he runs toward battle when others retreat. He is not content with lukewarm faith or feel-good slogans. He wants the real thing. And he wants you to want it too. And because I know Malachi, I know that what he writes is not just words. He has lived this. He's the real thing.

If you're weary of the noise, the accusations, the endless cycle of fear and failure— this book is for you. If you've been wounded by the church or tempted to weaponize your wounds against it, this book is for you. And if you suspect deep down that God is calling you to rise up in this hour—not with bitterness but with boldness—then you've found your marching orders.

Malachi writes like a man possessed, to use the cliche. But it's true. He writes as a man possessed by the love of Jesus, by the power of the Holy Spirit, and by a holy disdain for the lies that hold God's people hostage. This is not something you can fake. And he doesn't merely diagnose a problem; he declares a remedy. That remedy is not a principle. It's a person. His name is Jesus. And He alone has the power to restore, to heal, to vindicate, and to raise the dead—including the spiritually dead.

I don't endorse books lightly. But *Time to Rise* is a book I believe should be shouted from pulpits and whispered in prayer rooms. It is confrontational, yes—but it is also

ix

deeply pastoral. It offers truth, but drenched in grace. It's the kind of book that just might save a life—or a church. It is filled with wisdom. As you will see.

So brace yourself. You're not just turning pages. You're stepping into a furnace. And if you're willing, that fire might just set you ablaze. And of course that's the point. Because it's God's glorious will for you. For *you*. What could be better?

—Eric Metaxas

New York Times Best-selling Author of *Bonhoeffer* and Letter to the American Church

AUTHOR'S NOTE

THIS BOOK ISN'T just meant to be read. It's meant to be experienced, because transformation doesn't happen passively. It happens when you fully engage your heart, mind, and spirit.

To take your reading experience to the next level, I've created something powerful and completely free. Text RISE to +1 (816) 727-7747 to register and unlock an unprecedented, immersive journey through this book. You'll get exclusive content designed to amplify what you're reading—and help you live it out in real time.

At the start of each section, you'll also find a QR code that gives you immediate access to a behind-the-scenes conversation. These videos will give you insight into the heart behind what you're about to read and how to apply it immediately.

Here's why I believe this book will change your life: I fasted and prayed over every chapter. I faced intense spiritual warfare while writing it. Hell doesn't fight what doesn't threaten it. That's how I know this message matters. I believe this is the book you've been waiting for.

So let's not waste another minute. Let's begin.

PREFACE

TIME TO RISE

In the land of liars, when truth is spoken, it will be received as a declaration of war.
—GARRETT J. WHITE

THIS IS NOT a normal book. This is a weapon, a call to rise as a dangerous man or woman of God—armed with truth, unshaken by lies, and unstoppable in your pursuit of who you truly are in Jesus Christ. This book exposes the darkest attacks facing this generation of the church. It is a war cry for the praying, fasting, worshipping, wild-eyed generational curse breakers to take their stand. The battle is against the lies, the deception, and the spirit of accusation that relentlessly come against the bride of Christ—His holy church.

The truth is this: You are never more like Jesus than when you intercede for others in prayer. You are never more like Satan than when you accuse others in pride.

> Then I heard a loud voice in heaven say: "Now have come the salvation and the power and the kingdom of our God, and the authority of his Messiah. For the accuser of our brothers and sisters, who accuses them before our God day and night, has been hurled down."
>
> —REVELATION 12:10

> Therefore he is able to save completely those who come to God through him, because he always lives to intercede for them.
>
> —HEBREWS 7:25

I am writing to *confront the lies*. The ones attacking the church and the ones whispering in your mind when no one else is listening. The ones that haunt you in the early hours of the morning, keeping you awake. *This is the hour the spirit of accusation falls.* This is the hour every lie inside of you is annihilated. This is the moment you rise, discovering the limitless potential within you—because the limitless God is your very life, identity, purpose, and being.

I hate the lies that hold people hostage—the ones that tell them they are unworthy, unloved, or unseen. The lies that sedate and domesticate a generation from their limitless potential in God. I hate the deception that causes people to partner with Satan in spreading falsehoods about others. I hate the lies that cause us to focus on the sin in others more than the sin in ourselves. The lies that excuse holiness for legalism and the lies that blind many to believe accusation produces accountability. Just as the serpent deceived Eve in the Garden of Eden, the enemy still whispers, twisting truth and sowing doubt. Enough.

There is a dry-bone army being commissioned once again:

xiii

xiv | TIME TO RISE

Then he said to me, "Prophesy to the breath; prophesy, son of man, and say to it, 'This is what the Sovereign LORD says: Come, breath, from the four winds and breathe into these slain, that they may live.'" So I prophesied as he commanded me, and breath entered them; they came to life and stood up on their feet—a vast army."

—EZEKIEL 37:9–10

My prayer is that this book becomes the *ruach*—the very wind of God—in the hands of every reader.[1] That it refreshes you, revives you, and calls you back to life. This is an Ezekiel 37 declaration over those who have been crushed by the words and attacks of others. Dry bones, awaken.

THE TSUNAMI HAS REACHED THE SHORE

On December 26, 2004, one of the deadliest natural disasters in modern history occurred. A tsunami, unleashed with terror-inducing waves up to a hundred feet high, violently struck unprepared and unsuspecting coastal communities across fourteen countries. Hardest hit were Indonesia, Sri Lanka, India, and Thailand. In just a few hours, over 230,000 lives were lost, and millions more were displaced. Entire villages were erased, infrastructure was destroyed, and survivors faced a long road to recovery. Almost everyone lost someone.[2]

Why so much damage and devastation? Because many were unprepared for what was coming against them. There was no warning system and no one was ready.

Likewise, the church today is facing a spiritual tsunami—one that has arrived silently, surging through social media, pulpits, and even our private thoughts. It is a tsunami of accusation.

This book serves as a warning. It addresses the tsunami coming against the church and coming against everyone on the inside. A tsunami of accusations. The ones we hear, the ones shared on social media, and the ones we believe internally.

Please consider that this is not just a book you can read—this is a battle cry you respond to. You cannot afford to stay passive. The enemy is relentless, and the time for silence is over. Rise up. Pray like never before. Speak truth in the face of lies. Intercede for those under attack. Reject the accusations, break the chains, and walk in the authority God has given you.

You were not made to live bound by fear, deception, or the words of the accuser. You were made to rise.

The relentless attacks of cynicism, sarcasm, and passive-aggressive statements from others are not the end of you. They are your promotion into the power of the resurrection.

Revelation 12:11 declares, "They overcame him by the blood of the Lamb and by the word of their testimony" (NKJV). This verse reveals the twofold power by which believers walk in victory.

The blood of the Lamb represents the finished work of Jesus on the cross. His sacrifice paid for our sin, broke the power of the enemy, and secured our authority as sons and daughters of God. We don't fight *for* victory—we fight *from* victory, standing in the righteousness and redemption His blood provides.

The word of their testimony is the spoken declaration of God's faithfulness. Our testimony is not just our past redemption but our ongoing witness of His power at work in our lives. By speaking truth—who God is, what He has done, and who we are in Him—we silence the accuser and walk in boldness.

Overcoming isn't passive; it's a passionate standing in Jesus' victory and proclaiming it fearlessly. While those given to the spirit of accusation deconstruct the work of the cross, those who do not succumb to its insidious evil prove in real time that by death He conquered death.

I have found that most people don't read books cover to cover. Even fewer remember what they read. And almost none take action. But this book isn't meant to be passively consumed—it must become a modern-day manifesto for the wild ones. The ones who burn for Jesus. The ones who refuse to settle for a bored, barren, powerless faith. I believe a dangerous, obsessed society is emerging that terrifies the very demons of hell itself. Those who truly know God and do exploits.

I am not here to convince you of what I believe—who am I to tell you what to believe? I am writing so the Holy Spirit will brand you with Jesus. I am writing to point you to Him—because He is more than you have ever experienced. And He is enough to transform every area of your life. It doesn't matter how long you've been in church or how many years you've followed Christ—there are deeper encounters.

Time to Rise is a wake-up call—a call to stand, to fight, to refuse the lies of accusation. You fail only if you stay down. You lose only if you quit. Victory is still possible, but you must rise.

No, this is not just another book. It is a declaration of grace, mercy, and truth—for you, right here, right now, today.

So hear my plea: It's time to rise. No more waiting. No more excuses. The breath of God is moving. Will you stand and become part of His vast army?

Run if you want to, run if you will
But I came here to stay
Now when I fall down I'm gonna try to get up
Because I didn't start out to play
It's a battlefield, brother, not a recreation room
It's a fight and not a game

Run if you want to, run if you will
But I came here to stay

—Camp Victory Chorus[3]

xvi | TIME TO RISE

I sang those lyrics at Camp Victory when I was thirteen years old, and Jesus called me to rise, surrender all, and preach the gospel. These words reverberate in my soul even now.

This truly is a fight and not a game. So I say to all: *fight, fight, fight.*

INTRODUCTION
ONE THING IS NEEDED

Burn any form of Christianity and church you don't see in Christ crucified.
—MICHAEL KOULIANOS

THERE IS SO much inside and outside the church that needs to be torched and incinerated with holy fire. So much in modern Christianity we don't see in Christ crucified.

We are in a defining hour of history. The Lord Jesus Himself is reshaping our understanding of what it truly means to follow Him. He is stripping away distractions, false comforts, and powerless religion to reveal this one truth: He alone is the answer.

> But *one thing is needed*, and Mary has chosen that good part, which will not be taken away from her."
> —LUKE 10:42, NKJV, EMPHASIS ADDED

He is calling us to a place few have been willing to go—a place where first love for Jesus fuels our every breath, where His presence is our very oxygen, and His Word is our unshakable foundation. This is not a casual invitation. It is a radical summons to surrender, to forsake every lesser pursuit, and to live consumed by the fire of His love.

This interaction between Mary, Martha, and Jesus is more than a message; it is a mandate, an invitation to powerful simplicity and clarity. There, in the place of holy first love, the greatest revelation of human activity is highlighted as both the solution and the answer for the church at the end of the age. *Jesus truly is looking for people who won't leave Him alone*—people of presence and obsession with Him.

It is also in this interaction that we discover how the spirit of accusation seeks to take the focus off Jesus and put it on oneself. While Mary is noticing Jesus, Martha accuses Jesus of not noticing her.

There is resistance to first love. The spirit of accusation has been unleashed against the church like never before. Lies, division, and deception seek to weaken the body of Christ from the outside—and from within. The enemy whispers to believers, distorting identity, fueling insecurity, and keeping them bound in fear and self-doubt. Many live under the weight of accusation, both external and internal, not realizing that Jesus has already shattered those chains.

Why is only one thing needed? Because only one person is the answer for all the pain, all the suffering, all the injustice, all the hate, all the lies, all the evil.

JESUS OUTWEIGHS THEM ALL

There is one thing you must have—not should have—to live a fulfilled and meaningful life. That one thing is revelation, and it comes only through the Holy Scripture—and the Holy Spirit—concerning who Jesus is in every way.

"Just be balanced and take it easy; you might burn out" is a cute, clever excuse for compromise. We must behold *Him*.

> You want to know how that one man, dying alone for a few short hours on a tree, can save a multitude of men from an eternity in hell? Because that one man is worth more than all of them put together. You take mountains and molehills, crickets and clowns—you take everything. Every planet, every star, every form of beauty. Everything that sings, everything that brings delight, and you put it all [on] the scale, and you put Christ on the other side, and He outweighs them all.
>
> —Paul Washer[1]

This book is a call to return—to rediscover the simplicity and power of a life wholly given to Jesus. In these pages, we will confront both the accusations attacking the church and the internal lies that keep us from stepping into our true identity in Christ. We will expose the tactics of the enemy, silence the voice of accusation, and learn to stand firm in the freedom, authority, and victory Jesus has already won for us.

Everything we need—every longing, every solution, every breakthrough—is found in Him alone. The question is, will we answer the call?

FALSE ACCUSATION IS REAL SPIRITUAL ABUSE— TERMS AND DEFINITIONS MATTER

I almost did not put this into the book, but after much prayer I must at least briefly approach the issue at hand.

There are many things being called spiritual abuse today that are not actually spiritual abuse. There are many things being called trauma that are not actually trauma. A friend of mine recently put it this way: We have a generation in a love affair with trauma. I am not saying it does not exist. What I am saying is that new definitions have exploded in recent days to match one's experiences. If we are not careful, we will allow ideology to shape our theology, what we believe and know about God. We will hand over authority to something other than the Word of God and Spirit of God.

False accusations will come into the life of a believer at the hands of another. This is spiritual warfare.

Please see that one's worldview shapes one's definition. This is why, when discussing issues of the day, it is critical that we understand what someone means. Cultural ideologies are shaping the church more than we know. Marxism and critical race theory have crept into the church in undeniable ways.

We must beware of the wolves that come into the church—not in shepherd's

One Thing Is Needed | xix

clothing but in sheep's clothing. Here are the facts: If you see the world as oppressed and oppressor, you will never discover the power of redemption and the power of the cross. You will excuse your actions of accusation because you no longer see God as the one who vindicates. Justice become your responsibility instead of God's.

We need to get back to the basics. What is sin? What is repentance? What is forgiveness? Many who want to talk about how leaders are not kings like David, and yet they see themselves as Nathans, who are supposed to speak correction (2 Sam. 12). Those who want to throw away the prophetic want to be prophets of a different kind. We do not need a certain type of YouTube prophet who can't wait to upload the next video attacking someone else. Truly, God is looking for intercessors more than influencers.

God does not use accusation to reform the church. Jesus—and Jesus alone—reforms the church. The church does not need to be trauma-informed. The church needs to be Jesus-consumed.

The churches in Revelation reveal clearly that Jesus is the answer to everything facing the church. His invitation for reform comes from within, not without.

I personally believe that Donald J. Trump overcoming the lies and accusations against him is a sign to the church and believers not to succumb to the lies and accusations facing them.

This book is a massive action plan designed to help us overcome the spirit of accusation and walk in truth. If you recognize these stages, you will be able to experience lasting transformation.

Listen, this isn't theory. This is war. Each of these five stages is a divine recalibration and realignment for the life you were called to live and the elite version of yourself God created you to be. The stages were designed to snap you out of confusion, strip off false identities, and awaken the unstoppable fire God put inside you. *Now* is the time to get back to who you really are in Christ—undeniable in His purpose in you fueled by limitless passion for Him. The kind of passion and fire that makes others uncomfortable. This is your time to rise.

Stage 1: Awareness Stage—Our Words Influence Us

- We must recognize the power of words in shaping our beliefs and actions.
- We must understand how words can either build up or tear down.
- We must overcome the negative impact of accusations, gossip, and destructive speech.

Stage 2: Wisdom Stage—Our Discernment Guides Us

- We must learn to distinguish truth from deception.
- We must develop spiritual and emotional discernment to avoid false accusations.
- We must cultivate wisdom to respond rather than react.

Stage 3: Foundation Stage—Our Identity Controls Us

- We must understand who we are in Christ—our core beliefs.
- We must recognize how accusations attack identity and create insecurity.
- We must stand firm in a truth-based identity, not others' opinions.

Stage 4: Action Stage—Our Choices Empower Us

- We must take responsibility for our responses and decisions.
- We must choose faith over fear, truth over accusation, and forgiveness over bitterness.
- We must walk in freedom by making intentional, empowered choices.

Stage 5: Growth and Transformation Stage—Our Questions Unlock Our Purpose

- We must ask the right questions to challenge false narratives.
- We must use questions to seek wisdom, clarity, and deeper understanding.
- We must transform accusations into opportunities for growth and breakthrough.

I don't know about you, but this sets my soul on fire. Why? Because I know real and lasting transformation that defies all logic and overcomes all critics is possible. It has nothing to do with talent, money, connections, or titles. It has everything to do with hunger and the answer to these simple questions: Will you decide today to rise? Will you decide to do very hard things? The things others won't? If so, let's run. Let's stop being the managers of our circumstances. Let's be the creators of our lives. Let's get ready to throw down in the battle we were born for.

Time is short. We don't know the day or the hour of Christ's return or when we will breathe our last breath, but we do know the mission. It's time to wake up, stand up, and show up with a fire that won't quit. The call of God isn't optional—it's urgent. Let's move with relentless passion to see His kingdom invade this earth and His bride rise in power, purified and unstoppable. This is your moment. This is our moment. Don't hold back. Burn the ships. Let's go.

PART I

THE POWER OF WORDS— SHAPING OUR REALITY

On October 7, 2022, I ran a marathon. Twenty-six point two miles. The next day I did it again. And the next day I did it again. And the next day I did it yet again. This continued for 153 consecutive days, and I finished on March 8, 2023. That's right—you read that correctly. For 153 days in a row, I ran a marathon distance outside. For five full months.

That is how I got the nickname "Dr. Run."

I had to run a marathon distance every single day for five full months. There was no other option. I didn't do it for a medal or a moment—I did it because I had been called by Jesus to do so. His words became my life.

We have no idea how powerful words truly are. Not just the words of the crucified carpenter and not just the words of Holy Scripture but also the words we say to and over others. These narratives are playing out in the recesses of our very being.

I ran when it was twenty degrees below zero in the mountains of Colorado. I ran when I had a 102-degree fever and could hardly stand. I ran on days I had no sleep. I ran in every weather imaginable. Rarely was it convenient. Few understood why it had to happen.

But in the dark of night, in those many hours alone running, I began to discover the power of words. I discovered that when we do not just hard things, but very hard things, we are transformed. The only things that can stop us are the words and lies we believe on the inside.

Running those 153 marathons, I began saying to myself over and over again, "I am Dr. Run. I am Dr. Run. Malachi may get tired. Malachi might quit. Dr. Run does not."

As you step into the first chapters of this manifesto, I want you to carefully consider the power of words. Not just your words but, more importantly, the words of Jesus. Truly only one thing is needed.

What you speak, what you believe, and what you constantly repeat matters more than you could possibly imagine. Change that, and you change everything.

bit.ly/4mwGPvx

CHAPTER 1

PROPHECY OR POISON?

The narratives we tell ourselves, whether positive or negative, shape our reality. What we declare either limits us or liberates us.
—JESSE ITZLER

I AM AN ULTRAMARATHON runner. Truthfully, I'm obsessed with running—all the time, everywhere. I know how insane this might sound. My friends joke that it might actually be a cause for concern.

My idea of a fun run isn't a casual jog—it's a hundred-mile endurance challenge that lasts for hours. People often ask me, "Do you ever feel like quitting when you're running?" My answer? Every. Single. Time.

But here's the key: I never give my pain or feelings a voice. I don't allow negativity to take root. The soundtrack in my mind is one of resilience, endurance, and unwavering determination. Success or failure. Victory or defeat. Life or death. It all comes down to mindset. We can allow either the words of the enemy to create a stronghold or the words of Jesus to create a mindset no voice can pierce with accusation.

In April 2025 I finished the Arizona Monster 300. A grueling 304-mile trail race through the deserts and mountains of southern Arizona. It took me over 160 hours, and I had only about six to seven hours of sleep. It was by far the hardest thing I have ever done in my life. Physically, spiritually, and emotionally. I almost quit. What kept me from quitting were the words of others and the words I spoke to myself. The words I sensed God was speaking to me.

Our words matter. The words we speak to ourselves, about ourselves, and about others—they shape our destiny. Let's be honest—you already know this. Accusations and attacks flood online platforms. YouTube videos, X posts, and so much more. There are a lot of trolls, or online "Karens" as I refer to them, who have become gold medalists in projecting a form of godliness but denying the power therein. The culture of call-out and cancel has even crept into the church. Worse than that, it has become celebrated. But there is no such thing as exposure ministry.

ACCUSATION IS NOT A MINISTRY—IT'S DEMONIC

Accusation is not about exposing darkness for the sake of truth—it is about weaponizing shame for the sake of destruction. And the Bible is clear on where it originates.

> For the accuser of our brothers and sisters, who accuses them before our God day and night, has been hurled down.
>
> —REVELATION 12:10

4 | Time to Rise

Satan is called the accuser of the brethren because accusation is his language. It is how he formats his fiery arrows. Please consider this: When you and I engage in accusation, you and I are speaking his language. You are likely familiar with the five love languages concept. Just as there are love languages that help us connect, there are opposing shame languages that the enemy uses to destroy. I have discovered five shame languages of the enemy:

1. Condemnation
2. Emotional manipulation
3. Sarcasm
4. Cynicism
5. Insinuation

Some might call it "accountability." Others might call it "discernment." But if the goal is to tear down rather than restore, we're no longer partnering with Jesus—we're partnering with the enemy. Let me say this clearly: Accusation does not lead to reformation in the church. Jesus does. Go read His letters to the churches in Revelation— reformation comes through divine revelation, not human retaliation. Two things belong to God alone: glory and vindication.

Can I ask you something hard? Have you ever inwardly considered someone else's failure to be worse than your own? Sadly, I have. And deep down, I knew it was a lie. While we feast on the failure of others, we become blind to the decay inside ourselves. Here's the sobering truth: When we focus on the sins and faults of others, we are not focused on the crucified Lamb.

JESUS RESTORES; ACCUSATION DESTROYS

Does it mean we ignore sin? Of course not. Does it mean we are silent about the things God demands we speak out against? Never. We mustn't forget the old axiom to be loud where God is loud, soft where God is soft, and silent where God is silent. Righteous correction is biblical. Accountability is necessary—and needed more than ever. But *accountability seeks redemption, not ruin.* Accountability has a process, and that process does not include YouTube, sleazy blog sites, or piranha-style vigilante "justice" on X.

In carrying this message, I know that I have wronged people who have attacked and condemned me every time I took my eyes off Jesus. You see, we don't always have to be right. We do, however, need to seek to be like the Righteous One—Jesus.

Consider this: Jesus seeks to restore. Accusation seeks to destroy. One is led by the Holy Spirit. The other is fueled by hell. Puritan preacher Richard Sibbes stated, "There is more mercy in Christ than sin in us."[1] True holiness does not ignore the sin of others; it moves us to mortify our own sins.

Take a moment with me and look at the woman caught in adultery. This story (John 8:1–11) is one of the most powerful examples of how accusation operates—and how Jesus responds to it. The religious leaders weren't interested in justice or repentance; they wanted to trap Jesus and use this woman as a tool for their own agenda. Accusation often disguises itself as righteousness, but its real intent is destruction, not redemption.

The woman was guilty—there was no question about that. But the law also required both the man and the woman to be punished (Lev. 20:10). The Pharisees selectively applied the law to serve their accusation—just as the enemy twists truth to bring condemnation rather than conviction. They wanted stones to crush this woman. Religiously camouflaged opinions and progressive ideologies make for easy stones to throw.

David took stones and took out a giant vomiting accusation against the God of Israel. Jesus, the greater David, took stones of mercy and grace and took down the giant of self-righteous hypocrisy. As you carefully consider this story, you'll discover that instead of engaging with their trap, Jesus responded with wisdom and grace: "Let any one of you who is without sin be the first to throw a stone at her" (John 8:7). This exposed their *hypocrisy* and reminded them that they, too, deserved judgment.

One by one, her accusers walked away. Jesus—the only one without sin and the only one with the right to condemn—chose instead to forgive and restore: "Neither do I condemn you; go, and from now on sin no more" (v. 11, ESV). Jesus didn't ignore her sin. But He didn't let accusation define her future. He called her into freedom, not shame.

Pause and let this truth settle in deep: Jesus, who sees the darkness inside all of us, still offers freedom from our accusers. My belief is that the woman caught in adultery had already been crushed by the spirit of accusation against her from within. There's a reason she continued in her sin—until she met Jesus. People are not free from sin because of our accusations. Neither are they healed. They're radically set free when they see how mercy truly does triumph over judgment—especially in the moments they need it the most and seemingly deserve it the least.

But wait, are not leaders in the church held to a higher standard? Yes, they are—and they will be, at the judgment seat. Leaders are accountable to the church, not to social media judges playing jury and executioner. When you don't know the full story, don't make up a nightmare fairy tale laced with religiously camouflaged hit pieces. God hates that.

We have far too many aspiring online "Nathan the prophets" in this hour. *So when would* now *be a great time to break free?* All of us in some way have been guilty of accusation. Every last one of us. You're not alone. Please—don't earn a PhD in people you've never even met. We've all rehearsed past hurts and offenses. The number one reason people leave a church is because of offense and an unwillingness to forgive. We've all been tempted to replay the attacks of others, keeping the wounds fresh. But here's the outstanding news: We can be free. We can resist this vengeance culture that lives in our hearts and the assumption culture that governs our screens.

So how do we resist this culture of accusation—in our inner lives and in the outer world?

1. Examine your heart in view of Jesus. Are you doomscrolling or creating content that thrives on the failure of others? Do you feel a sense of satisfaction when someone falls? If so, it's time to repent.

2. Filter your words through Jesus. Before you post, ask these questions: Does this build up or tear down? Is it the truth or just my opinion? Would I say this if the person was in front of me?

3. Fight for restoration in Jesus. True accountability is rooted in love. If correction is needed, do it privately, biblically, and with the goal of restoration.

4. Refuse to engage in the industry of shame, which is not found in Jesus. Unfollow the pages, the blogs, the accounts that feast on failure. Don't share the hit pieces. Stop giving clicks to the cartel as prophetic declarations or poisonous limitations.

This isn't about ignoring reality. It's not about pretending everything is fine or faking positivity. That's weak. That's artificial. Fake positivity is like sugar—it might give you a quick high, but it won't sustain you. This is not about being "happy-clappy." This is about truth—raw, unfiltered, undeniable truth. The words you choose determine whether you rise or remain stuck in a cycle of defeat.

In *Soundtracks*, Jon Acuff writes, "If your day is spent overthinking broken soundtracks, your thoughts can be your worst foe, holding you back from ever taking action on the things you want in life."[2] By default, we drift toward negativity—unless we actively fight against it. And here's what Jon found. Our minds reinforce negativity by doing three things:

1. Lying about memories—twisting past events to fit a negative narrative.

2. Confusing fake trauma with real trauma—making small offenses seem like massive betrayals.

3. Believing what they already believe—searching for evidence to support a false bias instead of seeking actual truth.

Here's the dangerous part: Accusation thrives on these distortions. When bias is believed, we don't seek facts—we seek validation for our negativity. That's how the enemy works. Satan's fiery arrows aren't just accusations against others—they are accusations against you. Every negative thought that keeps you stuck? *It's not from God.*

Your words have the power to bend reality, reshape your identity, and create your future. This is why Jesus declared, "And you shall know the truth, and the truth shall make you free" (John 8:32, NKJV).

Freedom isn't found in emotionalism or opinion. Freedom is found in facts. But most people aren't free. They are trapped in their broken soundtracks—held captive by lies they've rehearsed for years.

ACCUSATION FOR ATTENTION IN THE BODY OF CHRIST

I've watched in horror as Christians tear each other apart online, ripping reputations to shreds just to gain a few likes and comments. It's as if we've confused destroying people with defending truth. If you do it long enough and loud enough, you might even get a plaque to hang on your wall.

Let me say this clearly: **The spirit of accusation is ravaging the church. It's doing more damage than false doctrine ever could.** This is Satan's scorched-earth strategy—divide ministries, derail destinies, and keep believers bound in offense and deception. I've watched the insinuations destroy lives. I've watched as well-meaning people say nothing out of fear while others are attacked. And I've watched people deconstruct into progressive, antigospel ideologies in defense of the indefensible.

The spirit of accusation is not just a bad habit—it is a *demonic principality*. Whenever I talk about this, the backlash is the same: "You're just trying to protect those who sin!" "You're just defending your friends!" "You're excusing corruption in the church!" No. I'm confronting the demonic strategy that is breaking the church from the inside out.

Accusation never leads to accountability. *It leads to condemnation.* It holds people emotionally hostage and paralyzes progress. I am an advocate for holiness. I long for righteousness to shine in the church like a thousand blazing suns. I believe in accountability that transforms—not accusation that tears down. And above all, I believe mercy triumphs over judgment.

What I am advocating for is the hard work of anyone who wants more of God.

WHAT IS THE SPIRIT OF ACCUSATION?

Read this slowly. The spirit of accusation thrives on false claims, partial truths, and emotional manipulation. It distorts reality, poisons relationships, and blinds people to redeeming grace. I believe it to be the driving force behind cancel culture in the church. It's more than finger-pointing. It's not purification—it's perversion.

It condemns rather than restores. It discredits rather than builds up. It traps people in past mistakes. It tears down identity with no regard for the damage caused. It sounds holy, but its fruit is anything but.

Please know and consider carefully that grace does not grow in a heart given to attacking others. It is not discernment. It is deconstruction. I'd like to share four signs for consideration that you may have become intoxicated by, and could be under the influence of, accusation:

Sign #1: You have become quick to accuse others through gossip, slander, strife, bitterness, and murmuring.

Sign #2: You are blaming instead of taking responsibility, shifting fault to others instead of growing.

Sign #3: Your focus is on past failures, using past mistakes to justify ongoing condemnation.

Sign #4: Your intent has become to harm or discredit, targeting someone's reputation instead of seeking reconciliation.

Sign #5: You no longer find yourself living in overwhelming gratitude for all the blessings you have been given. You can't focus on the positive because your emotions are driving you to focus on the negative.

THE BATTLE FOR YOUR WORDS

You have a choice—and it always begins in your heart. I like something John Bevere once said in his book *Bait of Satan*: "Often we judge ourselves by our intentions and everyone else by their actions. It is possible to intend one thing while communicating something totally different. Sometimes our true motives are cleverly hidden even from us."[3] Have you ever done this? Judging others by actions and yourself by intentions? I know I have.

Your words will eventually reveal your true motives. Sometimes it takes a while, because we're good at projection and self-protection. But eventually, the mask wears thin.

You can partner with the accuser—joining in the chorus of cynicism, negativity, and division. Or you can partner with the Advocate—aligning your words with truth, restoration, and breakthrough. Because here's the truth: *The Holy Spirit does not anoint the hypercritical.* He anoints the hungry. The surrendered. The ones consumed with Jesus.

So I ask again: Will you be the one to stop revival? Will you let skepticism silence what God is doing? Will you let criticism keep you from participating in the move of God? Will you let accusation steal your calling?

Or will you rise?

Don't criticize—contribute. Don't tear down—build up. Don't stop revival—fan the flames. It's time to take back your words, take back your thoughts, take back your destiny. It's time to reject the soundtrack of shame and rise into truth.

This is your time to rise.

CHAPTER 2

THE POWER OF PERSPECTIVE

You are entitled to know that two entities occupy your body. One of these entities is motivated by and responds to the impulse of fear. The other is motivated by and responds to the impulse of faith. Will you be guided by faith or will you allow fear to overtake you?
—NAPOLEON HILL

IN OUTWITTING THE DEVIL: *The Secret to Freedom and Success*, Napoleon Hill argues that most people fall into a state of drift—a life of passivity, mediocrity, and wasted potential—because they allow external forces to shape their beliefs and choices. To outwit the devil, you must become a *non-drifter*—someone with a definite purpose, control over their mind, and the refusal to let fear dictate their life.[1]

Very few non-drifters exist today. Russell Brunson calls these non-drifters the "driven."[2] These rare individuals live with clarity and intentionality. *Winning the daily war in your mind is the single greatest factor in your happiness and fulfillment.* If you want to rise above accusation and walk in victory, mastering your mind is not optional—it's essential.

Are you a drifter—or are you driven?

AM I THE ONLY ONE?

I live an over-caffeinated life. I'm an ultrarunner, a pastor, and an entrepreneur, and I work in politics. On top of that, my most important roles are being a husband and a father. With so much going on, I have to win the war in my mind. It's not a suggestion—it's survival.

As an ultrarunner, I run for days on end. As an entrepreneur, I run a digital media business that helps others bring neon-clear clarity into their communication and reach millions of people online. As a pastor, I am committed to leading Presence Church with one ambition: Jesus. As someone who works in politics, I am committed to bringing Christ into every sphere of policy. I must master my mindset in every area of my life. I must bring insane amounts of energy to the table every day. However, there are days I don't heed my own advice.

I don't always win. I've found myself drifting more times than I'd like to admit.

Have you ever been there? Woken up in the middle of the night, unable to sleep because your mind won't stop racing? Ever received a text or email from a friend, client, or family member that sends anxiety surging through your chest? That creeping dread. The tightness. You know the feeling. Maybe I'm the only one. But I doubt it.

Let me be vulnerable. There are moments—sometimes weekly, sometimes daily—when I feel overwhelmed, negative, like a fraud. Imposter syndrome. Failure. As if everything is falling apart and I'll never be enough. There are days my thoughts are dark. Those days are fewer now, but they still come. I am learning to discipline my disappointments and shift my state of mind quickly.

You wouldn't know that from what I post online. Social media has become a place where we showcase our external victories while hiding our internal battles. And when we do share struggles, it's often to seek validation, not breakthrough.

SO WHY DOES THIS HAPPEN?

The enemy doesn't just use words from others—he downloads accusations into our minds. Every dark thought you have about yourself or others did not originate from the Holy Spirit. Thoughts are words without sound. They form the soundtrack of your soul. Accusations are thoughts amplified by negative emotion. Just the other day I had someone I trusted dearly say some of the harshest and most critical words to me over the phone. Then the next day a well-known pastor did the very same thing. If we are going to be like Jesus, we must remember that none of us are immune to betrayal and attack. Those attacks become spiritual warfare, and they are fought with spoken words and internal thoughts.

And make no mistake—Satan understands the power of words. He has studied human behavior for centuries. He knows that words don't just describe reality; they shape it. So he deploys them as weapons, laced with deception. Lies, negative beliefs, and toxic narratives are his ammunition. And here's the kicker: *If you accept them, they don't just stay in your mind—they become your life.*

> For as he thinks in his heart, so is he.
>
> —Proverbs 23:7, nkjv

That verse isn't just poetic—it's a law of reality. Your dominant thoughts create the filters through which you experience life. If you believe you are unworthy, your mind will find proof everywhere. If you accept the identity of failure, you will unconsciously make choices that reinforce it.

That's why Satan doesn't need to attack your circumstances—*he only needs to influence your perception.* If he can get you to agree with the wrong thoughts, he's already won.

THE POWER OF PERSPECTIVE

Perspective is simply the way in which we see things. Perspective is the glasses we wear to filter the thousands of messages we receive and thoughts we entertain.

Personally, I receive dozens of vicious comments daily. People question my character, my faith, even my worth. Does it bother me? Ninety-nine percent of the time it does not. Because I've learned a crucial truth: What people say about you says more about them than it does about you.

The Power of Perspective | 11

And the same is true for you.

When someone speaks accusation and hate, they have partnered with the enemy. That, again, is the spirit of accusation. They have aligned themselves with the accuser of the brethren rather than the Great Intercessor of our souls. But here's where it goes even deeper—you don't have to be the one attacking to be in agreement with the enemy. If you replay those words in your mind…if you meditate on the accusation…if you let it take root…then you have partnered with the lie just as much as the person who spoke it.

It's time to take dominion over your mind.

You are not powerless against your thoughts. The Word of God is sharper than any double-edged sword, and it has the power to demolish strongholds. But it requires action. You must become aggressive about guarding your mind. You must speak the truth louder than the lies. Please hear me right now. I know that this is hard work. However, we have been called to do very hard things. The most successful people throughout history have learned the secret to doing this work.

Here's my challenge to you: Start paying close attention to the words you entertain. When a thought enters your mind, ask yourself, "Who said that?" If it doesn't align with God's voice, cast it out immediately. Don't coddle it. Don't analyze it. Replace it. Speak truth over it.

You don't just *hope* for a strong mind—you *build* one. Not through wishful thinking or motivational mantras but through intentional, relentless repetition of God's Word. Not just by verse-of-the-day reading but by saturation. Tidal-wave levels of holy Scripture. Because the loudest voice in your life isn't the enemy's—it's yours.

The question is which kingdom you are amplifying.

Allow me to be honest again. I can't tell you how many times I have let the words of others dwell in my mind and heart for days and weeks. It's not what they said—it's what I started saying. It wasn't their comments that had power—it was my agreement with them. I am probably again the only one who has ever done this. Or am I?

Let me ask you this: Have you been replaying someone's accusation, criticism, or misunderstanding—letting it shape how you see yourself, your calling, or even your faith? Have you allowed the words of others about others shape your opinions? Have you reread that text or email a thousand times? Have you relived that failure over and over again? Have you allowed yourself to listen to people tear others down? Let me encourage you right now. You're not alone. But this is the moment to rise. This is the moment to take your thoughts captive and remind your soul who you really are. It is time to be different from the crowd. Different people do the uncommon, and even now there is a voice rising inside you telling you it is time to rise above the noise of accusation.

Because the voice that defines you is not the outer voices of accusation or the inner voice of accusation. It's the voice of your Father. The voice of truth.

CHAPTER 3

THE INDUSTRY OF SHAME

"What can men do against such reckless hate?"
"Ride out with me. Ride out and meet them."
—J.R.R. TOLKIEN, *LORD OF THE RINGS: THE TWO TOWERS*

PLEASE READ WHAT I am about to say and consider my words carefully. This is a "ride out and meet them" moment. Right now, an entire industry exists solely to tear people down. It's made up of self-appointed "reformers," bloggers, and social media opportunists who thrive on exposing others—not to bring truth, not to restore, but to destroy.

This Failure Porn Cartel (FPC) has turned accusation into a business. With its small conferences, viral toxic posts, and hit-piece podcasts, it's an economy of outrage fueled by selective storytelling, half-truths, and outright lies. Every ministry and leader needs to hear this: If you haven't been targeted yet, it's only a matter of time.

THE SHAME PORTFOLIO

What's the currency of this shame economy? Cynicism, sarcasm, and passive-aggressiveness—all under the guise of "discernment." This isn't discernment. This is digital assassination.

Allow me to illustrate without naming names. I know of bloggers posing as journalists, who carefully craft narratives to manipulate perception. One of them said this: "Demand resignation in a message to someone else. You need to irritate folks there. Make a scene and videotape it. I have given you the ammo. Now you need to use it." This same blogger doxxed my address online last year in an attempt to attack.

I know of people posting secret audio recordings, taken out of context—not to bring clarity, but to weaponize words and destroy reputations. Yet these same people have their own shortcomings—just like I do—that they really don't want to become headlines.

I know of a pastor who lied on a podcast about another leader. He insinuated a belief that simply was not true. When confronted biblically, he dodged every attempt at accountability. I know of another pastor—attacked repeatedly by the mob—whose church cultivates a culture of mercy and is doing some incredible things for the kingdom that few are doing in this hour. This same pastor showed mercy and grace to a brother in Christ and was met with a YouTube video "calling him out." You can't make up the weaponized morality in this hour, which is nothing more than pharisaical grandstanding.

I know of another pastor, and friend, who walks in the Word yet faces the same types of attacks. That friend of mine told me of a blogger encouraging people to lie so that a newspaper would run the story. I know of several ministries and leaders that have come under the spirit of accusation, and the accusations are blatantly false. Even when the truth is revealed and the case is closed, the haters won't accept the truth.

A pastor in Alabama whom the Lord is using in a powerful way who went through a season of the most unreal accusations that were propped up by his denomination. He would not bend and he would not bow. He stood, and God has elevated his platform to a whole new level. I like what I heard my friend Landon Schott of Mercy Culture church state recently: "There was a death threat from Goliath to David, and that threat put David on the map." There is probably someone reading this right now who needs to know that God will use the attacks of others to elevate you to impact when you refuse to retreat. The battle belongs to the Lord.

Let me give you another example that is impossible to make up. I witnessed firsthand an offended leader fire off an email to another leader at 3:00 a.m. and cc dozens of others. I know this because I am on this email thread. Then some who received the email jumped on the bandwagon to viciously attack the same leader the email was sent to without ever hearing the full story. It was calculated. It was cruel. And it's happening more than you think. It's evil.

Remember this quote from Garrett J. White? "When speaking truth in the land of liars, it is received by those liars as a declaration of war."[1]

So right now, I am declaring war by speaking the truth. When the digital assassination begins, there will be moments when you'll feel intense pressure to stay silent. You'll be asked to agree with someone's narrative or join their ranks. Please hear me. You must refuse with fierce conviction. Courage is contagious. And it's rare. Let me encourage you—stand with your friends. Stand with them in prayer. Stand with them publicly when you must. Don't believe what you see online simply because it's online.

ACCUSATION IS BUILT ON FEELINGS, NOT FACTS

> But if you harbor bitter envy and selfish ambition in your hearts, do not boast about it or deny the truth. Such "wisdom" does not come down from heaven but is earthly, unspiritual, demonic.
>
> —JAMES 3:14–15

The cartel doesn't deal in truth—they deal in emotion. They record, post, and write not the truth that God knows but the truth they feel. And in the process, they leave a trail of wreckage—ministries shattered, reputations ruined, families devastated. Why? Because clicks, comments, and controversy pay. In a world drowning in weapons of mass emotion, where outrage is currency, the real question isn't who's guilty. It's who benefits.

Please consider my next words carefully: Betrayal is prophetic. Don't be shocked when people turn against you. As a pastor I've found that one of the hardest seasons of ministry has come not when people have left the church, which I hate deeply. The hardest season has been when former leaders have risen, left, and taken people with them.

Jesus said that part of the end times drama would be just that: "Brother will betray

14 | TIME TO RISE

brother to death, and a father his child; children will rebel against their parents and have them put to death" (Matt. 10:21). This verse is part of Jesus' warning to His disciples about the attacks they would face for following Him. It speaks to the division and betrayal that would come—even within families—as a result of the gospel.

SHAME SELLS; REDEMPTION DOESN'T

I was talking to a pastor friend recently who shared that those in the failure porn industry basically want those they attack to commit suicide or go to hell. Redemption is on their terms, not God's, and repentance has to meet their standards, not the Bible's. I don't disagree with him. He knows what the cure truly is in this hour. That cure is Jesus.

Mainstream media has taught us this: Scandal is profitable. Restoration and good news are not. They don't care if it is true. They just care that you think it could be true.

A pastor caught in a moral failure? The views skyrocket. The comment sections explode. The podcasts dissect every detail and twist the story for maximum impact. But what happens when that same pastor repents? When he walks through restoration? Silence. Crickets. No one cares.

Because redemption doesn't sell.

That's why accusation thrives. It feeds off destruction. The cycle of outrage continues because there's always another target. And when that pastor, leader, or individual repents? It's usually met with a "wait and see" response—or worse, outright rejection. It's almost like we're reliving the Salem Witch Trials. It is almost as if the very idea of honor has been cast aside. Almost as if no one wants to assign heaven's values over people.

Since we are having this candid conversation, please consider that never is the initial accusation from the cartel completely true. Rarely does a third-party investigation ever reveal the full truth. Only law enforcement and legal entities have the ability to get to the truth.

The FPC, driven by false justice, is preaching a punishment gospel. Sadly, when others are attacked, many stay silent because they know what could happen to them if they say anything. But I would rather stand with friends than stay silent in the face of accusation.

Does this mean we should jump into the comments of social media nonstop? It does not. A great friend of mine has encouraged me often in the wisdom of silence. While I have not always heeded that advice, I have come to believe that more often than not emotional reactions are not redemptive.

Let me ask you this: Does anyone care anymore what God thinks? Does anyone ask, "What does Jesus think and feel about this conversation? What does Jesus feel and know about us?"

We have to ask ourselves, "Does what I'm saying, posting, or consuming grieve the Holy Spirit? Have I traded truth for entertainment?"

Why do we crave stories of failure? Maybe, for a moment, they make us feel better about our own sins, our own struggles, our own shortcomings. But what if, instead of tearing people down, we interceded for them? What if we became a people known for grace instead of gossip? Because here's the truth: You can't partner with the accuser and the Advocate at the same time. You have to choose.

WOULD NOW BE A GOOD TIME TO WAKE UP?

The industry of shame will always exist—because the world loves scandal. But as followers of Jesus, we don't have to buy in. We don't have to feed the beast. We don't have to partner with accusation. Instead, we can be people of truth, of mercy, of restoration.

At the end of the day, the real question isn't who's guilty. The real question is, Who will choose grace? Who will fight for redemption instead of ruin? Who will walk in discernment instead of accusation? And most importantly—who will refuse to let the enemy use their words as weapons?

Wake up. The spirit of accusation is a demon. And it's time to cast it out.

CHAPTER 4

WHISPERS OF THE ENEMY: HOW ACCUSATION FUELS DOUBT

Doubt kills more dreams than failure ever will—believe in your potential and take action.
—ELON MUSK

FROM THE VERY beginning, Satan's strategy has been to twist, challenge, and distort God's words—leading people into doubt and deception. He doesn't just attack what God has said; he attacks God's will. It was God's will for Adam and Eve to refrain from eating the forbidden fruit, yet Satan planted doubt and manipulated truth until disobedience seemed like the better option.

We need deliverance from doubt.

In Genesis 3:1, we see the accuser at work, casting doubt on the Word of God: "Now the serpent was more crafty than any of the wild animals the LORD God had made. He said to the woman, 'Did God *really* say, "You must not eat from any tree in the garden"?'" (emphasis added).

That same spirit of accusation is at work today. It rises up to stop movements, kill callings, and paralyze purpose. It lures us into uncertainty, casting doubt where there was once faith. It convinces us that we are not enough, that we are unworthy, and that we are destined to fail. Those lies—though subtle—are some of the most powerful weapons in the enemy's arsenal.

THE ORIGIN OF ALL DOUBT

Reflect on your own life. How many times has doubt crept in, tempting you to question your calling? How often have you wrestled with questions about whether you are truly capable, truly chosen, truly enough? And here's the real question: Where did those doubts come from? From the Great Advocate—or from the accuser?

Accusation isn't just about words—it's about identity. In the Garden of Eden, Satan didn't simply challenge God's instructions; he challenged Eve's sense of completeness. He made her feel like she was lacking something, like she wasn't enough as she was. This is the root of every lie the enemy tells us today.

He whispers, "Are you really called? Are you really chosen? Do you really have what it takes? Did God really say that? You will always be a failure. No one sees what you are doing." His goal is to make you second-guess yourself until you disqualify yourself—before you ever step into what God has prepared for you.

16

THE PARALYZING POWER OF ACCUSATION

Accusation paralyzes. It makes us hesitate when we should take action. It makes us retreat when we should advance. It makes us shrink back in fear instead of rising up in faith. Sadly, I have allowed accusation to paralyze me. I have replayed conversations repeatedly in my mind. That never is productive, and we know it. So here's the truth: When you recognize where the doubt is coming from, you take back your power. We have to take ownership in our lives. We have the power to create. We have self agency. We can do that with truth or with lies.

Instead of entertaining the lies, replace them with truth. Declare what God has spoken over you. Stand firm in your calling. The enemy wins when you listen to his voice, but he loses the moment you start believing what God has already said about you.

When Jesus was tempted in the wilderness, Satan used the same strategy he used on Eve. Twisting God's words, he tried to plant doubt while even quoting Scripture out of context to manipulate Jesus into questioning His very identity and authority: *Did God really say?* (Matt. 4:1–11). But Jesus didn't engage with the lies. He responded with the unshakable truth of God's Word: *It is written.* That was His defense. And it must be ours as well.

THE ENEMY'S STRATEGY: ISOLATION AND ACCUSATION

The enemy's accusations are often most effective when we feel alone. He waits until we are alone, vulnerable, exhausted. He preys on our vulnerability, knowing that when we are disconnected from others, discouraged in spirit, or weary from the fight, we are far more likely to believe his lies.

This is why community is so important. We were never meant to fight these battles alone—but as one body, unified in Christ. When Elijah was overwhelmed by fear and ran to the wilderness, God didn't just give him a word of encouragement—He sent an angel to strengthen him and reminded him that he was not alone. There were still seven thousand in Israel who had not bowed to Baal (1 Kings 19:5–7, 19:18).

The enemy wants you to think you're the only one struggling, the only one battling doubt, the only one facing fear. But I'm here to remind you—you are not alone. The body of Christ is full of warriors who have walked through the same struggles and come out stronger on the other side.

BREAKING AGREEMENT WITH THE ACCUSER

Here's the hard truth: The enemy can work with only what we agree to. When we agree with the lie, we empower it. When we dwell on the accusations, we strengthen them.

But the moment we break agreement with the enemy and align ourselves with God's truth, everything changes.

18 | Time to Rise

So how do we do this?

1. **Identify the lie.** Recognize the accusations that have taken root in your mind. What negative beliefs have you been replaying?

2. **Replace it with truth.** Find the scriptures that directly counter those lies. If the enemy says you are unworthy, declare that you are fearfully and wonderfully made (Ps. 139:14). If he says you are weak, declare that God's strength is made perfect in your weakness (2 Cor. 12:9).

3. **Speak truth daily.** The enemy doesn't stop whispering, so we can't stop declaring truth. Speak God's promises over your life every single day.

4. **Stay in community.** Surround yourself with people who will remind you of God's truth when you forget it. Isolation is the breeding ground for deception.

5. **Pray with authority.** Rebuke the voice of accusation in Jesus' name. Stand firm in the authority God has given you.

LIVING IN VICTORY

When we learn to recognize the whispers of the enemy for what they are, we take back our power. We step out of doubt and into faith. And finally, we stop allowing the enemy to dictate our stories and start walking in the confidence of our callings once and for all.

Jesus didn't die for us to live in constant fear and self-doubt. He died to set us free. And part of that freedom means silencing the voice of accusation in our minds.

You were never meant to live under the weight of doubt. You were never meant to question your worth, your calling, or your purpose. The One who created you has already spoken over your life. His words are final. His truth is unshakable. And the enemy's lies hold no power in the light of God's voice.

So today, make a choice. Choose truth over lies. Choose faith over fear. Choose to silence the whispers of the enemy and walk in the fullness of who God has called you to be.

Because the truth is, the loudest voice in your life isn't your enemy's—it's yours. The question is, Which kingdom are you amplifying?

CHAPTER 5
SLANDERED AND SILENCED

In the spiritual realm, a man who will lead a rebellion has already proven, no matter how grandiose his words or angelic his ways, that he has a critical nature, an unprincipled character, and hidden motives in his heart....No, God never honors division in His realm.
—GENE EDWARDS

HAVE RUN SOME incredibly long ultraraces. Some over one hundred miles, one over three hundred miles, and many until I quit. I almost never ran my second ultramarathon race after I DNF'd (did not finish) my first one. I was running a fifty-mile race in 2012. At that time, I did not understand the difference between ultrarunning and regular running. The week earlier, I had run my fastest marathon of 3:14. So when I lined up to run the fifty-mile race, I assumed speed would be my ally. It was not. At mile 38, I was hurting and injured, and I had to pull out of the race. I was so embarrassed and so ashamed that I refused to wear the race shirt from that event or even talk about it with others. The voice in my head said I was a failure. However, years later, the voice of truth revealed to me that I was not a failure. That race was necessary—for the races to come.

Just like ultrarunning has prepared me for future endurance, David's battles trained him for greater trials. In the life of David, we discover how his dealings with Saul prepared him for his dealings with Absalom in 2 Samuel. The story of David and Absalom is more than a historical tragedy—it's a masterclass in how accusation warps the soul. What begins as a wound festers into bitterness, and bitterness, left unchecked, breeds rebellion. Absalom, a prince with much promise, became a rebel carrying much resentment, and in the end, his war against his father led to his own destruction.

This travesty began with injustice. Tamar had been violated and Absalom burned for justice, but when it didn't come fast enough, he took matters into his own hands. He murdered his brother Amnon, thinking it would bring him peace. But vengeance never heals—it only deepens the wound. And the longer Absalom sat in his pain, the more his grief turned into something darker.

Resentment became a lens. He no longer saw David as a father or a king but as a failure, an obstacle, an enemy. The voice of accusation whispered, "He's unfit to lead. He's unworthy of honor. He's lost the right to rule." And Absalom believed it. The same deception that poisoned his heart became the tool he used to poison a nation.

He positioned himself at the city gates—not as a servant, but as a thief of loyalty. He flattered. He manipulated. He murmured to the people, "If I were king, I would bring you justice." And just like that, he turned their hearts—not toward righteousness, but toward rebellion.

This is the nature of accusation—it doesn't just expose wrongs; it recruits you into war. It doesn't seek truth; it seeks division. And it always demands you take a side.

Absalom's mistake? He didn't simply address an issue; he hijacked it. He didn't just call out injustice; he used it as a weapon to justify his ambition. The spirit of accusation is never content with correction—it wants control. And control, cloaked in self-righteousness, will always lead to destruction.

And in the end? Absalom didn't find a throne or justice. He simply found death.

THE POWER OF A SHARED OFFENSE

Accusation rarely works alone. It spreads. It recruits. It doesn't just poison the accuser—it infects those who listen. How many times have you heard someone's grievance, their pain, their offense, and before long, it became your own? You weren't there. You didn't witness what happened. But the way it was told, the fire behind it, the raw emotion—it pulled you in. And suddenly, their battle became yours.

This is how division is born. This is how loyalty is stolen. One whispered offense at a time.

Absalom didn't just rebel—he built an army of the offended. He stood at the gates, speaking half-truths, fanning the flames of discontent. He didn't just recruit soldiers; he recruited hearts. He turned pain into a weapon, bitterness into a tool for harm, and whispers into war cries. And what about those who followed him? Sadly, they thought they were fighting for justice—but instead, they were marching toward destruction.

Please take a moment to pause and reflect: What if the story you're believing is only half the truth? Is it possible you've taken up an offense that isn't even yours to carry?

Here's the thing: Absalom's rebellion didn't end in victory. It ended with him hanging from a tree, pierced through the heart. A man who once had the favor of the king, the love of a father, and a future full of promise—undone by a lie he let fester.

THE COST OF ACCUSATION

Accusation is not merely an action—it's a spiritual force. It doesn't just turn people against each other; it steals destinies. It silences voices meant to bring truth, healing, and hope. It blinds people to grace and binds them to deception.

If you allow accusation to take root in your heart, it will change how you see everything. Friends become enemies. Leaders become villains. Differences become battle lines. And soon, the mission God gave you is abandoned—because you're too busy fighting a war He never called you to.

So ask yourself, "Am I being pulled into a battle that isn't mine? Is the offense I'm carrying leading me toward purpose or away from it? Is my heart aligned with truth, or am I reacting to pain?"

WHEN ACCUSATION COMES FOR YOU

But what happens when *you* become the target? What do you do when false accusations try to silence your voice?

David knew this pain well. He was the anointed king, yet he spent years running from Saul, enduring slander, betrayal, and rejection. And even after Saul was gone, the attacks didn't stop. His own son led a revolt against him.

Maybe you've been there—accused, misrepresented, slandered. Maybe people have believed lies about you. Has this ever happened to you? Perhaps you felt the weight of false narratives being spun about you, or the sting of betrayal from someone close to you. What about the frustration of being misunderstood?

It's important to remember this: You cannot control what people say about you. But what you can control is whether or not you allow their words to define you.

Jesus Himself was accused, mocked, and sentenced based on false accusations and lies. But He did not defend Himself in anger. Nor did He retaliate. He entrusted Himself to His Father—the One who judges justly. And because He endured the accusations, He secured the ultimate victory.

YOUR VOICE MATTERS

If the enemy can't destroy you, he'll try to silence you. He'll use accusation to make you doubt yourself, question your calling, and retreat in fear.

Don't let him.

Your voice is needed. Your testimony is powerful. Your mission is vital.

The spirit of accusation will try to tell you that you are disqualified, that you are not worthy to speak, that you should shrink back. But the Spirit of God declares the opposite.

Rise up. Speak truth. Refuse to be silenced.

The enemy's ultimate goal is not just to accuse—it's to destroy. He doesn't just want to steal your confidence; he wants to steal your calling. He doesn't just want to silence your voice; he wants to erase your impact.

But accusation has no power over a surrendered life.

David didn't fight Absalom with slander. He didn't engage in the same tactics his son used against him. He entrusted his cause to God, and in the end, it was God who brought justice.

The same will be true for you. Stand firm. Let God defend you. And never, ever let accusation steal your voice.

CHAPTER 6

THE HIDDEN AGENDA BEHIND ACCUSATION

The truly mature and godly have the most sensitive awareness of
their sins, and are the humblest before God because of it.
—JOHN MACARTHUR

THE CROSS OF Jesus stands in vivid contrast to envy and selfish ambition. Where Christ gave His life to redeem, the spirit of accusation seeks to destroy. And behind many accusations lies a hidden force, one that has existed since the beginning: envy.

Accusation does not always arise from a pursuit of truth or justice. More often than not, it is rooted in something far more sinister: the resentment of another person's favor, success, or righteousness. When people give themselves over to the spirit of accusation, they often believe they are serving a higher purpose. In reality, they are being driven by the very envy and selfish ambition that James warns will lead to disorder and every evil practice.

> For where you have envy and selfish ambition, there you find disorder and every evil practice.
> —JAMES 3:16

JEALOUSY, ACCUSATION, AND THE LION'S DEN

The story of Daniel provides one of the clearest examples of how accusation is often fueled by jealousy. Daniel was blameless, faithful, and trustworthy. His wisdom and integrity brought him favor in the kingdom of Babylon, earning him the king's trust. But this very favor made him a prime target.

Intimidated, Daniel's enemies searched for any fault they could find in him—but they found none. To their dismay, his character was beyond reproach, and his work was excellent. They decided that the only way to bring him down was to manipulate the law itself. They couldn't care less about justice; their goal was to destroy Daniel.

To that end, they convinced King Darius to sign a decree that no one could pray to any god except the king himself. They knew exactly what they were doing—because they were confident that Daniel's unwavering faith in God would no doubt cause him to break the law.

And they were right. Daniel did not waver. He continued to pray as he always had. And when he did, his enemies pounced—dragging him before the king, with their accusations in hand. Darius, who was bound by his own decree, reluctantly sentenced Daniel to the lions' den.

The reality is that this was never about righteousness. It was about power. It was about taking down a man whose excellence and favor exposed their own corruption. Jealousy is not content with mere opposition; it seeks annihilation. Daniel's accusers weren't satisfied with tarnishing his reputation. They wanted him gone. But God had the final word.

THE STRATEGY OF THE ACCUSER

Jealousy and accusation most often go hand in hand. They are the weapons of the insecure—the tools people reach for when they'd rather tear someone down than face what they need to build in themselves.

When people see God's favor on your life, they have two choices—they can celebrate it, or they can attack it. The ones who are confident in their own calling? They'll cheer you on. But the ones wrestling with insecurity or comparison? They'll see your success as a threat. And instead of rising, they'll try to tear you down.

The enemy knows this tactic well. He doesn't always come at you head-on—sometimes he just turns others against you. He whispers in their ears, fuels their doubt, stirs up old wounds, and convinces them that your breakthrough somehow takes something away from them. Before you know it, they're criticizing you—not because you did anything wrong but because you remind them of everything they haven't yet dealt with.

Have you ever felt that? That moment when your obedience made others uncomfortable? When your favor stirred up resentment—or maybe not-so-silent opposition? It's not always about what you do. Sometimes, it's just about *who you are*.

Daniel's story reminds us of this. He wasn't accused because he failed—he was accused because he stood out. Because he walked in excellence. Because his life carried weight. And the same might be true for you.

STANDING IN THE FIRE

Daniel's story could have ended in death. But thankfully, God does not abandon His own. He is full of mercy and love. I've often wondered what Daniel was thinking when he was heading to the lions' den. Was it fear? Anguish? Or was it faith that God would pull him through—as only He can? I know what I would have been thinking. Let me be very real: I would have thought that this was not fair. I would have thought God had abandoned me. I want to get to a place in my life where I see every "lion's den" as a divine appointment to see God show Himself strong and mighty. I want to get more excited the more difficult and challenging life gets.

Daniel was indeed facing a very real danger. The lions were real—and likely hungry. But as real as the threat was, so was the God who shut the lions' mouths. Daniel stood firm in the face of the accuser and moved forward in faith, grounded in his convictions.

So while the enemy may plot and the jealous may scheme—God still holds the final verdict.

Tests will come. You will have moments when you are forced to decide: Do you fear the lions, or do you trust the Lion of Judah to make a way where there seems to be no way? Yes, the world will pressure you to bow, to compromise, and to conform. The accusers will watch—waiting for your downfall. But faith refuses to yield. Faith stands tall, believing that even in the face of destruction, God is sovereign.

Jealousy and accusation may throw you into the den. But faith will bring you out.

Because here's the thing: Daniel wasn't just delivered from the lions—he was delivered long before that. He was delivered in his heart and mind the moment he chose to stay faithful, no matter the cost.

THE DANGER OF FALSE ACCUSATION

> At the king's command, the men who had falsely accused Daniel were brought in and thrown into the lions' den, along with their wives and children. And before they reached the floor of the den, the lions overpowered them and crushed all their bones.
>
> —Daniel 6:24

Daniel's accusers learned the hard way that the spirit of accusation doesn't stop with the guilty—it devours everything in its path. And here's the thing: Most accusers don't see it that way. They think they are serving a greater good. They've convinced themselves that their words are righteous and their actions are justified. But in the end, the very trap these accusers set for Daniel became their own downfall.

That's the danger of false accusation. It may feel holy in the moment. It may even feel *necessary*. But eventually, it leads to a path of destruction. And it rarely travels alone. Accusation breeds more accusation, pulling others into its grasp. Those who give themselves over to it usually pull others in—seeking validation, gathering allies, trying to build their case. The more voices they enlist, the more confident they feel in their cause.

But here's what we have to remember: Numbers don't determine truth, and consensus doesn't equal righteousness.

Daniel's story reveals a sobering reality: The cost of false accusation is high. It doesn't just harm the accused—it brings ruin to the accuser. And in trying to shut Daniel down, trying to draw attention away from God Almighty, they ended up doing the opposite. God was glorified all the more. Their wickedness was exposed. Their plan backfired.

Because the truth always rises. And so do God's people.

CHOOSING A DIFFERENT PATH

So where does this leave us? I believe this understanding invites us to ask some hard heart-level questions: Do I celebrate others' success—or do I secretly resent it? Do I allow envy to shape my words, my tone, my posture? Have I ever jumped into an accusation without knowing the full story?

We have to be vigilant. The spirit of accusation is subtle. It doesn't show up waving red flags. It disguises itself as justice, as discernment, as righteous anger. The problem is, underneath it all, it's fueled by envy and selfish ambition. And its agenda is always the same: to divide, to control, to destroy. We must reject it—every time.

So what is the antidote? Gratitude. And gratitude is a choice. It won't always feel natural. But it's always powerful. Instead of tearing others down—lift them up. Instead of listening to the lies of the enemy—tune your ear to the voice of God. It may feel awkward at first. It may even feel like you're forcing it. But trust this: God is gracious. And He always meets us when we resist the pull of accusation and choose gratitude instead.

Will jealousy and accusation disappear completely? Probably not. But you don't have to partner with them. You can choose, daily, to walk a different path. A path marked by honor, integrity, and love. This is what we see reflected in Daniel's story. The accusations were fierce. The opposition was powerful. But God showed up in greater measure. And as you stand firm in Him, no lion, no scheme, no accusation can prevail.

In the end, as we choose gratitude, envy won't win. Ambition won't win. Accusation won't win. God wins.

CHAPTER 7

THE ENEMY OF GOD'S WORK

The man who has God for his treasure has all things in One.
—A. W. TOZER

IN THE MIDST of accusation the presence of Jesus is needed the most. And in the midst of walking in obedience to God's call, you can expect the attacks to come. You're not crazy. You're not imagining it. When God is moving, opposition is not far behind. This is the price of being used greatly by God.

Take Nehemiah. When he set out to rebuild the walls of Jerusalem, he wasn't just restoring broken stones—he was reviving a people, a calling, and a promise. But wherever God is at work, the enemy is plotting. Opposition arose in the form of Sanballat, Tobiah, and Geshem, men who saw Nehemiah not as a leader, but as a threat (Neh. 2:17–19).

These men didn't attack him with weapons. They came with words. They hurled accusations at him of seeking power, rebelling against the king, and having selfish motives. They twisted his motives, stirred up rumors, and crafted narratives designed to intimidate, discredit, and manipulate. Why? Because when the enemy can't stop the work of God by force, he'll try to stop it with fear.

ACCUSATION: THE WEAPON OF THOSE INSECURE ABOUT THEIR CALLING

The enemy's playbook has never changed. When he can't shut down God's plans, he goes after the person carrying them. Nehemiah didn't just face opposition—he faced a targeted, relentless assault on his character.

Sound familiar? Maybe you've been there. You said yes to God, and suddenly, the arrows started flying. False assumptions. Character attacks. Gossip disguised as concern. Misunderstandings that spread like wildfire. And the harder you tried to stay focused, the louder the noise became.

Why? Because accusation is Satan's most effective weapon against forward movement. And it's often launched not with swords, but with suspicion.

False accusations aren't rooted in truth—they are rooted in fear. They're fueled by insecurity and often come from people who feel threatened by what God is doing in you. When others don't understand the vision God has given you, they assume the worst. When they can't explain your favor, they call it ambition. When they see your progress, they try to stop it. The enemy uses insecurity as a breeding ground for slander.

REFUSING TO BE DISTRACTED

What I appreciate most about Nehemiah is that he didn't take the bait. The attacks on his life weren't subtle. His enemies sent messages, spread rumors, and tried to manipulate him into stopping the work.

In Nehemiah 6:5–9 (emphasis added), we see just how relentless they were:

> Then, the fifth time, Sanballat sent his aide to me with the same message, and in his hand was an unsealed letter in which was written: "It is reported among the nations—and Geshem says it is true—that you and the Jews are plotting to revolt, and therefore you are building the wall. Moreover, according to these reports you are about to become their king and have even appointed prophets to make this proclamation about you in Jerusalem: 'There is a king in Judah!' Now this report will get back to the king; so come, let us meet together."
>
> I sent him this reply: "Nothing like what you are saying is happening; you are just making it up out of your head."
>
> They were all trying to frighten us, thinking, "Their hands will get too weak for the work, and it will not be completed."
>
> *But I prayed, "Now strengthen my hands."*

The enemy's goal is always the same: to make your hands weak so that the work stops. Satan doesn't need to destroy you—he just needs to distract you. If he can keep you tangled in the web of defending yourself, proving your innocence, and managing the opinions of others, he wins.

Nehemiah shows us the right response: He didn't waste time arguing. He didn't call a meeting to set the record straight. He didn't let fear or false accusations slow him down. Instead, he prayed, "Now strengthen my hands."

And that's my prayer for you as you read this book—that in the face of accusation, God would strengthen your hands. That you would stay focused and finish the work He has called you to do.

THEY DID NOT START YOU. THEY CANNOT STOP YOU.

Let's get something straight—especially if you're feeling the immense weight of the fight as some of you are feeling this very moment: The people coming against you didn't breathe life into your purpose...so they can't shut it down. They didn't call you, they didn't anoint you, and they don't get the final say. Their opinions? Irrelevant. Their resistance? Powerless. The assignment for your life was forged by God, and no amount of noise or opposition can cancel what heaven has already declared. So rise up and lock in.

One of the biggest mistakes we make when faced with accusation is forgetting who called us. When God initiates something in your life, only He can complete it. The voices of opposition didn't ignite your mission—so they can't extinguish it either. Nehemiah

28 | TIME TO RISE

had to make peace with this. He had to reach a point where he was no longer concerned with what others thought; he had to remain focused on obedience. The only thing that mattered was what God had asked him to do.

The thing with accusation is this: It doesn't usually stop you externally first. It works from the inside out. The real battle isn't in the rumors or the lies—it's in whether or not you allow them to take root in your heart. The moment you start believing the accusations, you've already lost. When the enemy convinces you to lay down your calling before you've even stepped into it fully.

Nehemiah gives a powerful road map for facing false accusation. He did three things that, if we do them too, will keep us rooted in truth:

1. **He prayed for strength.** He didn't look for validation. He didn't go on defense. He simply asked God for strength. When you're under attack, don't pray for revenge—pray for endurance.

2. **He refused distraction. He didn't answer every lie or try to defend his reputation.** He stayed focused on the wall. You don't need to vindicate yourself when God already knows the truth.

3. **He remained focused on the assignment.** Nehemiah just kept building. He didn't stall out or change direction. He remained focused on the wall until he was finished. Because the work matters more than the whisper of doubt.

STAY ON THE WALL

Nehemiah never stopped building. His enemies tried everything—rumors, letters, threats—but he refused to come down. He didn't descend into arguments or defend himself against false claims. Instead, he declared, "I am doing a great work, so that I cannot come down" (Neh. 6:3, NKJV).

That line isn't just a clever comeback. It's a posture of the heart. It's what it sounds like when someone refuses to let accusation steal their focus. The enemy wants to get you so caught up in proving yourself that you stop pursuing your purpose. But you don't have time to entertain distractions when God has called you to build.

Here's what Nehemiah understood: You don't owe everyone an explanation. Not every critic needs a reply. Not every rumor deserves your time. You don't need to vindicate yourself when God has already called you. Stay on the wall.

This is the moment where many people give up—not because they're out of strength, but because they're out of focus. If the enemy can't stop your mission, he'll try to derail your attention. That is why this decision matters.

We often waste energy trying to convince people of our integrity when the truth is, their minds are already made up. You cannot reason with someone committed to misunderstanding you. Nehemiah understood this and made a decision that changed everything—he kept building.

Your destiny is too valuable to be sidetracked by the opinions of those who never supported you in the first place. Remember, the critics didn't start your calling—so they can't stop it either. If the enemy can't stop the work of God, he will try to stop the worker. His tactics remain the same: fear, slander, intimidation. But the strategy to overcome remains the same too: faith, focus, and perseverance.

So let the accusations come. Keep building anyway. Let the voices rage. Because in the end, when the wall is finished and the dust settles, it will be obvious who had God's hand on them all along.

And in the end, Nehemiah's faithfulness paid off. The wall was completed in just fifty-two days—despite all the opposition. And what happened to the accusers? They were humiliated. Nehemiah 6:16 says,

> When all our enemies heard about this, all the surrounding nations were afraid and lost their self-confidence, because they realized that this work had been done with the help of our God.

The very people who tried to discredit Nehemiah had to acknowledge that God's hand was on him. The same will happen for you. Your accusers may talk, plot, and attempt to derail you. But if you stay faithful, your work will speak for itself. The voices will fade, but your fruit will remain. Truth always has the last word.

KEEP BUILDING

The enemy will always oppose what God is doing through you. That's a given. But when accusation comes, you have a choice: descend into distraction or stay on the wall and finish the work.

Don't let fear dictate your focus. Don't let accusation steal your energy. Don't let the enemy convince you to abandon what God has called you to build.

Because in the end, your work is bigger than their words. Keep building.

CHAPTER 8

JESUS AND THE SPIRIT OF ACCUSATION

The vision is JESUS—obsessively, dangerously, undeniably Jesus.
—Pete Greig

A RESURGENCE IS HAPPENING. A revolt of another kind. People are waking up to the reality that the Jesus they hear snippets about on Sundays is not the Jesus who is returning for His bride. They're done with the spiritual hospice care the Sunday club has provided. They're tired of the saline drip they've been given—just enough to survive, never enough to revive. They are desperate for the tsunami of Jesus.

This is a turning point.

Because here's the thing—if we're honest, the only reason we keep believing the lies that keep us bound in our graveclothes like Lazarus, or the only reason we could possibly feel compelled to fire off words as virtual spears like a mad King Saul throwing them at a worshipping David, is this: We've grown disconnected from our first love.

A belief is a terrible substitute for an experience. Jesus—the Galilean God-man with eyes of fire—invites you, right now, to feel what He feels, know what He knows, and think what He thinks.

THE CROSSROADS OF WANT AND NEED

Pause here. Ask yourself this: "What if what I want and what I need are actually two completely different things?" What if you want vindication—but He knows you need to bear His reproach? What if there's a deep work He desires to do in you—and there is no other way forward except through your own personal crucifixion?

He knows what it is like to be betrayed, hurt, accused, despised, rejected, depressed, anxious, pained, grieved, tired, hungry, and forgotten. He understands every human agony. And yet—He remained sinless. That's the Lamb we follow. That's the One who leads us not away from pain but through it. And this is the invitation: to walk the path of the Lamb who was slain.

What if—just for a moment—He is drawing you into a place where you can minister to His heart? What if He's calling His bride, His shepherds, and His friends into a garden—a garden filled with both roses and thorns? A place of solitude, where the mysteries of all time can be revealed?

ACCUSED FOR THE COMPANY HE KEPT

Jesus was accused of being a drunkard—not because He partied with sinners but because He refused to avoid them. He was present where the religious elite refused to go. He sat

Jesus and the Spirit of Accusation | 31

at tables they considered defiled. And the accusations? They were strategic. They weren't about justice—they were about discrediting Him.

And isn't that still happening today?

One way you can spot accusation in the body of Christ is this: when someone tries to accuse you of sin because of whom you choose as friends. Accusers want to dictate the terms of your contact list. They want to limit your interaction to their approved list of "safe" or "socially acceptable" sinners.

Jesus was also accused of colluding with demons. They claimed the only reason He could cast out demons was due to Him being under demonic influence. Pause and let that sink in. The religious crowd accused the Son of God of being in league with hell.

And that same spirit is alive today. We see it rise up in subtle, insidious ways—especially in how some try to discredit the supernatural or attack deliverance ministries. It reframes the miraculous as being manipulative. And those who speak against it often don't even realize they are aligning with the same spirit that once stood opposed to Jesus Himself.

THE FREEDOM OF FORGIVEN PEOPLE

Here's the truth: When we recognize the depth of our own personal sin and brokenness—and realize that Jesus has completely forgiven us and called us sons and daughters—we no longer have time to focus on the sins and failings of others. Every second spent in that effort is a second not spent in extravagant devotion to Jesus.

Basilea Schlink wrote in *Repentance: The Joy-Filled Life*:

> Sinners with broken and contrite hearts have but one desire. Filled with thanksgiving, they want to love Him who loved them so much. They are so overwhelmed that He has borne their sins and carried them away.
>
> When we receive forgiveness, our hearts are so filled with joy that we cannot help but love Him with a lavish love. We cannot help but give our lives to Him who gave His life for us and set us free from the prison of sin. We cannot stop thanking Him, and so we do everything possible to bring Him joy and to bestow our gifts upon Him, serving Him with all our talents and strength.
>
> And this is what heaven is all about: centering upon Jesus and loving Him above all else.[1]

When we have truly encountered Jesus, we don't have time to waste in the trenches of gossip and accusation. We are consumed by His love, overwhelmed by His grace, and undone by His great mercy. The spirit of accusation loses its grip when we fix our eyes on the One who first loved us.

THE OVERCOMERS—LAMBS WITH THE FACES OF LIONS

I recently had a conversation with the daughter of one of the most well-known preachers of a generation, and she shared with me something profound: She has never heard her dad talk negatively about another minister of the gospel. Not once. Maybe, just maybe, the reason why God uses some people more than others is because they choose to be radically different from almost everybody else. Maybe it is because they choose the way of Jesus. We overcome the spirit of accusation—both internally and externally—by following the Lamb wherever He goes. And when we do, something supernatural happens: We become lambs with the faces of lions. We are baptized with liquid ferocity, ready to rise as the redeemed.

I don't know what exactly is missing in your life right now. I don't know what has held you back in the past or what an extraordinary life looks like for you. But here's what I do know: The shift that changed everything for me was realizing I could stop believing the lies and, from this day forward, make loving Jesus my ultimate goal.

In my personal life, my business, my politics, my ultrarunning, my parenting, my marriage, and my ministry—the foundation of it all is this: loving Jesus.

So let me ask you—what would your life look like if you made that same shift? What would change if you were consumed by love? How would you live, speak, respond, if His voice became the loudest one in your life?

This is the antidote to accusation. Not defending yourself. Not proving your worth. Not retaliating against those who misunderstand you. Just loving Jesus with everything in you—and trusting Him to handle the rest.

Because in the end, it won't matter who accused you. It won't matter what was said. It won't even matter what you lost along the way. The only things that will remain are these three questions: Did you love Him? Did you follow Him? Did you stay faithful to the end?

The Lamb among wolves was never afraid of the accusations hurled at Him. He just kept loving. He kept healing. He kept restoring. And in the end, He was vindicated by resurrection power.

And so will you be.

CHAPTER 9

THE CHEAP SEATS BELONG TO THE CRITICS

It is not the critic who counts; not the man who points out how the strong man stumbles, or where the doer of deeds could have done them better. The credit belongs to the man who is actually in the arena, whose face is marred by dust and sweat and blood.
—THEODORE ROOSEVELT

THERE WILL ALWAYS be critics. They sit in the cheap seats, far removed from the blood, sweat, and sacrifice required to step into the arena. Their voices ring louder than the rest. Their judgments are harsh. And their courage—nonexistent. They are spectators, those who sit on the sidelines and never participate, yet freely offer opinions on battles they've never fought. They mock the wounds they've never endured and condemn efforts they've never dared to make themselves.

These words above, drawn from Teddy Roosevelt's famous quote, remind us that history does not actually remember the critic. So who does it remember? Those who fight. The risk takers. The ones who rise and fall—and rise again. The critics? Well, they fade off into irrelevance, their voices carried away like dust in the wind.

But make no mistake—criticism still has power. If you allow it, the words of the critic can steal your courage, paralyze your purpose, and keep you sitting on the sidelines of your own destiny. The enemy doesn't need to destroy you if he can simply make you afraid to act.

THE SPIRIT OF ACCUSATION

Criticism isn't always just an opinion. Sometimes it's an assignment. The enemy thrives on accusation—it's his native language. As we've discussed throughout this book, Revelation 12:10 calls him "the accuser of our brethren" (NKJV). He doesn't just accuse you before God—he accuses you to yourself, to others, and often *through* others.

And many times those "others" are well-meaning. They're not necessarily evil or scheming. They've likely, and unknowingly, come into agreement with the wrong voice. Yet through them the enemy whispers doubt. And when we repeat those whispers aloud, the damage multiplies.

You've heard the voice: "Who do you think you are?" "You'll never succeed." "You're not qualified." "You're going to fail, and everyone will see it." "You are a terrible _____ (fill in the blank)."

These lies aren't just about insecurity—they're part of the demonic strategy to stop your forward motion. The enemy doesn't need to blow up your life—he just needs to

33

keep you quiet. Keep you on the sidelines of your own destiny long enough that he can tangle you up in second-guessing and shame. It's there—in that hesitation and heaviness—that the work God has called you to never even gets off the ground.

And here's the irony: The ones doing the accusing are rarely doing anything themselves. They're not even in the arena. They're not taking any risks. They're not the ones paying the price for obedience. They just want to make sure you never take a swing that they weren't brave enough to try for themselves.

But let me remind you: The critics don't define you. God does. They didn't start your calling—so they don't get to stop it either.

THE ONE IN THE ARENA

So what is the arena, exactly? The arena is our place of struggle. It's where our very real battles are fought—and our victories are won. It's the arena of life. It's the place where the dreamers dream, the builders build, the warriors fight, and the pioneers gather.

It's also where mistakes happen. The learning curve of trial and error lives here. It's where our plans don't always work out the way we once hoped. In the arena, failure isn't just possible—it's inevitable. But it's also where transformation takes place. Because the one who steps into the arena—regardless of the outcome—will always come out stronger and more resilient than the one who stands on the sidelines and spectates.

And the greatest example of someone living in the arena? Jesus.

He wasn't preaching from the sidelines or shouting commands from a distance. No—He walked among the broken. He touched those the world deemed untouchable. He stood firmly against the religious leaders who aimed to silence Him completely.

And what about His critics? They attacked Him relentlessly. Calling Him a blasphemer. They falsely accused Him of being a drunkard. They twisted His friendship with sinners into something scandalous. They nailed him to a cross. Their accusations crucified Him.

But the best news of all? The critics didn't have the final say. No. Because the grave ended up empty. Victory belonged to the Lord. And because of Him, it belongs to us too.

So expect this: The moment you decide to step into the arena, the critics will come. Expect opposition. Expect misunderstandings. Expect betrayal. Expect people to talk. But also expect this—they don't matter. Their opinions need not hold any weight. Their words do not dictate your destiny.

Look at history. Every great leader, every innovator, every world changer had critics. Jesus had them. Paul had them. Martin Luther had them. William Wilberforce had them. Abraham Lincoln had them. Every person who ever did something worth remembering had a chorus of voices telling them they couldn't, shouldn't, or wouldn't succeed.

And yet—they did.

YOUR ASSIGNMENT

Be encouraged today: Your job is not to silence the critics. Your job is to ignore them.

Your focus belongs on the mission God has placed before you. Keep your eyes fixed on the author and finisher of your faith. Keep your feet moving, even when doubt tries to paralyze you. Keep your heart guarded, knowing your identity is secure in Christ—not in the approval of man.

Don't waste your energy defending yourself to those who were never meant to—nor could they ever—understand your calling. Become obsessed with the Crucified One and allow the fear of criticism to fall away. No longer should it rob you of the joy of your obedience. No longer do you need to let the voice of the enemy be louder than the voice of your Father.

My advice: Own your story. Refuse to defend it.

This may sound conflicting—but it's not.

When you feel yourself falling, remember to fall forward. If you feel like you're failing, fail while daring greatly. If you're struggling, struggle with purpose. But whatever you do—stay in the arena.

Because in the end, the critics will fade. The cheap seats will empty.

And the only thing that will matter is this:

You fought the good fight. You finished the race. You kept the faith.

CHAPTER 10

THE POWER OF WORDS: PRINCIPLES FOR LIFE AND VICTORY

When you are deeply hurt, no person on this earth can shut out the inner-most fears and deepest agonies....Only God can shut out the waves of depression and feelings of loneliness and failure that come over you.
—David Wilkerson

Words hold an incredible power. They have the power to build up or to tear down, to bring life or cause destruction. Scripture repeatedly reminds us of the significance of our words—they shape our reality. Our words influence others, and ultimately, they can determine the course of our lives. Not just the words we speak aloud, but also the words we whisper to ourselves in silence. The thoughts we ruminate on. The truths we cling to—or the lies we let take root. I don't know about you, but as a runner, I've learned to rely on the words I declare over myself. They keep me going. They carry me forward—especially when I'm quite literally running the race before me, mile after mile. Words give me endurance and enable me to persevere.

I want to share ten key principles I have discovered in Scripture about the power of our words—how they can be used to live a godly life and walk (or run) in the victory Jesus secured for us on the cross. I am referring to spoken words, words in our mind and hearts, words sent through text, email, and social media. All words.

Please look carefully at these principles. They are not a call to be silent or retreat in the face of lies. They are a call to move forward in the Spirit of the Lord, following the pattern God set in Genesis—speaking light into the darkness.

PRINCIPLE 1: WORDS CARRY LIFE OR DEATH

Death and life are in the power of the tongue, and those who love it will eat its fruit.

—Proverbs 18:21, nkjv

Let's be honest—every word we speak carries weight. Whether we realize it or not, we're planting seeds with what we say. And what we sow, we're also going to reap. Speak life, and you'll harvest peace. Speak doubt, negativity, or slander, and you'll eventually see destruction show up in your life—or someone else's. So before you allow the words to leave your lips, pause and ask, "Is this bringing life, or is it bringing death?"

PRINCIPLE 2: OUR WORDS WILL JUDGE US

> But I tell you that everyone will have to give account on the day of judgment for every empty word they have spoken. For by your words you will be acquitted, and by your words you will be condemned.
>
> —Matthew 12:36–37

This one should stop us in our tracks. Jesus said every careless word—every cutting joke, flippant comment, or passive-aggressive jab—will be brought into account. That's a sobering thought. It means our words aren't just temporary; they echo into eternity. So let's slow down and speak like heaven is listening. Speaking with intentionality and wisdom is crucial, as our words reflect the condition of our hearts and our relationship with God.

PRINCIPLE 3: WORDS HAVE THE POWER TO BUILD OR DESTROY

> Likewise, the tongue is a small part of the body, but it makes great boasts. Consider what a great forest is set on fire by a small spark. The tongue also is a fire, a world of evil among the parts of the body.
>
> —James 3:5–6

You know how just one spark can start a wildfire? That's how our words work. One sentence can either spark peace or burn everything down. And it doesn't take a loud voice to do damage—sometimes, it's the subtle sarcasm or quiet criticism that does the most harm. But the flip side? One word of love or truth can shift the atmosphere. So use your words to build, not burn.

PRINCIPLE 4: OUR WORDS SHOULD HEAL, NOT HURT

> The soothing tongue is a tree of life, but a perverse tongue crushes the spirit.
>
> —Proverbs 15:4

We all know what it feels like to be lifted up by someone's words—and we all know what it feels like to be crushed by them too. Your words can be a safe place for someone's heart, or they can be what finally breaks them. So be intentional. Choose to be a source of healing by speaking words that offer nourishment, encouragement, and strength.

PRINCIPLE 5: SPEAK TO BUILD OTHERS UP

> Do not let any unwholesome talk come out of your mouths, but only what is helpful for building others up according to their needs, that it may benefit those who listen.
>
> —Ephesians 4:29

38 | TIME TO RISE

It's all too easy to slip into venting, complaining, or gossip when we feel frustrated or justified. But as Paul reminds us in Ephesians 4:29, let us be a people who speak only what is helpful. If our words aren't helping someone grow, why say them? Are we bringing encouragement? If your speech is filled with negativity, ask the Holy Spirit to reshape your vocabulary so your default becomes one of encouragement rather than critique.

PRINCIPLE 6: WORDS SHOULD BE FULL OF GRACE AND WISDOM

Let your conversation be always full of grace, seasoned with salt, so that you may know how to answer everyone.

—COLOSSIANS 4:6

Grace doesn't mean sugarcoating the truth—it means we speak the truth in love. Salt adds flavor, but it also preserves. Our words should aim to do both—make the truth easier to receive and carry lasting value. Before you jump into a difficult conversation, take a breath. Pray. And speak with grace and wisdom.

PRINCIPLE 7: RECKLESS WORDS CAUSE DAMAGE

The words of the reckless pierce like swords, but the tongue of the wise brings healing.

—PROVERBS 12:18

We've all been on both sides of this. We've felt the sting of someone else's reckless words—and likely been the one who caused the wound too. Often it happens in the heat of the moment, or through something small we didn't think much of. But either way, the impact lasts. So let's be the ones who aim for healing, not harm.

PRINCIPLE 8: GUARD YOUR MOUTH

Set a guard over my mouth, LORD; keep watch over the door of my lips.

—PSALM 141:3

This is one of my favorite prayers. It's simple, honest, and necessary. Because let's face it—sometimes our mouths want to run ahead of our spirits. David's prayer should become our daily request. Asking God to help us guard our words isn't weakness—it's wisdom. Let your words be a reflection of Christ in you by inviting the Holy Spirit into every conversation.

PRINCIPLE 9: SPEAK KIND AND HEALING WORDS

Gracious words are a honeycomb, sweet to the soul and healing to the bones.

—PROVERBS 16:24

Words can literally feel like honey. You've felt it when someone spoke something that lifted the heaviness right off your chest. You've probably delivered that kind of healing to someone else too. Kindness doesn't just sound nice, it does something deep in the soul. Let's be generous in choosing words that bring sweetness and healing.

PRINCIPLE 10: WORDS REVEAL THE HEART

> A good man brings good things out of the good stored up in his heart, and an evil man brings evil things out of the evil stored up in his heart. For the mouth speaks what the heart is full of.
>
> —Luke 6:45

If you want to know what's really going on inside someone, listen to how they talk. And if you're wondering what's going on in your own heart—listen to your own words. They'll tell you the truth. When bitterness or sarcasm starts slipping out, it's often a sign something in us still needs healing. Our words are a direct reflection of our inner lives. So instead of just filtering our speech—let's invite God to transform our hearts.

Words aren't just sound waves—they're spiritual seeds. Words are more than sounds—they are tools that shape reality. The Bible teaches us that words create, heal, and influence the world around us.

To walk in victory, we must do the following: Speak life—not death. Build up rather than tear down. Speak with purpose. Speak with power. Let your words carry the love of Jesus—seasoned with truth and saturated in the authority given to us by God Almighty.

This is a journey, but let us daily aim to grow in our understanding of the power of our words. Let's position ourselves for victory by pausing before we speak—especially in moments of confrontation. Because your words don't just reveal who you are. They help shape who you—and the people around you—are becoming.

Let this be a call to rise, speak with purpose, and use your words as a force for good in the world. Just as Jesus spoke clearly and loudly, "Lazarus, come forth," I believe He is speaking to you right now as you read this to "come forth." The real you. The you He has destined and called you to be.

PART II

THE GIFT OF PERCEPTION—NAVIGATING TRUTH AND DECEPTION

AT TWENTY-SEVEN YEARS old, I should have been thriving. I was in seminary, deep in ministry, living the life I had always imagined. On the outside, everything looked right. But on the inside? I was dying.

I had reached the point of no return spiritually. I wasn't running from God—I was just numb. I had lost my hunger, lost my fire, lost the edge that once made me pursue Him at all costs. I was on autopilot, going through the motions, living a life that felt like a hollow shell. And I knew something had to change.

Then, in the middle of a winter class on spiritual formation, God shattered my complacency.

That day, I watched a video about revival at First Baptist Church of Springdale, Arkansas, in 1995. Their pastor, Dr. Ronnie Floyd, had just finished a forty-day liquid fast and stood before his church as a different man.[1] The presence of God was on him in a way I had never seen before. It wasn't emotional hype. It wasn't human effort. It was raw, unshakable hunger for Jesus.

And in that moment, I knew—I had a choice.

I left class, walked straight to my wife, and said, "Tomorrow, I start a forty-day liquid fast." No hesitation. No second-guessing. Just desperation.

That fast changed my life. There are things God did in me during those forty days that are too sacred to even write about. It wasn't about discipline or willpower. It was about hunger—the kind of hunger that makes you leave everything behind. That moment in my life gave to me the greatest gift I could have been given. It changed the way I viewed everything. It changed my perspective. What we need to win against the spirit of accusation both internally and externally is perspective.

This next section deals with the gift of perception—how to navigate truth and deception.

bit.ly/4mxh0vo

CHAPTER 11

LIFE IS NOT WHAT HAPPENS TO US

The last of the human freedoms: to choose one's attitude in any given set of circumstances, to choose one's own way.
—Viktor Frankl

THERE IS A quiet yet fierce strength found in perspective. It shapes our ability to respond proactively rather than reactively. I've found that living reactively gives too much weight to our emotions, our circumstances, and the words of others. We end up letting those things dictate how we feel—and how we respond. But as we embrace the perspective Jesus offers, we rise above the noise. We begin to see through the distractions. We learn to drown out the accusations.

Jesus, through His life, shows us how to rise above it all—and ignore the opinions of man. He perfectly modeled the way forward. He wasn't swayed by public opinion or shaken by false accusations. Instead, He lived connected to the heart of the Father. And that's what He's inviting us into now. God is not looking for people who merely repeat what they've heard. He's seeking those who know His heart—and who trust His voice.

YOUR PERSPECTIVE SHAPES YOUR REALITY

Your life story changes once you realize *life is always happening FOR you, not TO you.*

— Tony Robbins[1]

Read that again. Slowly. Because this is one of the most powerful shifts you can make: You are not a victim of your circumstances—you are the author of your perspective.

Think about that. What you believe about your setbacks and suffering has the power to shape your future. Your perspective holds the key to walking in faith or in fear. It's the difference between confidence or insecurity. Between living in freedom—or staying stuck in bondage.

The enemy? He's after your mind. He wants you to believe your hardship *is* your identity. That your past defines your future. That your failure gets the final word. But as for Jesus—He's after your heart. He longs for you to see what He sees: that every setback is an invitation for growth. Every closed door is His protection. And every moment of pain? A stepping stone to something greater.

REFRAMING TRIALS AS OPPORTUNITIES

What if you stopped seeing your problems as barriers and started seeing them as gifts? What if that betrayal you experienced was actually a setup for a breakthrough? What if that loss you endured was clearing the way for new life? And what if that closed door was a reflection of God's mercy?

Think of Joseph. His brothers' betrayal could have defined him. He could have chosen bitterness. He could have lived for revenge. But instead, he embraced the bigger picture. He allowed God's perspective to reign in his life: "You intended to harm me, but God intended it for good to accomplish what is now being done, the saving of many lives" (Gen. 50:20).

Joseph let God reframe his pain—and that led to his promotion.

I have to wonder: How often do we forfeit what God is calling us into because we're unwilling to change our perspective? How many times do we allow offense to take root in our hearts, clouding the way we see God? That kind of distortion doesn't stop there—it spills into how we see others. And even how we see ourselves.

I believe accusation thrives in our hearts when our perspective is limited. When we believe only what we feel, rather than seeking to see what God is doing, we get trapped in a cycle of offense and bitterness. But when we pause and ask God for His vision—His eyes—and take a step back, letting Him redefine our reality? That's when we step into freedom. What if all the conflict we are facing right now is something made up in our heads because of the stories we tell ourselves?

ACCUSATION SEEKS TO CONTROL YOUR THOUGHTS

Let's discuss something we all face—those moments when accusation doesn't come for your name but comes for your mind.

Those given to accusation aim to impose their views as your views. They look to control the narrative. They have formed strong opinions—and they're determined to make you agree. They're not looking for feedback; they're looking for submission. To put it simply—they're picking a fight. And if you're not careful, these encounters will drain your energy and distract you from God's call on your life.

But this behavior is not a reflection of Christ.

Jesus does not impose—He invites. He calls you to see beyond the temporary by calling you higher.

This reminds me of Stephen from the book of Acts, the first martyr of the church. After being falsely accused and condemned, he was being stoned—but instead of giving in to fear or defeat, he looked up and saw heaven open. His eyes weren't fixed on his accusers; they were focused on Jesus. Stephen had a unique perspective—one not bound by the limitations of the flesh but anchored in eternity. And in that moment, instead of cursing those who were killing him, he prayed for them.

Now that is a powerful portrayal of the importance of a renewed perspective.

Today, let Stephen's story serve as an important reminder. Have you allowed

Life Is Not What Happens to Us | 45

accusations to consume you? Have you been replaying conversations in your mind? Rehearsing offenses? Dwelling on injustices? When we live this way, we give room for the enemy to control our thoughts. Don't give in. Fix your eyes on Jesus. Choose today—and each day forward—to see from His vantage point. When you do, everything shifts.

I must confess to you that I have all too often allowed perceived offenses and injustices to create anger and frustration in me that I took out on others. I am not proud of this but am just being real with you. I have allowed it to rob me of time and moments. Fixing our eyes on Jesus is not simply a clever mantra; it is the only way. It is warfare worship that leads us through the storms. We become all that God calls us to be not by avoiding the fire but rather by walking through it. Choosing a different perspective is a constant act of the heart, soul, mind, and strength within each of us. It is how we love Jesus practically.

So whose perspective will you choose? Jesus'—the lover of your soul? Or the accuser of the brethren's? The accuser says, "You are disqualified." Jesus says, "You are chosen." The accuser says, "You will never overcome this." Jesus says, "I have already overcome for you." The accuser says, "You should hold on to offense." Jesus says, "Forgive as I have forgiven you." Remember, the perspective you choose will shape your future.

Choosing to live from the perspective of the accuser means you will always see yourself as a victim. You'll easily find reasons to be offended, carrying the weight of bitterness around like a ball and chain. But choosing to live from the perspective of Jesus means those chains break. You will move forward in freedom. God's peace becomes your portion. And your confidence? Unshakable.

SHIFTING YOUR PERSPECTIVE DAILY

Shifting your perspective is not a onetime decision—it's a daily choice. Every day, the enemy presents you with opportunities to be offended, to react in anger, to dwell in fear. And every day, Jesus invites you to see differently. This is how we rise above the noise.

Jesus was falsely accused, misunderstood, rejected, and condemned. Yet He never allowed the voices of accusation to define Him. He stayed focused on His mission, unmoved by human opinion. And the same is true for us—when we know who we are in God, when we stand on the truth of His Word, accusation loses its grip.

So how do we make this shift daily? We fix our eyes on Jesus. Just as Stephen looked up in the midst of accusation, we must train our hearts to focus on Him rather than our circumstances. We speak truth over ourselves, rejecting the lies of the accuser and declaring what God says is true. We guard our thoughts, paying attention to what we dwell on. Are we replaying offenses—or meditating on God's promises? We pray for those who accuse us, knowing nothing silences accusation like blessing those who've wronged us. And we seek the bigger picture, asking God to show us how He's working in the midst of it all—because sometimes what looks like an attack is actually preparation.

The enemy's goal is to entangle you in offense and accusation, so you never step into the fullness of what God has for you. Not just offenses and accusations you face without and within, but also the offenses and accusations of others that we are tempted to pick up and carry. Again, the enemy wants to trap you. But when you shift your perspective—when you refuse to live from a place of reaction—you disarm the enemy's greatest weapon. So, the next time accusation comes, whether from the enemy, from others, or even from within, take a step back and ask, "Am I reacting, or am I choosing God's perspective? Am I allowing the enemy to control my emotions, or am I fixing my eyes on Jesus?"

When you change your perspective, you change your life. And when you choose to see through the lens of heaven, you rise above the noise, above the distractions, above the accusations. The choice is yours. What perspective will you live from today?

CHAPTER 12

WHY PEOPLE DO WHAT THEY DO

Slay the dragon in his lair before he comes to your village. If you run from the things you are afraid of, you run from what you need, in fact, to find.
—JORDAN B. PETERSON

HAVE YOU EVER found yourself wondering why people do what they do? More specifically, have you ever questioned why *you* do what you do? I know I have. The thing is, most people don't realize that a vast majority of their actions are subconscious. Our experiences shape our beliefs. Over time, we become conditioned. In my experience, one of the most powerful subconscious drivers we face is how we respond to negativity.

Left unchecked, negativity can spread faster than wildfire. It infiltrates our conversations, taints our perspective, and poisons our relationships. Just turn on the news—and you'll find negativity dominating the headlines. So I have to ask, Why are we so drawn to it? Why do we buy into the negative spin so quickly? Why is it so easily shared? In my research, I've found the answer is both physiological and spiritual.

THE PHYSIOLOGICAL PERSPECTIVE: HARDWIRED FOR SURVIVAL

Whether we realize it or not, our brains are designed to keep us safe, not necessarily to keep us joyful. This means we are naturally wired to detect threats. We are better at spotting danger than we are at discerning peace. Our instinct is for survival, which is not so great for spiritual growth.

Your brain is constantly scanning the environment for what's wrong, not what's right. That's why one negative comment can stick with you longer than ten compliments. It's why bad news pulls you in faster than a feel-good story. It's also why painful memories often feel sharper than happy ones. Psychologists call this *negativity bias*—the brain's tendency to give more attention and weight to negative experience than positive ones.[1]

Negativity bias explains why

- a single harsh word replays in your mind long after the conversation ends,
- one bad review can overshadow dozens of encouraging ones, and
- you remember the embarrassment from years past but forget the encouragement you received last week.

47

48 | TIME TO RISE

Social media, gossip, and accusation exploit this negativity bias. Think about it: When you hear about a scandal, or see a controversial headline, or witness someone being torn down, are you drawn to hearing more? This is because the more emotional the information is, the more compelled we feel to react to it.

And here's where it gets even deeper: Even when engaging in a negative activity such as doomscrolling, we are hit with a dopamine release.[2] That's right. Engaging in these matters causes a chemical reaction in your brain that rewards you with a tiny hit of pleasure. It's the same chemical involved in addiction. Unfortunately, engaging in too much of this can leave you feeling emptier than ever before.

Negativity may feel powerful in the moment, but it only deepens disconnection in the long run. But here's the good news: Just as the brain can be conditioned toward fear, it can also be renewed by truth (Rom. 12:2).

Negativity is not just a brain thing—it is a battle thing.

From the very beginning, we see the enemy using accusation to drive a wedge between God and His people. The serpent's words to Eve in the garden—"Did God really say...?" (Gen. 3:1)—were full of subtle accusation. That one question planted doubt in her heart and distorted how she saw God. And the enemy hasn't changed his tactics since.

Why does the enemy love negativity?

+ It creates division—"For where you have envy and selfish ambition, there you find disorder and every evil practice" (Jas. 3:16).

+ It diminishes faith—negativity fosters doubt, keeping people from trusting God's promises.

+ It distracts from purpose—the more focused we are on gossip, offense, and negativity, the less focused we are on our calling.

This is why negativity resonates so deeply. It's not just a chemical response; it's a spiritual assault. When we partner with that voice, we're not just expressing opinions—we're echoing the language of hell.

BREAKING FREE FROM THE NEGATIVITY TRAP

For us to rise above negativity, we must train our minds and guard our spirits. We don't merely slip in and out of negativity—we either resist it or partner with it. It takes intention. Scripture calls us to "take captive every thought to make it obedient to Christ" (2 Cor. 10:5). You have been given authority through Christ to interrupt unhealthy patterns, tear down toxic strongholds, and replace them with truth.

Here's how:

+ **Take control of your thoughts.** When negativity rises, don't let it pass through unchecked. Call it out and speak truth over it.

Why People Do What They Do | 49

- **Refuse to share what does not build up.** "Do not let any unwholesome talk come out of your mouths, but only what is helpful for building others up" (Eph. 4:29).

- **Ask yourself these questions before you speak or post:** Is this true? Is this helpful? Is this necessary?

Remember this and choose wisely: Negativity feeds our flesh, but truth feeds our spirits.

A few years ago, I had the privilege of being on my friend Jon Gordon's podcast while I was in the middle of running 153 consecutive marathons. Jon—a best-selling author and one of the clearest voices on the power of positivity—said something that stuck with me:

> We have the power to improve our lives, relationships, and teams by cultivating and experiencing more positive thoughts and emotions. We have the power to influence how we think and feel and thus influence the direction of our careers [and our lives].[3]

Let that sink in: You have power. You're not at the mercy of your emotions. You're not a victim of your past or the voices around you. You get to choose what kind of atmosphere you carry.

Side note: If you haven't read Jon's books or listened to his podcast, I highly recommend them. His insights carry what I believe are divine downloads—especially when it comes to leading with optimism and overcoming adversity with faith.

Have you ever considered what life could look like if you chose to focus on the positive instead of the negative? I'm not saying ignore the hard stuff or pretend it doesn't exist. But there's power in choosing to see what God is doing—even in the midst of difficulty. I am not just talking about the power of positivity. I am talking about the power of promise.

You were created to speak life. To walk in truth. And to reflect the voice of your Father. So the next time negativity comes knocking—don't answer. You can break the pattern today. Call out the lie and replace it with the truth. You've been given the authority; it's time to use it.

YOUR CHOICE: POSITIVE OR NEGATIVE?

If negativity is an addiction, then positivity is a discipline—a choice we make moment by moment.

- Negativity is quick to react, but positivity takes a breath and responds.
- Negativity tears down, but positivity builds up.
- Negativity fuels fear, but positivity stirs faith.

One is easy. The other is intentional.

50 | Time to Rise

Every day, you get to choose which voice you'll listen to. You decide whether you'll be a resounding voice of division or a carrier of the sound of truth.

So, the next time you feel the pull to dwell on wrong, pause and ask yourself, "Is this the story I want to tell?" Because the story you tell yourself becomes the life you live.

CHAPTER 13

THE SIX HUMAN NEEDS AND THE POWER OF ACCUSATION

All dysfunctional behaviors arise from the inability to consistently meet these core needs. But people's needs aren't just behind the bad decisions we make—they are also behind all of the great things humans accomplish. Understanding your own needs and psychology can not only help you avoid toxic behaviors and habits but can also help you achieve your goals.
—TONY ROBBINS

THE QUOTE ABOVE highlights Tony Robbins' teaching on the Six Human Needs.[1] These are core drivers that influence every one of us. These needs shape our decisions, stir our emotions, and even impact our relationships. When we feel unfulfilled in these areas, we are often looking for ways to fill the void—sometimes in destructive or misguided ways.

Whether we're seeking redemption, identity, or a sense of belonging, we can easily fall into the trap of accusation. Why? Because accusation offers us a false promise: that if we label others, or expose their flaws, we'll finally feel secure. But I have to tell you—it's a lie.

Let's take a closer look at each of these needs—and how accusation twists what God intended to be fulfilled in healthy, life-giving ways.

The Six Human Needs are these:

1. Certainty—the need for security and stability
2. Variety—the need for excitement and change
3. Significance—the need to feel important
4. Love & Connection—the need for deep relationships
5. Growth—the need to develop and improve
6. Contribution—the need to give and impact others[2]

Something we need to remember—an important truth we must consider—is that people will almost always sacrifice their own personal values as a means of meeting their needs, especially their top two: certainty and variety. Research shows that men are most often driven by the need for significance, while women are primarily driven by the need for certainty, which is most often met through a sense of safety.

With that in mind, I believe it's important to take a closer look at each of these six needs in greater depth to see how they connect to the spirit of accusation. As we do,

51

52 | Time to Rise

you'll begin to see how accusation subtly creeps in, offering a false sense of fulfilment in the very places where God intended us to experience true wholeness.

1. CERTAINTY: ACCUSATION CREATES FALSE SECURITY

We all long for a sense of safety—knowing that things are stable and under control. That's the very heart of certainty. We crave it. It's the need to feel secure and have some sense of predictability in the ever-changing world around us. And when this need goes unmet, we often become anxious—grasping for control anywhere we can find it.

This is where the spirit of accusation often sneaks in.

We want to feel like we understand the world—to know who the "good guys" and "bad guys" are. Accusation offers a false sense of security by labeling people as "right" or "wrong," "holy" or "heretical." It offers us neat little categories to place people in, which in turn makes us feel safe and in control.

The Pharisees in Jesus' time thrived on this kind of certainty. They were quick to accuse Him of blasphemy because His unpredictable nature disrupted their rigid system. Their rules brought them comfort—a sense of control—so even if it meant falsely condemning the true Son of God, they were okay with it.

Accusation might make us feel in control, but what it's actually doing is blinding us to the truth. It becomes an obsession. We convince ourselves that we must have certainty—no matter the cost.

But when that need is met by a counterfeit—accusation—we miss what God is actually doing. How do we miss it? Because we are too busy trying to fit Him into our preconceived categories.

2. VARIETY: ACCUSATION FUELS DRAMA AND EXCITEMENT

As much as we crave stability, we also need variety. It's the desire for change, excitement, and stimulation—something new to break up the routine. God wired us this way. Variety, in its healthiest form, invites us into creativity. It feels adventurous. It awakens possibility.

But when we're dissatisfied with life, we often go looking for stimulation in all the wrong places. That's where the spirit of accusation creeps in—offering just enough drama for us to feel alive.

Scandals, outrage, and controversy keep people hooked. Social media thrives on it. Accusation becomes an emotional roller coaster that keeps us engaged. Think about the times you've been pulled into online debates or controversies. There's an adrenaline rush in "exposing" someone's perceived wrongdoing. It pulls on our flesh and makes us feel powerful—or worse, purposeful.

But here's the truth: It's a counterfeit. Instead of finding healthy variety in adventure, creativity, spiritual growth, or God's presence, many stir up conflict just to break the monotony.

What if, instead of feeding on negativity, we sought our excitement in discovering more of God's presence—and His divine purpose for our lives? What if we let holy wonder lead us, instead of our perceived "righteous" outrage?

Accusation may offer us drama. But God offers us divine adventure.

3. SIGNIFICANCE: ACCUSATION CREATES AN ILLUSION OF IMPORTANCE

At the core of every human heart is the desire to matter. We want to be seen. We want to feel valued. This is the need to feel significant—the belief that our life has meaning, that we are important to someone, somewhere.

When that need goes unmet, we often try to fill the void with whatever gives us a sense of being "somebody." And that's where the spirit of accusation can be so deceptive.

Accusation offers a shortcut to significance. By pointing out someone else's flaws, we position ourselves as more insightful. A sense of self-righteousness rises within us. We might not say it outright, but the inner message is clear: "I am better than them. I see what others don't." It creates a false sense of superiority.

And while it can feel powerful to expose someone else's failures, it's an illusion. A mirage. We feel elevated above the rest, and a false sense of power begins to grow. We feel noticed, even validated—but for all the wrong reasons.

This is why social media has become a breeding ground for accusation. People build platforms by attacking others. They mistake criticism for wisdom and controversy for influence.

But here's the truth: That kind of significance is hollow. It's the counterfeit. It's rooted in pride, not purpose. I caution you: Accusation may feed the ego, but it doesn't feed the soul.

Real significance doesn't come from being louder, smarter, or more "discerning" than others. It comes from knowing who we are in Christ. It's built on humility, not self-promotion. It's lived in surrender to God and service to our brothers and sisters in Christ.

When we rely on accusation to feel important, we miss the true identity God has given us—one that doesn't require tearing others down to stand tall.

Scripture calls us to "honor one another above yourselves" (Rom. 12:10). That's not weakness—it's strength rooted in our true identity in the Lord.

4. LOVE & CONNECTION: ACCUSATION CREATES TRIBALISM

Every human heart longs to belong. We were created for love—for real connection with God and with one another. This need runs deep. It's not just about being liked; it's about being known, accepted, and safe in relationship.

But when that need goes unmet, we often reach for whatever offers a counterfeit version of closeness. This is where the spirit of accusation can feel deceptively communal.

One of the fastest—and saddest—ways to bond with others is through a shared enemy. Over the years, I've witnessed many friendships that weren't built on love; they were built on mutual hatred. I caution you: If your relationship is centered on tearing someone else down, it's not real connection—it's toxic.

There are many religious and political groups out there, often fueled by the spirit of accusation to strengthen their ranks. Their message is clear: "We are the good ones, and they are the bad ones." But this is a tribalistic mindset—loyalty to a group especially when combined with strong negative feelings for those outside the group.[3] It doesn't unite the church; it fractures it. It doesn't promote righteousness; it breeds self-righteousness.

This is precisely what the accuser wants—to isolate people from true love and replace it with counterfeit relationships: connections built on division instead of grace.

Jesus, on the other hand, modeled radical love. He ate with sinners, embraced outcasts, and refused to let religious leaders dictate who was worthy of grace. He showed us that love is built not on shared hatred but on a shared passion for God and His truth.

5. GROWTH: ACCUSATION STUNTS SPIRITUAL MATURITY

So what does growth really look like? I'm talking about *real* growth—in the face of rising hostility and a culture obsessed with reckless exposure. Real growth requires humility and self-examination. But the spirit of accusation shifts the focus outward. Instead of asking, "How can I grow?" those under its influence become addicted to asking, "What's wrong with them?"

Accusers feel powerful when they expose the faults of others—but they remain blind to their own. True spiritual growth begins not with accusation but with repentance.

When was the last time you examined your own heart with the same intensity you once used to evaluate someone else's flaws?

Growth doesn't happen when we magnify others' shortcomings. It happens when we humble ourselves before God—allowing Him to do the deep work in us first.

6. CONTRIBUTION: ACCUSATION PRETENDS TO SERVE A CAUSE

One of our greatest needs is to know that our lives make an impact. It's woven into us—we long to contribute to something meaningful in the world. But instead of offering love, service, and truth, many have been deceived into thinking they're helping by tearing others down.

There are many false ministries of "exposure" that claim to protect people from deception, but their goal is rarely restoration—it's destruction. Yet God calls us to build, not destroy.

If you truly want to make an impact, consider this: Are you building something meaningful, or simply tearing others down? Are you restoring people, or just pointing out their failures? Are you leading with love or with fear?

The greatest contribution you can make to the world is to reflect the character of Jesus. He didn't come to accuse. He came to save: "For God did not send His Son into the world to condemn the world, but that the world through Him might be saved" (JOHN 3:17, NKJV).

YOUR CALL TO RISE

We have made remarkable progress in exposing the root of accusation—laying the groundwork for understanding the deceptive nature of the beast that is the spirit of accusation.

While it falsely promises to meet our deepest needs, accusation will always leave us feeling empty. Like anything the world offers that claims to "save the day" or "fill the void," it's counterfeit. It will never satisfy.

Only Jesus can fill that void. Only His words, His presence, and His promises can meet the needs of the human heart. He says, "Let anyone who is thirsty come to me and drink" (John 7:37). Only in Him are we truly filled. Outside of Jesus, every promise of fulfillment is smoke and mirrors—a carefully constructed lie designed to drive a wedge between you and the Father.

Accusation may offer a sense of certainty, but certainty through the world's lens only breeds fear. It may produce a fleeting thrill, but it fosters division. It may give you a momentary sense of importance, but it isolates and leaves you alone. It creates a counterfeit form of connection that ultimately destroys real relationships. It stunts personal growth and replaces true contribution with destruction.

But Jesus offers a better way. Instead of certainty He gives faith. Instead of variety, He gives purpose. Instead of false significance, He gives true identity in Him. Instead of toxic connection He offers authentic love. Instead of tearing down, He builds up.

So which path will you choose?

It's time for us to love generously. To build with humility. To serve with boldness. And to grow with joy. It's time to rise above all the noise and chaos of accusation— and leave it behind for good. I fully believe a greater measure of the Spirit of God is going to be poured out on those who choose to become the dangerous obsessed ones. Those who refuse to play Satan's games. Those who choose the way of Jesus. Holiness. Redemption. Mercy. Grace. Forgiveness. Hope.

CHAPTER 14

THE MINISTRY OF EXPOSURE: A DEMONIC COUNTERFEIT

A lie will go round the world while truth is pulling its boots on.
—CHARLES SPURGEON

WE ADDRESSED A very similar topic earlier in this book when we explored the power of our words. But now let's examine it from a different angle—our perspective. Carefully consider the posture of the self-righteous Pharisee in Luke 18:11, who prayed, "God, I thank you that I am not like other people—robbers, evildoers, adulterers—or even like this tax collector." That same spirit is alive and well today.

Sadly, I have seen a new counterfeit ministry emerge in the body of Christ—one obsessed with exposing rather than redeeming. These self-appointed watchmen parade under the banner of truth while leaving a trail of destruction in their wake. While some may have true intentions, many—if not most—appear to have an agenda. Their words? They don't heal; they cripple. And their actions? They don't restore the church; they bring ruin. Though they claim to operate with a "right heart" as defenders of the faith, their behavior tells a different story—one that mirrors the Pharisees, who weaponized law and leveraged condemnation to elevate themselves at the expense of others.

This so-called "ministry of exposure" feels more like an oxymoron. After all, how can *ministry* and *exposure* truly go hand in hand? Aren't we all called to the same ministry of reconciliation? As 2 Corinthians 5:18 reminds us, God "gave us the ministry of reconciliation." That's the heart of true ministry—restoration, not destruction.

These "exposure ministries" claim to call for repentance, but in reality, it feels more like a death sentence—a modern-day stoning with words. Their passive-aggressive attacks aren't born from a love of truth, and certainly not from a love of their brother or sister in Christ. They're fueled by a hunger for attention. It seems to me that they believe it's their duty to "call out" what others won't, but in doing so, they leave behind wrecked reputations, crushed spirits, and broken lives. Nothing about it resembles Jesus.

THE TRAP OF PUBLIC EXECUTION

Once again, Jesus provides the perfect model for how we are to approach those caught in sin. Take the woman caught in adultery—He didn't humiliate her. He didn't stand beside her accusers, hurling stones. He stood between her and her would-be executioners and said, "Let him who is without sin cast the first stone" (John 8:7, paraphrased).

But this is not what we see exemplified through the modern-day ministry of exposure. Quite the opposite, in fact. These so-called "ministers" seem to thrive on public execution. Their method feeds outrage, leveraging platforms to strip people of dignity under the guise of "discernment." And I have to wonder—do they ever stop to consider the people they're attacking? Do they think about their families—their mothers, fathers, sons, daughters, or spouses? Or have they set their sights on one goal: to cast stones at the accused, no matter the cost? I must say it plainly—hate disguised as discernment is still hate. And Scripture calls it demonic.

I know a few will read and hear this and say that if someone does not call others out, then who will? How will the church ever walk in holiness if we are not willing to stand and speak? How will we ever have real accountability if everything is hidden? My answer is simply this: Whom does this authority belong to? Who has the authority to call out faults and failures of others? Those not under authority and those who do not understand biblical authority will assume authority never given to them.

Jesus warned us in Matthew 7:3–5 about the hypocrisy of pointing out the speck in someone else's eye while ignoring the plank in our own. Yet those who engage in the ministry of exposure often refuse self-examination. While they're busy scrutinizing the failures of others, they seem to excuse their own shortcomings. "At that time many will turn away from the faith and will betray and hate each other" (Matt. 24:10).

And social media? It's become the perfect breeding ground for this kind of betrayal. A seemingly digital mob lies in wait—hungry, eager, and watching for the next leader to fall, the next scandal to erupt, the next opportunity to tear someone down and grow their own platform. It doesn't matter how many YouTube subscribers they have or how many likes they rack up—hate attracts hate. And in the end, they don't just destroy others—they destroy their own souls.

They seem to have an intimate understanding of the power of repetition. If you tell a lie long enough, people will eventually believe it. This psychological phenomenon—known as the *validity effect* or *reiteration effect*—explains why most people believe something is true simply because they've heard it multiple times, even if it's false.[1]

WHEN EXPOSURE BECOMES A TOOL OF THE ENEMY

It's difficult for me to imagine a person devoting their life to accusing, exposing, and tearing down others in the body of Christ. And yet, in doing so, they advance the enemy's agenda. They become his hands and feet—or worse, his mouthpiece—instead of answering the call to be the hands and feet of Jesus. Think about it for a moment: The devil no longer needs to whisper lies when there are people willingly—and loudly—spreading destruction in the name of "truth."

This isn't to say correction isn't biblical—it is. But there is a stark difference between biblical correction and satanic accusation. Biblical correction happens within the life of a local church and through those in spiritual authority in our lives. Its intention is redemption, not humiliation. Biblical correction is rooted in love, seeking to restore (Gal. 6:1). Satanic accusation is rooted in pride and seeks to destroy. Biblical correction invites repentance and healing. Satanic accusation invites shame and division.

58 | TIME TO RISE

Remember: If the goal is exposure rather than restoration, it's not of God.

True discernment is meant to lead people to Jesus, not push them into condemnation. Consider the example of Nathan and David in 2 Samuel 12. Nathan confronted David about his sin with Bathsheba, but his goal wasn't ruin—it was repentance. And look at how Jesus handled Peter in Luke 22:31–32. He warned Peter of Satan's coming attack, not to shame him, but to prepare him for restoration.

Now contrast that with the modern "ministry of exposure," which seeks to make a spectacle out of someone's failure. Instead of pointing people to the cross, it drags them to the gallows. If you are someone who feels called to call others out, let me be the first to tell you that it was not God who called you and that you are not a modern-day Paul addressing Peter. This is a moment for the sake of your soul to repent. The darkness you want exposed is in you as well.

THE CALL TO BE LIKE JESUS

Jesus' ministry was built on redemption. And while He never ignored sin, He addressed it in a way that called people to transformation—not condemnation.

If you find yourself drawn to "discernment" channels, controversy-driven ministries, or gossip cloaked as concern, ask yourself, "Does this produce love or division in my heart? Does this encourage restoration or destruction? Would Jesus speak this way?"

A ministry led by condemnation instead of love is not a ministry of Jesus. The world does not need more Christians functioning as critics—we already have plenty of those. What it needs is more Christlike leaders—men and women who restore, heal, and lift others up through love and truth walking together.

Let us reject the counterfeit ministry of exposure and embrace the true ministry of reconciliation (2 Cor. 5:18). The church will be known not by its ability to expose darkness but by its ability to radiate the light of Christ—where truth and love walk hand in hand.

CHAPTER 15

WEAPONS OF MASS EMOTION

My feelings are not God. God is God....My feelings are echoes
and responses to what my mind perceives. And sometimes—
many times—my feelings are out of sync with the truth.
—JOHN PIPER

W E LIVE IN a world where emotions aren't just expressed—they're weaponized. More than ever, people are using what I call "weapons of mass emotion" to sway public opinion and shape narratives. And it's working. To me, this is sounding more political in nature than reflective of the church Jesus died for us to have. Many are using weapons of mass emotion to manipulate perception, control narratives, and shape reality.

When emotions are weaponized, compassion gets pushed aside. Criticism is rebranded as discernment. And discernment—a powerful tool given to us by the Holy Spirit—is dressed in trendy packaging to mask the ugliness of impure motives underneath. Before you know it, what began as a moment of tension becomes a full-blown wave of deception.

One of the most effective weapons in the enemy's arsenal is accusation. Why? Because it aims straight for the heart, triggering an immediate emotional response. When we're accused, it stirs something deep inside us. Feelings like anger, fear, outrage, or shame surge from within. And once those emotions take over, it becomes hard to slow down and ask, "What's actually true?" The enemy takes great pleasure in this kind of emotional manipulation because it leaves little room for true spiritual discernment. We become distracted and overwhelmed. These emotions seem to demand an immediate response, pulling us into impulsive decisions before we've had a chance to think. And when we are emotionally manipulated, we become blinded to truth—often making choices we later regret.

Fear, outrage, shame, and victimhood—each of these has become a weapon of mass emotion, spiraling into one great whirlwind of emotional manipulation that is bringing significant turmoil within the church today. When left unchecked, these emotions begin to shape how we see ourselves, how we see others, and even how we see God. In the sections that follow, we'll take a closer look at each one—not to condemn, but to expose the enemy's schemes and reclaim our ability to discern his wiles.

FEAR: THE ULTIMATE CONTROL MECHANISM

Fear is one of the strongest weapons of mass emotion. It's subtle but strategic—and when used effectively, it makes people easy to control. Fear of rejection. Fear of failure.

Fear of punishment. Fear of being labeled. These fears might not always be loud, but they're deeply rooted, and they shape how we respond to pressure.

We see this weapon used everywhere. Governments use fear to enforce compliance. News outlets thrive on it, keeping people addicted to crisis headlines. Some churches have even used fear to modify behavior. And on social media, fear is weaponized through cancel culture—punishing those who dare to step out of line, whether intentionally or unintentionally.

What concerns me deeply is how quickly people are led by the emotions of others—especially when it comes to how they feel about someone else. The Pharisees did the same thing with Jesus. They hurled accusations of blasphemy in an attempt to silence Him. But Jesus never bowed to fear. He walked in truth—steady, anchored, and unshaken by the emotional manipulation surrounding Him. Even when He stood before Pilate, knowing death was near, He refused to let fear dictate His response.

Fear has been a tool of control since the very beginning. Adam and Eve hid from God in fear after their disobedience. Fear has the power to paralyze or push someone into decisions they were never meant to make. When we fear rejection, we conform. When we fear punishment, we submit.

But Jesus came to set us free from the bondage of fear. While fear aims to force us into submission, the truth will set us free.

OUTRAGE: THE ADDICTIVE TRAP

Outrage is one of the easiest emotions for us to justify—and one of the hardest to let go of. It feels powerful. It feels righteous. It feels like action. But outrage is a cheap substitute for real authority. It doesn't build anything. It just burns.

It's a highly addictive weapon of mass emotion, giving people a sense of moral superiority. I've seen outrage fuel movements, inspire headlines, and spread as viral tweets. It offers a false sense of justice, causing those who are outraged to justify their actions, believing they are fighting for a worthy cause. But in reality, many are simply reacting to a clever narrative spin.

The problem? Once outrage is triggered, facts go out the window. Truth becomes an illusion, while people attack freely without seeking full understanding. Our critical thinking isn't engaged—our impulses are. We feed hunger for justice on partial information, misrepresentation, or outright lies.

We see this clearly in the story of Stephen found in Acts 7:54–60. The religious leaders were so enraged by his words that they stoned him to death. Their emotions clouded their judgment and overpowered their ability to wait, reason, and discern. That's what outrage does—it blinds us to truth. Instead of responding with wisdom and discernment, we react with violence and destruction.

Today, social media amplifies outrage like never before—creating digital mobs that cancel individuals based on rumors. Once someone is accused, they're often condemned without a fair hearing. The culture of outrage demands instant judgment, leaving little room for grace, redemption, or truth.

Outrage doesn't create solutions. It creates divisions and destruction.

But Scripture calls us to something better: "Let every person be quick to listen, slow to anger, for human anger does not produce the righteousness of God" (Jas. 1:19–20, paraphrased).

SHAME: THE SILENT KILLER

Shame is another one of the enemy's most destructive weapons—and one of the least talked about. It doesn't just wound you emotionally; it attacks your very identity. Unlike fear or outrage, which are more externally expressed, shame has the power to paralyze internally. From deep within, it convinces us we are unworthy, broken, and irredeemable.

The accuser (Satan) is a master at using shame. He whispers,

- "You're not good enough."
- "You will always be defined by your past."
- "You can never be used by God."

Shame causes people to hide—like Adam and Eve in the garden. It makes them withdraw from community, purpose, and even from God Himself. It convinces us we're beyond redemption, keeping us trapped in cycles of guilt, isolation, and self-loathing.

But Jesus exposes and destroys shame. His actions toward the woman caught in adultery in John 8:1–11 are a reflection of Jesus' posture toward accusers. Jesus refused to condemn her. Instead, He set her free. He didn't ignore her sin—but He gave her an opportunity for transformation.

In contrast the Pharisees tried to use shame as a weapon, publicly humiliating her to trap Jesus in a legal dilemma. But Jesus turned the tables—not just on their judgment, but on their hearts—revealing their hypocrisy.

We all have shortcomings. We are all flawed. But where the enemy uses shame as a tool to focus us inwardly on our sin, God uses conviction as a tool to bring restoration and free us from sin. The difference is profound. Shame leads to hopelessness, while conviction leads to repentance and change.

Shame enslaves. Grace restores.

VICTIMHOOD: THE POWER OF BLAME

Victimhood is yet another weapon of mass emotion. It convinces us that our pain is our identity and that we have no responsibility for our future. It shifts blame to others, creating a cycle of resentment and powerlessness. Accusation fuels victimhood. Instead of encouraging us to heal and rise, it keeps us stuck in anger and self-pity. Remaining in a victim mentality rejects personal responsibility and seeks validation through suffering.

But Jesus never called us to stay victims—He called us to overcome. The man at the pool of Bethesda had been paralyzed for years, blaming his circumstances. Jesus asked him, "Do you want to be healed?" (John 5:6, ESV). Isn't it interesting that Jesus asked

62 | TIME TO RISE

the man whether he wanted to be healed? It almost seems like an unnecessary question—yet it reveals something powerful: The power to rise was in the man's hands.

The enemy would love nothing more than for us to remain stuck—dwelling on past wounds and living as victims forever. But God calls us to healing. He calls us to freedom. Victimhood may bring temporary sympathy, but it will never lead to true restoration.

BREAKING FREE FROM THE WEAPONS OF MASS EMOTION

If you're living controlled by fear, outrage, shame, or victimhood, you are not living in truth. The spirit of accusation thrives in these emotions because they distort reality. So how do we break free?

It begins with awareness. Recognize emotional triggers as they arise—when you feel fear, anger, or shame rising, pause and ask, "Is this truth, or is it an emotional reaction?" Discernment begins in the pause.

Then choose wisdom over impulse. Proverbs 4:7 reminds us, "Wisdom is the principal thing; therefore get wisdom" (NKJV). Instead of reacting impulsively, seek God's wisdom and guidance. Let the Holy Spirit filter your thoughts before your emotions carry you away.

We must refuse to engage in emotional manipulation. Just because an emotion feels strong in the moment doesn't mean it is justified. There's a difference between holy conviction and manipulated outrage—and the difference matters.

Galatians 5:16 reminds us to "walk by the Spirit, and you will not gratify the desires of the flesh." The flesh thrives on fear, pride, and anger. But the Spirit leads us in truth and peace. As we follow Him, we begin to replace emotional distortion with grounded discernment.

And when the lies of the enemy rise up—combat them with truth. When fear tries to grip your heart, declare the words of 2 Timothy 1:7: "For God has not given us a spirit of fear, but of power and of love and of a sound mind" (NKJV).

Above all, choose love. When outrage demands reaction and accusation seeks to divide, the love of Jesus restores all. Cultivate a heart of love and grace. "Love covers over a multitude of sins" (1 Pet. 4:8). Love repairs what the spirit of accusation tries to destroy.

Jesus is calling us to rise above emotional manipulation to walk in clarity, wisdom, and love. Emotions are meant to be felt, but they should never control us. It's time to lay down the weapons of mass emotion and take up the armor of truth. The world doesn't need more emotionally reactive people—it needs those who can discern beyond emotion, seek truth, and extend grace. Freedom isn't found in reacting. It's found in responding—with wisdom.

CHAPTER 16

NO PROBLEM IS PERMANENT

No problem is permanent, only your soul is permanent.
—TONY ROBBINS

LIFE IS FULL of problems. Some are just minor frustrations—a missed appointment, a flat tire, a rough day at work. But others? They hit hard. The kind of problems that keep you up at night. The kind that make it hard to breathe—financial pressure, fractured relationships, unexpected illness, betrayal from someone you trusted, or just that gnawing feeling of uncertainty about what's ahead in your life. And in those moments, we often feel stuck—like there's no way out. We wonder whether this is how it's always going to be.

But here's what I want you to hear: No problem is permanent. And more than that—every challenge you face is an invitation to grow. God doesn't waste pain. Problems aren't punishments. They're teachers. They stretch us. They refine us. And they shape us into the people God created us to be. Through them we walk in greater purpose and deeper faith. They call us to trust God to do what seems impossible in our lives—because only He can.

THE TEMPORARY NATURE OF PROBLEMS

Every problem you're facing right now has an expiration date. Pain fades. Circumstances shift. What feels unbearable today will one day be just a part of your story. But when you are in the thick of it—when the pressure is real and the weight is heavy—it's easy to believe the lie that this is how it's always going to be.

Take a moment and look back. Think about where you were five years ago. What were you carrying that felt overwhelming then? Maybe it resolved. Maybe it changed. Maybe it just lost its power over you. Where are those problems now? What once felt permanent was actually temporary.

But while problems come and go, your soul doesn't. Your soul lasts forever. That's why Jesus said, "What good is it for someone to gain the whole world, yet forfeit their soul?" (Mark 8:36). The soul—that eternal part of you made in the image of God—is the only thing that truly remains when everything else fades.

Life can touch your finances, your reputation, even your health—but it can't touch your soul unless you let it. And that's what gives you the power to endure. When you know who you are—and whose you are—you can face temporary hardship without losing your eternal hope. Understanding this truth gives you the power to endure. Your problems don't define you. And they certainly don't have the final say over your life.

64 | Time to Rise

PERSPECTIVE DETERMINES POWER

How you see your situation can either keep you stuck or move you forward. Most of the time, we feel trapped not because the situation has no way out but because we're looking at it through the wrong lens. When we view life only through a temporary, earthly lens, our problems look enormous—immovable. But when we ask God for His perspective—an eternal one—everything begins to shift.

It's important to remember God sees the full picture. He's not bound by time the way we are. He knows the beginning, middle, and end of your story—and He's already working in all three. What feels impossible to you right now is being woven into something greater than you can imagine.

Consider this: When Jesus was crucified, the disciples thought it was over. They saw only His suffering, His betrayal, and His death. But three days later, everything changed. What seemed like a permanent defeat was actually a temporary moment in God's greater plan. In the same way, your current situation may feel overwhelming now, but in light of eternity, it's small. This isn't to minimize your pain, but to remind you of the incredible hope you have in Christ. Your suffering is not the end. No matter what you're facing, resurrection is always on the other side of surrender.

That's what faith does. It reminds us that what we see isn't the full story. It lifts our eyes from the ground to the heavens. It shifts our focus from what's happening *to* us to what God is doing *in* us and *through* us.

You are not stuck. You are in process. This season isn't the end—it's part of your preparation for something greater. And the God who started a good work in you? He's faithful to finish it (Phil. 1:6).

THE ENEMY WANTS YOU TO BELIEVE IT'S PERMANENT

This is where the enemy goes to work. Right in the middle of your pain, when you're vulnerable, weary, just trying to make sense of it all. That's when he whispers lies meant to keep you stuck. "You'll never be free. You will always struggle. This situation is hopeless." The spirit of accusation thrives in these moments, speaking not just to your situation but to your identity. He wants you to believe the hardship is permanent so you'll stop hoping and give up.

Satan wants you to magnify your problems instead of magnifying God. If he can convince you that your situation will never change, he knows you will stop fighting. You'll stop believing. You'll stop praying. And once your focus is fixed only on what's wrong, you'll never see what's possible. But Jesus always calls us to rise above the temporary and fix our eyes on eternity: "So we fix our eyes not on what is seen, but on what is unseen, since what is seen is temporary, but what is unseen is eternal" (2 Cor. 4:18).

The greatest battles are won in the mind. If the enemy can control your thoughts, he can influence your future. That's why Scripture urges us to "be transformed by the renewing of your mind" (Rom. 12:2). When we dwell on the idea that things will never change, we begin to live as though they never will. But when we believe that God is truly working all things for our good—just as He promises—we begin walking in greater faith and hopeful expectation of what's ahead.

PROBLEMS ARE GIFTS THAT CAUSE US TO GROW

It might sound strange, but problems—yes, even the hard ones—can be a gift. They challenge us. They wake us up. They shake us out of comfort and into dependency on God. The problems we face in life aren't just obstacles—they're catalysts for growth. And the Father loves when His children draw near to Him. Speaking from experience, I've grown the most in seasons of trials. I have learned more through the fires of life than I ever have when things were going well. Think about the hardest moments in your life. Didn't they teach you something? Didn't they leave you stronger?

- ✦ Financial struggles teach us stewardship and reliance on God.
- ✦ Betrayal teaches us discernment and forgiveness.
- ✦ Delays teach us patience and trust.
- ✦ Hardships teach us endurance and faith.

It's important we stop viewing problems as pointless—they have a purpose. When Joseph was betrayed, sold into slavery, falsely accused, and imprisoned, God positioned him for his ultimate purpose: to save a nation. What if your problems aren't barriers but stepping stones? What if, instead of breaking you, they're actually building you into the person you're becoming?

> Consider it pure joy, my brothers and sisters, whenever you face trials of many kinds, because you know that the testing of your faith produces perseverance. Let perseverance finish its work so that you may be mature and complete, not lacking anything.
>
> —James 1:2–4

Maturity is established through trials. Strength is built in struggle. Faith is forged in fire. And the problems you are facing today? They're equipping you for the future God has for you.

THE ROLE OF FAITH IN OVERCOMING CHALLENGES

Faith provides a bridge between your current struggles and your future victory. It's the ability to trust in what we cannot see while offering hope for what is possible. Without faith, our problems often feel final. But with faith, those problems become mere tests paving the way for profound testimonies of the goodness of God.

Scripture defines faith as "confidence in what we hope for and assurance about what we do not see" (Heb. 11:1). So let me ask you—what are you hoping for? Do you believe your best days are still ahead? Or have you settled into a life dictated by fear and doubt?

Faith is one of those powerful tools we carry in our spiritual arsenal. It refuses to accept the lie that things will never change. It's faith that rises from deep within our souls, boldly declaring that God is greater than any obstacle. Faith can move the mountains before us. It breaks the chains of doubt. It shifts hopeless circumstances into hopeful opportunities. It doesn't ignore the problem—it just doesn't bow to it. Faith keeps you going when everything in you wants to give up.

YOUR SOUL'S ETERNAL DESTINY

If only your soul is permanent, then the real question is not "How big are your problems?" but rather "How is your soul?" Are you anchoring your soul in the truth of Christ? Are you living in the reality of eternity—or are you letting temporary problems control you?

One of the greatest deceptions is to spend your entire life focused on temporary problems while ignoring the eternal condition of your soul. It's possible to win every earthly battle and still lose the war for your soul. That is why Jesus said:

> "Do not store up for yourselves treasures on earth, where moths and vermin destroy, and where thieves break in and steal. But store up for yourselves treasures in heaven, where moths and vermin do not destroy, and where thieves do not break in and steal. For where your treasure is, there your heart will be also."
>
> —MATTHEW 6:19–21

No problem is permanent—only your soul is. I urge you—live today with eternity in mind. Refuse to allow your temporary struggles to define you. Instead, fix your eyes on Jesus, who is the pioneer and perfecter of your faith (Heb. 12:2). The problems you're facing today will pass but the condition of your soul? It lives on forever.

So let's keep choosing faith over fear. Say goodbye to panic and hello to perseverance. The troubles of this life are temporary. But truth? Truth is eternal.

CHAPTER 17

UNDERSTANDING THE PATTERNS OF ACCUSATION

Hard times create strong men. Strong men create good times. Good times create weak men. And, weak men create hard times.
—G. Michael Hopf

ACCUSATION IS NOT random. It's calculated. It follows patterns, strategies, and cycles that are meant to wear us down—to break people apart, stir division, and twist truth until it no longer resembles what it once was. If you've ever found yourself under the weight of accusation, you know how disorienting it can be. That's because the enemy of our souls isn't just throwing darts in the dark. He's methodical. He's strategic.

But here's the good news: With the help of the Lord, we can recognize the patterns and break free from their grip. The more we learn to see the enemy's tactics for what they are, the more equipped we become to stand firm in truth and walk in the freedom Jesus died to give us. So while the enemy may be subtle, he's certainly not original. He's been using the same tactics since the beginning of time. Let's take a closer look at how accusation takes shape—and how we can dismantle it before it takes hold of us.

1. Accusation plants doubt: The first pattern of accusation is planting a seed of doubt. We see this strategy in the Garden of Eden when the serpent asks Eve, "Did God really say…?" (Gen. 3:1). The goal of this question was not just to gather information—it was to create uncertainty.

This same tactic is still in play today, often beginning with a subtle suggestion: "Are you sure they really care about you?" "Is God really with you in this season?" And once that doubt takes root, it doesn't stay small for long—it grows quickly into full-fledged accusation. Before we know it, our faith is weakened and we start second-guessing everything—our relationships, our purpose, our calling, and even the character of God.

2. Accusation twists truth: Accusation doesn't necessarily rely on blatant lies. In fact, it often hides behind partial truths—just enough accuracy to sound convincing, but twisted in a way that distorts reality. This is one of the enemy's most deceptive and effective tactics.

We see this clearly in the story of Nehemiah. His enemies accused him of wanting to be king—something he never said or intended—using partial information to discredit his calling and distract him from his mission (Neh. 6:6–7). How crafty of the enemy—to mix truth with assumption as a way to provoke fear and confusion.

This same thing happened during Jesus' trial. Religious leaders took His words about the temple and twisted them to serve their agenda: "We heard Him say, 'I will destroy this temple made with human hands and in three days will build another, not made with hands'" (Mark 14:58). They weren't quoting Him directly—they were twisting His words out of context to justify their accusations.

That's how the enemy works. He'll take what's been said or done and bend it just enough to make you question someone's motives—or even your own. This is why discernment is so critical. When accusation shows up dressed as truth, we need the Holy Spirit to help us recognize the difference.

3. Accusation is strengthened in groups: Accusation rarely stays isolated—it seeks agreement. It spreads through groups, gaining momentum as more voices come into agreement with it. When Satan accused Job before God, he didn't do it alone. Others joined in—including Job's own friends, who added to the accusations instead of offering support (Job 1:9–11; 2:4–5, 11–13; 22:5–10).

We see this pattern in mob mentality, social media outrage, and gossip circles. Once an accusation gains traction, it becomes harder to stop—even if it's false. The more people believe it, repeat it, and react to it, the more "real" it begins to seem. Public perception becomes louder than the truth.

That's why false accusations often escalate. What starts as a single doubt or suspicion can snowball into widespread condemnation, fueled by speculation and emotion rather than truth. And by the time facts come to light, the damage has already been done.

4. Accusation isolates: One of the enemy's main goals in accusation is to separate people—both from community and from the presence of God. When someone is falsely accused, they often feel misunderstood, abandoned, and painfully alone.

We see this in David's life when he was on the run from Saul. Though innocent, he was hunted like a criminal (1 Sam. 24:11). The same was true for Joseph—who was falsely accused by Potiphar's wife and thrown into prison for a crime he didn't commit (Gen. 39:11–20). Both men were isolated—not just physically, but emotionally and spiritually.

That's the enemy's strategy. Accusation doesn't just aim to discredit—it aims to disconnect. Isolation can bring about a weakened state in us, making us more vulnerable to self-doubt and spiritual attack. When we withdraw because of accusation, we cut ourselves off from the very things we need most: encouragement, truth, wisdom, and support.

Satan knows this. If he can get you alone, he can get you to question your worth, your calling, and even your faith. But God's heart is always to restore—to bring us back into our community, back into truth, and back into His presence.

5. Accusation destroys identity: Perhaps the most dangerous pattern of accusation is that it attacks identity. It's not just about making someone feel guilty—it's about redefining who they are.

We see this clearly when the enemy accused Jesus, "If you are the Son of God..." (Matt. 4:3). The implication was that if Jesus was truly God's Son, He would prove it

Understanding the Patterns of Accusation | 69

by performing a miracle. Satan's strategy wasn't just temptation—it was about warfare. He wanted Jesus to question who He was and respond out of insecurity rather than obedience.

The enemy did the same with Job: "He only serves God because he is blessed" (paraphrase of Job 1:9–10). Satan was trying to discredit Job's identity as a faithful servant of God, suggesting that his devotion was conditional rather than genuine.

Accusation is never just about what you've done—it's about who you are. The enemy's ultimate goal is to get you to believe you are what you've been accused of. If he can label you a failure—and get you to agree with it—then the real damage isn't just the accusation; it's the distortion of your identity in Christ. This is why the greatest accusations internally are the ones that attack who you are more than simply what you do.

But here's the truth: In Christ, your identity is secure. You are chosen. You are redeemed. You are loved. While accusation may challenge your character, it can never undo God's divine purpose for your life.

FREEDOM FROM THE PATTERNS OF ACCUSATION

If we want to overcome accusation, we must learn to respond with wisdom and spiritual authority. Here's how:

- **Recognize the pattern.** Don't fall for the enemy's century-old schemes. Once you learn how to recognize how accusation works, you can break the cycle and counter it with truth.

- **Hold on to truth.** God—not accusation—defines your identity. No matter what's said about you, your worth and purpose are secure in Christ alone.

- **Stay in community.** Accusation thrives in isolation. Surround yourself with people who speak life—those who remind you of what's true when your mind is under fire.

- **Respond in faith, not fear.** Fear fuels accusation, but faith disarms it. When false claims arise, choose to trust in God's justice and timing rather than reacting out of panic or anger.

- **Follow Jesus' example.** Jesus endured constant accusation, but He never let it define Him. He stayed rooted in His Father's love and purpose—refusing to be controlled by the lies of His accusers.

The enemy may accuse—but Jesus is our great intercessor (Rom. 8:34). While Satan tries to condemn, Christ declares freedom. The question is, Whose voice will you believe?

When you recognize the patterns of accusation, you can rise above them. Accusation is designed to weaken, isolate, and destroy—but truth, faith, and godly community will always overcome it. Stand firm in your identity. No accusation can undo what Jesus has already secured in you.

CHAPTER 18

NOT EVERYTHING THAT GLITTERS IS GOD

*The ticket to victory often comes down to bringing
your very best when you feel your worst.*
—DAVID GOGGINS

HAVE YOU EVER noticed how often feelings of failure and attacks of the enemy repeat themselves predictably? When you really look at it, the enemy's playbook isn't all that creative. In fact, it's predictable. And once you recognize the pattern, you can prepare for it in advance. Those who walk in victory are often the ones who've learned to quickly spot the mental and emotional cycles that lead to accusation—both from the inside and from the outside.

Let's talk about the voice inside your head—the one that shapes how you see yourself, your future, and even God. Every single day, you are bombarded with thoughts. Some are rooted in truth. Some are blatant lies. And some are subtle—half-truths that sound wise but are really deception in disguise. If we don't learn to discern which voices we're listening to, we'll spend our lives chasing what looks good, sounds good, or even feels good—but it isn't from God.

The enemy is clever. He knows he can't destroy you outright, so he deceives you with counterfeits. He whispers things that sound like truth—but they're twisted just enough to make you stumble. And if he can get you to believe the wrong voice? He doesn't even have to fight you anymore. You'll chain yourself.

THE ENEMY OF YOUR DESTINY SPEAKS IN DECEPTION

Jesus said in John 10:27, "My sheep listen to my voice; I know them, and they follow me." That means there's another voice competing for your attention—the voice of confusion, accusation, fear, and doubt. It shows up when you feel called to something new and suddenly hear, "Who do you think you are?" Or when you start to feel the love of God but hear, "You'll never be enough." Or when you're right at the edge of breakthrough and fear says, "What if you fail?"

These aren't obvious attacks—they're subtle distortions. That's how the enemy works. He doesn't shout, "God isn't real!" He whispers, "God doesn't really care about you." He doesn't scream, "You're a failure!" He speaks quietly to your soul: "You'll never get past this."

So how do we fight back? By learning to recognize the counterfeit voices that hinder our momentum—and replace them with the truth.

THREE COUNTERFEIT VOICES THAT KEEP YOU STUCK

1. The Voice of Accusation

This is one is relentless. It reminds you of every failure. It insists that your past disqualifies you from your future. It says, "You're too broken for God to use" or "You'll always struggle with this." But here's the truth: "There is now no condemnation for those who are in Christ Jesus" (Rom. 8:1). If God says you're forgiven, you are. Period. Accusation keeps you looking backward instead of forward. It chains you to who you used to be and blinds you to who God is calling you to become. So the next time you hear that voice, reject it with the truth of God's Word.

2. The Voice of Distraction

This one's sneakier. It doesn't attack you head-on—it just keeps you busy. Not every good opportunity is a God opportunity. Some things are designed to keep you occupied but not fruitful—pulling you away from your purpose. This voice says, "Chase success. Chase approval. Chase comfort." But if you'll pause for a moment to listen, I'll bet you'll hear God saying, "Chase Me, and I'll take care of the rest."

Distraction isn't always obvious. It can show up as being a workaholic, endlessly scrolling, or even pouring energy into things that feel productive but aren't aligned with your true calling. When Martha was distracted by preparations, Jesus gently redirected her, "You are worried and upset about many things, but few things are needed—or indeed only one" (Luke 10:41–42). That one thing? It's Jesus. We get so distracted by the perceived inactions of others that we fail to take critical actions God has called us to take.

So pause and ask yourself, Are you focusing on what truly matters—or are you being pulled in a hundred directions by things that don't lead to spiritual growth?

3. The Voice of Doubt

This one is sharp. It cuts like a knife. This voice keeps you playing small. It halts your progress, convincing you that you're not ready—or worse, that you'll never measure up. It festers in the lie that others are more qualified. It whispers that stepping out in faith is too risky, so you stay put.

But here's the truth. God doesn't call the qualified—He qualifies the called.

Moses doubted himself, saying, "Who am I that I should go to Pharaoh?" (Exod. 3:11). But God didn't let Moses' insecurity define his destiny. Gideon saw himself as the least in his family, yet God called him a mighty warrior (Judg. 6:15–16). Over and over in Scripture we see a pattern: God calls the unlikely and empowers them to do the impossible.

If you wait until you feel "ready," you'll never move. Faith requires action, even when doubt tries to hold you back. When I was in the three-hundred-mile ultramarathon in April 2025, there were many clear moments of doubt that I had what it took to finish the race. If I had listened to the voice of doubt and the voice of pain, I would have quit. And for a moment quitting would have felt good. However, it would not be long before

72 | TIME TO RISE

the pain of quitting would be worse than the pain of staying in the race. Don't quit your race because of doubt.

HOW TO TUNE IN TO GOD'S VOICE

How do we silence those negative voices so we can hear what God is saying?

- **Check the source.** If the voice in your head leads to fear, confusion, or shame—it's not from God. His voice leads to peace, conviction (not condemnation), and clarity. God's voice will never make you feel unworthy or hopeless.

- **Compare it to Scripture.** God will never contradict His Word. If the voice you're hearing goes against what He has already said, reject it. For example, if you hear, "God will never forgive you," you can immediately know that's a lie because "if we confess our sins, he is faithful and just and will forgive us" (1 John 1:9).

- **Pay attention to the fruit.** Jesus said, "A tree is recognized by its fruit" (Matt. 12:33). A voice aligned with God produces confidence, purpose, and spiritual growth. A counterfeit voice produces anxiety, hesitation, and guilt. Here's how you can tell the difference: If a thought leaves you paralyzed with fear instead of moving forward in faith—it's not from God.

- **Spend time in God's presence.** The more deeply you know someone, the more easily you recognize their voice. The same is true with God. The more time you spend in prayer, worship, and the Word, the more familiar His voice becomes to you. "My sheep hear My voice, and I know them, and they follow Me" (John 10:27, NKJV). Just like a child can recognize their parent's voice in a crowded room, you can learn to recognize God's voice in the noise of life.

I cannot stress this enough: Nothing is more important in your life than time alone with God. And yet—how often we neglect it. Don't let busyness steal the one thing that makes everything else make sense.

THE VOICE YOU BELIEVE DETERMINES YOUR FUTURE

What if the biggest battle you're facing isn't about your circumstances but about the voice you've chosen to believe? The enemy will always makes the counterfeit sound close to the truth—but the real voice of God leads you to life, freedom, and purpose.

Every major decision you make—whether stepping into your calling, forgiving someone, or choosing not to give up—hinges on which voice you choose to follow. If you believe the voice of accusation, you'll shrink back in shame. If you believe the voice of distraction, you'll waste time on what doesn't matter. If you believe the voice of doubt, you'll never step into the fullness of what God has for you.

Not Everything That Glitters Is God | 73

But if you believe the voice of God? You will walk in boldness. You will rise above fear. You will step into everything God has called you to do.

Today, you decide. Whose voice will you choose to listen to? The one that keeps you chained to fear and accusation—or the One calling you to rise up, step forward, and walk in the power God created you for? Your destiny is determined by the voice you follow. Choose wisely.

CHAPTER 19

THE POWER OF PERSONALITY

Your focus on hating yesterday is killing your opportunity to love tomorrow.
—GaryVee

As we've discussed so far, perspective carries power. It shapes how we see the world and determines how we engage with it. Will you rise above the challenges—or allow them to crush you? Will you stand firm on truth—or succumb to the lies of the enemy? And when it comes to deception—will you recognize it for what it truly is, a counterfeit truth? Will you allow the Holy Spirit to embolden you, giving you strength to stand firm on the unshakable Word of God?

Here's something we don't talk about often enough: Our perspective is directly tied to our personality.

I have a confession to make—I'm addicted to personality tests. I haven't found one yet that I didn't take. I find them dangerously accurate, and for that reason, I'm hooked. But the real value, in my opinion, isn't just what I learn about myself. It's what I come to appreciate in others. God made each one of us unique, and these tests are just one more reminder of how beautifully different we all are.

It's no wonder we become frustrated when others don't respond the way we do in certain situations. But here's the truth: They weren't meant to. God wired each of us with unique strengths, specific struggles, and a distinct way of interpreting the world.

Over the years of studying human behavior and spiritual growth, I started noticing something most personality tests completely miss: the powerful link between how we're wired and how we discern spiritually. That insight sparked a personal mission—to create a simple symbolic personality framework that's rooted in Scripture and designed for transformation. This isn't recycled theory. It's a tool I developed to help you recognize how your God-given design influences your perspective, your relationships, and even the way you fight your spiritual battles.

If we each don't understand our personality—and how it affects our perception— we risk falling for deception. We may stumble into spiritual traps, or even operate as wolves in sheep's clothing without realizing it. But when we embrace how God designed us, our discernment is sharpened, our wisdom deepens, and our lens is adjusted to see as Jesus sees.

As we'll explore in this framework below, some of us are drawn to leadership like Fire—bold, passionate, and unafraid to take charge, but sometimes at risk for acting too quickly or harshly. Others refine truth like Diamonds—sharp, analytical, and precise in their thinking, but sometimes overly skeptical. Some are steady and faithful like Gold—loyal, dependable, and committed through hardship, but often resistant to

The Power of Personality | 75

change. And then there are those who move with the flow of Water—relational, peace-seeking, and flexible, yet sometimes vulnerable to compromise or conflict avoidance.

Let's explore these four symbolic personality types—each revealing how God has uniquely wired us to perceive the world, respond to those in our lives, and grow in Him.

TIME TO RISE ARCHETYPES

1. Fire—the passionate leader

Fire—it burns bright. It ignites. It consumes. It spreads. If this is you, you likely feel a deep drive to lead, to build, to move things forward. Those with Fire personality are natural-born leaders. You're driven, charismatic, and relentless in your pursuit of purpose. You don't just talk about change—you *become* it. You inspire others, blaze trails, and refuse to settle for mediocrity.

How Fires see the world

- Fire personalities perceive challenges as opportunities.
- They're drawn to vision, revolution, and shaking things up.
- They have strong convictions and little patience for passive living.

The danger of Fires

- Without wisdom, fire can destroy instead of refine.
- A fiery person can be quick to speak, slow to listen, and resistant to correction.
- Their passion can blind them to deception if they listen to voices that only fuel their fire rather than challenge them.

How Fires discern truth

If you identify with Fire, it's important to balance your intensity with humility. Your passion is a gift—but it's truly powerful only when it's anchored in godly wisdom. Don't let your fire run wild. Seek the Holy Spirit daily, and allow Him to guide your zeal, not just fuel it. When your fire is surrendered, it doesn't just burn—it builds.

2. Diamond—the analytical thinker

A diamond is rare. It's valuable. It's formed under immense pressure. It reflects light with incredible precision. If you identify with this personality, you're likely a deep thinker—logical, analytical, and hungry for truth. You crave understanding and are often driven by a need to *know* before you move.

How Diamonds see the world

- They analyze everything, breaking down arguments to uncover truth.
- They question emotions, preferring reason over impulse.

76 | TIME TO RISE

+ They see deception as a problem to solve rather than a feeling to navigate.

The danger of Diamonds
+ They can become overly skeptical, doubting even when faith is required.
+ Their love for logic can make them resistant to experiences of the supernatural.
+ They may struggle with trusting God when things don't make sense.

How Diamonds discern truth
As a Diamond, your clarity and discernment are a gift—but truth isn't always something to figure out. Sometimes it must be received. Faith isn't always logical, and not everything about God can be fully understood. Some things must simply be *encountered*. The challenge for you is to hold truth and mystery together in tension. When you allow both to work together, your insight becomes not just sharp—but Spirit-led.

3. Gold—the loyal and steadfast
Gold is stable. It's enduring. It's unshakable. If this is you, you're likely the steady one in your circle—the faithful, the dependable, the committed. You hold strong when others falter. You don't chase trends or waver with every new wave of thought. You're grounded, and your consistency is a gift to those around you.

How Golds see the world
+ They value tradition, stability, and reliability.
+ They trust authority and are slow to be swayed by new ideas.
+ They see deception as a slow drift rather than a sudden fall.

The danger of Gold
+ They can resist necessary change, holding on to old ways even when God is doing something new.
+ Their stability can turn into stubbornness, making them inflexible.
+ They may be slow to recognize deception if it's wrapped in something familiar.

How Golds discern truth
As someone wired for loyalty and strength, you must be intentional about staying open to fresh revelation from the Lord. While your love for structure and tradition is valuable, remember this: Your loyalty must be to God first, not to systems or patterns of the past. The Holy Spirit may lead you into something unfamiliar—but if it's Him, it's trustworthy. Stay rooted, but stay responsive.

4. Water—The Adaptable Peacemaker

Water is gentle. It moves with grace, adapts to its surroundings, and brings life wherever it flows. If you resonate with this personality, you're likely the peacemaker—the one who smooths rough edges, brings people together, and senses what others are feeling even before they say a word. You're relational, empathetic, and deeply compassionate.

How Waters see the world

- They perceive truth through relationships—who is speaking matters just as much as what is said.
- They are compassionate and tend to see multiple sides of an issue.
- They are quick to forgive, often preferring reconciliation over confrontation.

The danger of Waters

- They can compromise truth to keep the peace.
- They may struggle with setting boundaries, allowing deception to creep in.
- Their adaptability can turn into passivity if they avoid necessary confrontation.

How Waters discern truth

Your discernment flows best when anchored in Scripture. Your sensitivity is a gift—but it must be guarded. Truth and love are meant to work together. Don't be afraid to stand firm, even when it creates tension. And remember: Peace isn't the absence of conflict—it's the presence of Christ. Let His Spirit lead your heart and guide your voice.

HOW THESE PERSONALITIES AFFECT SPIRITUAL DISCERNMENT

Every personality type has unique strengths and blind spots when it comes to perception. Some are naturally discerning. Others struggle to spot deception right away. Neither is better—it just means we must be aware of how our God-given wiring interacts with truth.

Here's how each type interacts with truth:

- **Fires** see deception as an enemy to attack—but must be careful not to be blinded by passion.
- **Diamonds** analyze deception with precision—but must remember that faith isn't always logical.
- **Golds** stand firm in truth—but must ensure they're not holding on to traditions instead of God's leading.
- **Waters** seek peace in the midst of deception—but must be willing to confront lies when necessary.

78 | TIME TO RISE

Understanding how you see the world is the first step to sharpening your discernment. If you know you're wired like Fire, you can temper your zeal with wisdom. If you're a Diamond, you can make room for faith beyond logic. If you're Gold, you can stay grounded while still remaining open to God's sudden directional shifts. And if you're Water, you can hold peace in one hand and boldness in the other.

Here's the thing: Your personality may shape your perspective—but truth should shape your personality.

At the end of the day, our personalities influence how we interpret the world—but they should never dictate how we respond to truth. Truth isn't subjective. It's not based on emotion, logic, tradition, or even relationships. Truth is a person—Jesus Christ (John 14:6).

The enemy will always try to use our strengths against us—pushing Fire personalities into reckless zeal, Diamond into doubt, Gold into stubbornness, and Water into passivity. But when we submit our personalities to the Holy Spirit, He refines us. He uses our strengths for His glory and guards us from our vulnerabilities.

So, which one are you? Fire? Diamond? Gold? Water? Know yourself. But more importantly, know the One who made you. Because when your perception is shaped by His truth—deception doesn't stand a chance.

CHAPTER 20

MONKS AND MYSTICS

*If you're torn between two paths, pick the harder path. Because if the
easier path were the right path, you would've picked it already.*
—ALEX HORMOZI

OFTENTIMES I WILL get asked why I run. Why do I run for hours and sometimes even days? The answer is simple for me: I am looking for something. I am looking for a fire deep within that I know is there but find only when I have nothing left to give. I truly believe all of us have a fire that accusations from within and without seek to extinguish.

Now I understand that this chapter title might sound somewhat odd at first, so please let me explain. I have always been intrigued by two groups throughout the history of the church: monks and mystics. However, in this hour I believe the Spirit is converging the deepest and most valuable aspects of both of them to give us a new perspective. A new holy order. A new way to live out the Word and the Spirit. I believe there are those who are of a dangerous obsessed order. The Order of the Flame.

The Order of the Flame is not for the faint of heart. It is not a community for spectators. It's not a place for the lukewarm. It is a brotherhood. A sisterhood. A fellowship of the few who have chosen to burn—with relentless passion, with unshakable truth, and with a purpose that refuses to be silent.

It's a people set apart. Forged in fire. Refusing to back down, even when the cost is everything.

To enter the Order is to embrace a life of transformation. To stay in the fire—to carry it—you have to live by its rules. Fire represents the Spirit. Fire represents revival. Fire represents a daily pursuit. Allow me to present some rules for this new order in this new hour. These aren't casual ideas or suggestions. They are sacred commandments of the flame, found in the Word of God. Forged for those who are willing to carry the fire into a dark world.

Let those who read with understanding weigh the cost. Because once you say yes to the fire, there's no going back. But if you're ready—truly ready—then come. And live by the rules that carry the flame.

RULE 1: THE FIRE MUST COME FIRST

No pursuit, ambition, or comfort shall ever take precedence over the fire within you. You are not called to mediocrity. You are not given breath to waste your days in passivity. The fire is your first devotion, your highest commitment, your defining pursuit.

Ask yourself daily, "What have I done today to feed the fire?"

RULE 2: BURN AWAY THE LESSER THINGS

The fire does not share space with what is unworthy. The distractions, the vices, the compromises—burn them. If it dulls your spirit, if it dims your clarity, if it makes you hesitant in your mission, it must be cast into the flame.

Nothing has the right to remain in your life if it keeps you from the fire.

RULE 3: SPEAK ONLY WHAT IS TRUE AND NECESSARY

Words are kindling. The careless tongue sets destructive fires, while the disciplined tongue ignites truth. Let no word leave your mouth unless it's true, necessary, and worthy of the fire you carry. Let no deceit touch your lips. No gossip. No compromise. No half-truths.

Guard your words, for they shape the world around you.

RULE 4: LIVE AS ONE WHO CANNOT BE SHAKEN

The Order of the Flame does not flinch in the face of adversity. It doesn't bow to fear. It doesn't surrender to the pressures of a world that demands compromise. Trials will come. Critics will mock. The weak will fall away. But you? You will stand. You will burn. You will remain unshaken.

RULE 5: REJECT LUKEWARMNESS

You have a choice: Will you react out of emotion or respond with wisdom? Will you let fear keep you silent, or will you speak when truth demands it? Will you trust God to fight for you, or will you take matters into your own hands?

Truth always wins. Whether you're called to speak boldly or stand silently, remember that your identity isn't shaped by accusations. It's shaped by the One who calls you His own. So stand firm. Stay wise. Never let a false word shake the truth of who you are.

KAIZEN AND JESUS: THE POWER OF DAILY, CONSISTENT GROWTH

At first glance, Kaizen—the Japanese philosophy of continuous improvement—might seem like just a business strategy or self-help concept.[1] But when you look closer, you'll find it mirrors something even deeper: the way of Jesus.

Jesus never demanded instant perfection from His disciples. He didn't expect them to get everything right overnight. Instead, He called them into a journey of daily transformation—one step, one choice, one act of surrender at a time. That's the heart of Kaizen—and it's the heart of following Jesus.

1. Small steps, big change. Kaizen teaches that lasting transformation doesn't happen all at once. It happens through small, steady steps—one decision, one adjustment, one act of faith at a time. And that's exactly how Jesus led His disciples.

Jesus didn't expect Peter, James, or John to become fearless leaders overnight. He didn't demand perfection from day one. He walked with them—daily—correcting, teaching, refining, and calling them higher every step of the way.

Luke 9:23 says it clearly: "Whoever wants to be my disciple must deny themselves and take up their cross daily and follow me.".

Growth in Christ isn't about a onetime emotional experience. It's about waking up every day and choosing Him again. Choosing to trust again. Choosing to follow again. Choosing to take the next small step toward the life He's called you to live.

2. Progress over perfection. Kaizen emphasizes continuous progress while rejecting the idea of perfectionism. Jesus demonstrated this principle with His disciples.

Peter was impulsive—cutting off ears, denying Christ, making bold claims. But Jesus patiently worked on him, and over time, Peter became the leader of the early church.

Paul had a violent past—yet Jesus didn't expect an instant transformation. Paul spent years growing before stepping into full-time ministry.

Philippians 1:6 says, "He who began a good work in you will carry it on to completion until the day of Christ Jesus." The goal isn't to be perfect overnight but to let God refine us step by step.

3. The power of daily habits. Kaizen emphasizes the power of small repeated actions to bring about transformation. Jesus reinforced this in His teachings on spiritual discipline.

- **Prayer**—Jesus withdrew to pray constantly (Luke 5:16), showing that intimacy with the Father wasn't a onetime event but a habit.

- **Scripture**—In Matthew 4:4, Jesus says, "Man shall not live on bread alone, but on every word that comes from the mouth of God." Just like we eat daily, we need daily intake of God's Word.

- **Community**—Jesus trained His disciples over time, investing in their growth. Hebrews 10:25 reminds us to keep meeting together and encouraging each other. Your spiritual strength doesn't come from a single encounter with God—it comes from daily seeking Him.

4. Eliminating what slows you down. One of the key ideas in Kaizen is removing inefficiencies—getting rid of things that slow growth. Jesus spoke about this repeatedly: "Every branch in Me that does not bear fruit He takes away; and every branch that bears fruit He prunes, that it may bear more fruit" (John 15:2, NKJV).

If something in your life is hindering your spiritual growth—whether it's pride, distraction, or unhealthy relationships—Jesus calls you to *cut it off* so you can bear more fruit.

5. A life of constant refinement. Jesus never called us to stagnant faith. He called us to *a life of continual learning, continual surrender, continual transformation.* Romans

82 | TIME TO RISE

12:2 says it like this: "Do not conform to the pattern of this world, but be transformed by the renewing of your mind."

The word *transformed* in Greek—*metamorphoō*—is the same word used to describe a caterpillar turning into a butterfly.[2] Real transformation isn't instant. It's a process. And that's exactly what Kaizen teaches too: No matter how much you've grown, there's always another level. There's always more God wants to do in you.

Those who carry the fire—the ones in the Order of the Flame—don't do anything halfway. If you worship, worship with passion. If you work, work with excellence. If you love, love fiercely. There is no space in the fire for the apathetic or the indecisive.

Either you are all in, or you are out. There is no middle ground.

RULE 6: FEAR NO OPPOSITION—IT IS THE PRICE OF THE FIRE

If you burn brightly, darkness will try to extinguish you. If you carry truth, lies will be thrown at you. If you move with power, the weak will try to pull you back down.

Let it be so.

The fire will not apologize for being fire. The flame does not ask permission to burn. Neither shall you.

RULE 7: ENDURE THE REFINING PROCESS WITHOUT COMPLAINT

Fire purifies, but it also burns. There will be seasons where the heat is intense, where your weaknesses are exposed, where you feel stripped of comfort and certainty.

This is good. This is necessary. The unrefined cannot carry the fire for long.

Welcome the refining. Do not resist it. It is making you into what you were always meant to be.

RULE 8: DO NOT SIMPLY KEEP THE FIRE—IGNITE IT IN OTHERS

The fire is not for you alone. If it remains within you and goes no further, it will die. Seek out those who hunger for it. Speak into lives that need it. Do not waste time on those who mock it, but always be ready to set ablaze those who are ready to burn.

A fire that does not spread will eventually go out.

RULE 9: MAKE WAR AGAINST DECEPTION

The world is filled with half-truths, empty promises, and counterfeit flames. The Order of the Flame discerns. The Order of the Flame sees through the illusion.

If it is not truth, it is not of the fire. If it deceives, expose it. If it manipulates, resist it. If it distracts, destroy it.

The greatest battle of fire bearers is against the shadow of deception.

RULE 10: NEVER ABANDON THE FIRE—NO MATTER THE COST

There will be days when you want to quit. When the cost feels too high. When the fire feels too heavy.

That is the moment of decision.

Either the fire owns you, or the world does.

To leave the fire is to return to the cold, to mediocrity, to a life of watching instead of burning. But those who endure? They will carry the flame until the end.

A FINAL WORD TO THOSE WHO WOULD BE FIRE AND BURN

These are the rules of the Order. They are not easy. They are not comfortable. They demand everything.

But if you choose to abide by them, if you choose to let the fire consume you and forge you, then you will walk in a power and clarity few ever know.

The world does not need more watchers. It does not need more hesitant voices. It does not need more people waiting for permission to step into their callings.

The world needs fire.

And if you have read these rules and found them resonating deep within you—then you already know who you are.

The fire is calling. The choice is yours.

Will you burn?

PART III

IDENTITY AND AUTHORITY— KNOWING WHO WE ARE

When I was in high school, I lived through a supernatural miracle that changed the direction of my life.

In my sophomore year, while heading to an Easter sunrise service, I was hit head-on by a drunk driver going seventy miles per hour. I should have died. The miracle is this: I was a teen with my first car, and I did not always wear my seat belt. Yet that morning, as I climbed into my car, I had a strong, overwhelming sense that I should buckle up. I now know why.

It was still somewhat dark outside, and rain was coming down when the crash happened. I was following my pastor to the lake where we were going to hold the sunrise service. We had just gotten onto the major highway near Lyndon, Kansas, and had reached full speed when I saw headlights coming straight at me—in my lane. The rest is a blur. I vaguely remember the paramedics pulling me from the car and the ride in the ambulance.

I am convinced that if I hadn't buckled my seat belt that day, I would have died.

But even in that moment, I made a choice: I chose not to become a victim of my circumstance.

The doctors told me I would never be able to run again. It took over a year of slow, painful healing before I could finally run. But my identity was not limited to their belief about my ability. My authority did not come from their expertise. My authority came from the One who kept me alive.

Now as I run hundreds of miles—and most recently the 304-mile ultramarathon run in Arizona called the Arizona Monster 300—I am more convinced than ever: Jesus wants to set people free. Not just to survive but to live fully alive in His identity and His authority.

bit.ly/4m4rOBf

CHAPTER 21

YOU ARE NOT YOUR PAST: YOU ARE WHO GOD SAYS YOU ARE

Many people are crucified between two thieves. The thief
of yesterday and the thief of tomorrow.
—Dr. Jay Strack

YOUR PAST MAY be a chapter in your story, but it is not your identity. Too many people carry the weight of who they used to be, allowing past mistakes, failures, and wounds to dictate their future. But here's the truth: You are not your past—you are a new creation in Christ.

The voice you listen to determines the life you live. If you keep replaying the old script in your mind—the one that says you're broken, unworthy, or forever tied to past failures—you will stay stuck. But if you choose to believe what God says about you, you can step into a completely new identity.

YOU HAVE NOT BEEN IMPROVED—YOU HAVE BEEN TRANSFORMED

Jesus didn't die so bad people could become good or that good people could become better—He died so dead people could live.

Second Corinthians 5:17 says, "If anyone is in Christ, the new creation has come: The old has gone, the new is here!" That means the old you—the one defined by sin, shame, and regret—no longer exists in God's eyes. When you surrender to Christ, He doesn't just fix your old self; He makes you brand new.

Yet many of us live as if we are still the old versions of ourselves. Why? Because we've spent years—sometimes decades—identifying with our past. We say things like "I've always been this way." "This is just who I am." "People will never see me differently."

But God is saying, "That's not who you are anymore!"

The real question is this: Are you going to agree with your past—or are you going to agree with God?

SHIFTING FROM A PAST-BASED IDENTITY TO A GOD-BASED IDENTITY

Your past is a terrible place to build an identity. Why? Because it holds only who you *were*, not who you're *becoming*. If you let it, your past will trap you in cycles of guilt, shame, and self-doubt, robbing you of the future God has already prepared for you.

88 | TIME TO RISE

But when you step into your God-given identity, everything shifts:

- Your past doesn't disqualify you—it prepares you.
- Your mistakes don't define you—they refine you.
- Your failures aren't your identity—they're stepping stones to growth.

Think about Peter. He denied Jesus three times. He blew it—badly. If Peter had let his past define him, he would have stayed buried in shame. But Jesus didn't leave him there. He restored him, He called him forward, and Peter became a foundational leader in the church.

And hear me on this—God is doing the same for you. He's calling you out of the identity of your past and into the identity of His purpose. Your story isn't over. It's just getting started.

HOW THE ENEMY USES YOUR PAST AGAINST YOU

The enemy knows he can't change what God has declared over you. So he does the next best thing: He works to keep you trapped in a false identity. He whispers lies that sound dangerously close to truth:

- "You will always be the same."
- "You are too broken to be used by God."
- "People will never see past your mistakes."
- "You don't deserve a second chance."

If you believe these lies, you will live beneath your calling. You will settle for less than God's best. You will keep returning to the very thing God has already freed you from.

But here's the truth: *Your past has no authority over you—unless you give it permission.*

HOW TO LIVE IN YOUR NEW IDENTITY

Agree with God, not your past.

Stop replaying the old script in your mind. Replace it with what God says about you. When the voice of shame speaks, answer with scripture:

- Shame says, "You're unworthy." God says, "You are chosen and dearly loved" (Col. 3:12).
- Fear says, "You will always be stuck." God says, "Who the Son sets free is free indeed" (John 8:36).
- Guilt says, "You are beyond redemption." God says, "There is no condemnation for those in Christ Jesus" (Rom. 8:1).

Speak life over yourself.

Your words shape your identity. Start declaring truth over your life:

+ "I am a new creation."
+ "My past has no hold on me."
+ "God is using everything for my good."
+ "I am forgiven, free, and walking in purpose."

Step forward in faith.

You don't have to feel different to start living differently. Faith isn't about feelings; it's about trust. Move forward, trusting that God has already made you new.

If you feel stuck, take a small step in obedience. If you feel unworthy, serve others and let God work through you. If you feel disqualified, remember this: God specializes in calling the unlikely and equipping the unqualified.

Surround yourself with truth.

The company you keep will reinforce either your old identity or your new one. Stay around people who see you through the lens of grace, not condemnation. Be planted in an environment where your faith is built, not torn down.

Find a community that speaks life over you. Avoid voices that drag you back into shame. Stay rooted in God's Word daily.

Live like you're free.

You are not bound to your past. Walk boldly in the identity Christ has already given you. Don't let old habits, old thoughts, or even old relationships pull you back into chains you've been set free from.

Stop apologizing for a past God has already forgiven. Stop waiting for people to validate your transformation. Stop believing that your best days are behind you.

Let me say it plainly: You are not the divorce. You are not the addiction. You are not the failure. You are not the mistakes you've made. You are a child of God—and your future is greater than your past.

CHAPTER 22

THE HERO'S JOURNEY: YOUR PATH TO TRANSFORMATION

All men dream: but not equally. Those who dream by night in the dusty recesses of their minds wake in the day to find that it was vanity: but the dreamers of the day are dangerous men, for they may act out their dream with open eyes, to make it possible.
—T. E. LAWRENCE

EVERY GREAT STORY follows a pattern—the hero's journey. You see it woven into ancient myths, blockbuster movies, and the lives of the most impactful people in history. But here's what most people don't realize: Your life is a hero's journey too.

At some point, you will be called to step out of your comfort zone, face obstacles, and become the person you were created to be. The question is, will you answer the call?

Now is the time to be what Donald Miller calls "a hero on a mission." Before we dive into the stages of the hero's journey, I want you to consider something crucial: There are four characters any one of us can choose to become in life.

- Victim—someone who has experienced pain and chooses to live in it
- Villain—someone who, out of their own pain, seeks to make others pay for it
- Hero—someone who has been transformed by their pain
- Guide (or hero maker)—someone who once walked through all the previous roles and now helps other heroes on a mission[1]

So pause for a second and ask yourself this: Which character are you living today? And which one is God inviting you to become?

THE CALL TO ADVENTURE

Every hero begins in the ordinary world—a place of familiarity, routine, and predictability. But then something happens. A challenge appears. A crisis erupts. A restlessness stirs. This is the call to adventure—an invitation to step into the unknown.

Most people resist this call. Fear kicks in. Doubt whispers, "Who do you think you are?" But deep down, the hero knows there is more.

In your own life, this might be the moment you realize your job is draining you, your relationships aren't fulfilling, or your purpose is calling you higher. But stepping into the unknown requires one thing: courage.

We see this pattern in Scripture. When God called Moses to deliver the Israelites, his first response wasn't excitement—it was self-doubt. "Who am I to do this?" (Exod. 3:11). The same hesitation showed up in Gideon, in Jeremiah, and in nearly every biblical hero. But here's the key: They stepped forward anyway. And that's what set them apart.

CROSSING THE THRESHOLD

Eventually, the hero takes the first step—leaving the old world behind. This is the moment of commitment—the crossing of the threshold. It's the entrepreneur quitting their nine-to-five. The addict finally reaching out for help. The believer surrendering fully to God's call.

But the journey is never easy. Obstacles arise. Doubts creep in. Opposition intensifies. And this is where most people turn back.

Think about Peter stepping out of the boat to walk on water (Matt. 14:29). As long as he kept his eyes on Jesus, he did the impossible. But the moment he focused on the storm, he sank. The lesson is simple but profound: Once you step into the unknown, resistance will come. But if you keep your eyes on Jesus, you will overcome.

THE BATTLE AGAINST ACCUSATION

Every hero must confront their deepest fears, including the voices of accusation—both external and internal.

+ "You're not strong enough."
+ "You'll never change."
+ "People like you don't succeed."

Sound familiar? These are the lies designed to stop you from becoming who you were created to be. In Scripture, the enemy has always been the accuser, trying to convince God's people that they are unworthy, incapable, or disqualified.

Job faced it. His friends told him his suffering was his own fault. David faced it. His own family doubted him before he ever fought Goliath. Jesus faced it. Religious leaders falsely accused Him, and even at the cross, bystanders mocked Him.

And you? You will face it too. But here's something you must know: Your greatest attacks will not come from strangers—they will often come from family and people you once called friends. If Satan can't get to you directly, he will get to you through those closest to you. Every time.

Please remember this: Accusation always intensifies when you're on the verge of transformation.

But the hero? They fight. They grow. They become.

THE TRANSFORMATION

In every hero's journey, there is a pivotal moment of transformation—a revelation, a breakthrough, a shift in identity. The hero realizes that the real battle was never about the external obstacles—it was about becoming the person they were always meant to be.

For you, this moment might be when you finally break free from past wounds, overcome limiting beliefs, or step boldly into your God-given identity.

Paul experienced this on the road to Damascus. He went from being a persecutor of Christians to one of the most influential apostles of all time. His encounter with Jesus changed everything.

And here's the truth: Your encounter with Jesus is just as real, just as life-altering, as Paul's was.

Transformation requires a new mindset. It demands letting go of old labels and lies—and embracing who God says you are. You are not your past. You are not your mistakes. You are not the accusations spoken over you. You are who God has called you to be—and no one, absolutely no one, gets to redefine that.

RETURNING WITH POWER

The final stage of the hero's journey is the return—but the hero is no longer the same person who began the journey. They come back with wisdom, strength, and a deeper understanding of their purpose.

And they don't return just for themselves—they return to impact others.

Moses returned to Egypt to set his people free. Joseph, after years of suffering, became a leader who saved nations. Jesus, after conquering death itself, returned to commission His disciples—and through them, the world was changed.

This is your story too.

You weren't called to stay stuck in fear—the fear that you will never be enough, or you will never be truly loved. You weren't created to live small, beneath your purpose. You were made to rise, to overcome, to transform—and to help others do the same.

HOW TO STEP INTO YOUR HERO'S JOURNEY

- **Recognize the call.** Pay attention to the restlessness in your spirit. That holy discomfort? It's God calling you to something greater.
- **Push through fear.** Fear will try to paralyze you. Move forward anyway. Courage isn't the absence of fear—it's moving forward despite it.
- **Fight the lies.** Accusation will come. Recognize it. Reject it. Replace it with God's truth.
- **Embrace the transformation.** Let go of who you used to be. Step boldly into who God is making you to be.
- **Return with purpose.** Your journey isn't just for you. It's for those you are called to impact.

The greatest tragedy isn't failing. It's never answering the call in the first place. There is someone who needs your story. There is someone who needs your courage. There is someone who needs the freedom your testimony will bring.

Will you step into your calling? Will you fight through the accusations? Will you rise and become the person you were created to be?

CHAPTER 23

KNOWING WHO YOU ARE IN A WORLD OF OPINIONS

Somebody may beat me, but they are going to have to bleed to do it.
—Steve Prefontaine

Every day, a battle takes place within you—a battle of voices. Some voices tell you that you are enough, that you are capable, that you are loved. Others whisper doubt, fear, and insecurity, questioning your worth and your place in the world. And the loudest voice? It's often the one you've unknowingly trained yourself to listen to—the internal dialogue that quietly shapes how you see yourself and how you live.

So let me ask you: What is that voice telling you?

For many of us it's a voice shaped by past experiences, by old wounds, and by others' expectations. It's the echo of hurtful words spoken in childhood, the replay of past failures, the constant pressure to be someone you were never meant to be. And when that internal voice is rooted in fear, comparison, and approval-seeking, life feels exhausting. You find yourself constantly adjusting. Constantly striving. Constantly trying to measure up—only to feel like you never quite do.

But what if the problem isn't the world around you? What if the real battle is within?

THE WAR OF IDENTITY

The truth is, the world will always have opinions. People will always have something to say about you—whether it's praise or criticism. But those voices have power over you only when they confirm what you already believe about yourself inside. That's why two people can receive the same criticism, yet one is destroyed by it while the other moves forward unfazed. The difference isn't what was said—it's what was already believed.

Jesus was unshaken not because the world was kind to Him—it wasn't. He was unshaken because He was secure in His identity. He didn't need the approval of others to validate Him, nor was He destroyed by their rejection. He lived from a place of deep certainty—anchored in the truth of who He was and whose He was.

Can you say the same about yourself?

For most of us, the answer is hard. We live in a culture where identity is built on fragile foundations—what people think, what we achieve, how we compare to others. But when identity is rooted in shifting sands, we are easily shaken.

One negative comment can send us spiraling. One failure can make us question our worth. One rejection can convince us we are unlovable.

But there's another way to live—a way that is unshaken, unmovable, and rooted in eternal truth.

BREAKING FREE FROM THE LIES

The enemy doesn't need to destroy you outright—he just needs to make you doubt. He whispers accusations in your mind, subtle lies that shape your perspective:

- "You're not good enough."
- "You'll always struggle."
- "You're a failure."
- "You're unworthy of love."

And when those thoughts go unchecked, they become your reality—not because they are true, but because you've allowed them to take root.

But here's the game changer: You have the power to shift the narrative. You are not obligated to believe every thought that enters your mind. You are not defined by past failures, by what others think of you, or by the insecurities that try to hold you back.

THE VOICE YOU CHOOSE

Living unshaken isn't about silencing the world—it's about choosing which voice you will listen to. Will you continue to believe the script of fear and inadequacy? Or will you replace it with the truth of who God says you are?

- You are chosen (1 Pet. 2:9).
- You are fearfully and wonderfully made (Ps. 139:14).
- You are more than a conqueror (Rom. 8:37).

When your internal voice aligns with God's truth, the opinions of others lose their grip. You don't have to live in reaction to every criticism or validation. You can move forward with confidence, knowing your worth is already established by the One who never changes.

HOW TO LIVE UNSHAKEN

So how do we move from simply hearing this truth to actually living it out? Here's how you can start:

- **Know the truth.** The only way to fight lies is with truth. If you don't know what God says about you, you'll believe whatever the world tells you. Spend time in Scripture. Let it reshape your thinking.
- **Guard your mind.** Not every thought deserves your attention. Filter your thoughts—if they don't align with truth, reject them immediately.

96 | TIME TO RISE

- **Stop seeking approval.** The need for approval is a prison. Break free by realizing that no amount of human validation can replace God's affirmation.
- **Build your foundation on Christ.** When your identity is rooted in Him, life's storms won't shake you. You'll stand firm, no matter what comes your way.
- **Speak life over yourself.** Your words shape your reality. Stop declaring doubt and insecurity. Speak truth over yourself: "I am loved. I am strong. I am enough in Christ."

THE FREEDOM OF LIVING UNSHAKEN

When you live unshaken, you stop striving. You stop performing for approval. You stop allowing fear to dictate your steps. Instead, you walk in freedom, purpose, and confidence. You begin to live the way God intended—fully secure in His love, unshaken by the opinions of the world.

The voices will keep coming, but they don't have to define you. The real question is—who are you becoming in the process?

The world doesn't need more people who live in fear, seeking validation from others. It needs people who are firm, unwavering, and confident in who they are in Christ. It needs people like you—who choose to live unshaken.

CHAPTER 24

ATTACKED AT THE CORE: WHY IDENTITY IS SATAN'S PRIMARY TARGET

Criticism is easier to take when you realize that the only people
who aren't criticized are those who don't take risks.
—DONALD J. TRUMP,

YOUR IDENTITY IS the lens through which you see the world, the foundation of your decisions, and the script that runs in the background of your mind. It dictates how you respond to challenges, how you treat yourself, and how you interact with others. But where does it come from? What shapes the way we see ourselves?

If you want to transform your life, you must first understand what has shaped your identity—and, even more importantly, who you are allowing to define you.

Because let's be clear: Your identity is built either on truth or on lies. And Satan's number one strategy? Attack you at the core. If he can get you to doubt your worth, your calling, your very existence—he's got you exactly where he wants you.

But here's the good news: You don't have to accept the lies. You have the power—through Christ—to rewrite the narrative. You have self-agency. He has given it to you.

THE WORDS WE HEAR

From the moment we are born, we are shaped by the words spoken over us. Parents, teachers, friends, and even strangers contribute to the narrative we tell ourselves. Encouragement builds confidence, but criticism can plant seeds of doubt.

If you were told "You are smart, capable, and strong," you likely carry confidence into new situations.

If you were told "You'll never amount to anything," that lie might still echo in your mind today, influencing your choices and limiting your courage.

Words have power. That's why Proverbs 18:21 warns, "The tongue has the power of life and death." The enemy knows this truth too. He will use the wrong words, spoken at the right moment, to create doubt, insecurity, and confusion. He will whisper accusations that *sound* like truth simply because they align with old wounds you've never fully healed.

But you don't have to accept every word spoken over you. You get to choose which words take root—and which ones you reject.

THE EXPERIENCES WE HAVE

Your past experiences—both good and bad—leave a deep imprint on your identity. Successes often affirm our abilities, while failures can make us question our worth. Trauma, rejection, and betrayal? They have a way of distorting our view of ourselves, making us feel unworthy or unlovable.

If you've ever been deeply hurt, you might have internalized a lie like "I'm not good enough" or "I don't deserve love." These beliefs don't just sit quietly in the background—they actively shape the choices you make and the risks you're willing to take.

But let's get something straight: *Your past does not define you.* Jesus came to heal the brokenhearted and set the captives free (Luke 4:18). Your identity is not in what has happened to you—it's in what God says about you. This is why we must confront the inner voice of accusation. Your freedom is won when you refuse to believe the lie about your past that ultimately controls your present and predicts your future.

So the real question is this: Will you let your past chain you, or will you let it propel you forward?

THE LABELS WE ACCEPT

Society constantly tries to label us—by our achievements, failures, social status, or even struggles. People often identify themselves by what they do, whom they're with, what they own, or how they look.

But none of these things are the foundation of who you truly are. If your identity is in your job, what happens when you lose it? If your identity is in a relationship, what happens when it falls apart?

Let me tell you something clearly: The only *unshakable* identity is the one rooted in Christ. The moment you accepted Him, your identity was rewritten:

- You are a *new creation* (2 Cor. 5:17).
- You are *not defined by your past* (Rom. 8:1).
- You are *adopted* into God's family (Eph. 1:5).

When you build your identity on anything else, you are standing on shaky ground. But when you stand on the truth of who God says you are—you become immovable.

THE THOUGHTS WE BELIEVE

Your mind is the battlefield of identity. Every single day, you are either reinforcing God's truth or agreeing with the enemy's lies. The enemy doesn't have to control your life if he can control your thoughts.

Ever heard that voice in your head whispering, "You're not good enough," "You'll always struggle," "You're a failure," or "You're unworthy of love"?

Those thoughts aren't random. They are strategic attacks designed to keep you stuck, small, and defeated. But here's the game changer: *You are not obligated to believe every thought that enters your mind. You get to choose what you agree with.*

That's why Romans 12:2 tells us to "be transformed by the renewing of your mind." When you change the way you think—you change the way you live.

And here's the secret most people miss: Your identity is built by the thoughts you consistently reinforce. If you want to live free, you must *choose—every single day*—to stand in truth.

WHO ARE YOU BECOMING?

The most important question you can ask is not "Who am I?" It's "Who am I becoming?" Because identity isn't just about where you are today—it's about where God is leading you.

You don't need to be defined by old wounds, past mistakes, or others' words. You can *rewrite the script.* You can step into the identity God has waiting for you.

I've discovered along the way that true happiness doesn't come from everything going perfectly. It comes from daily progress—becoming the person God created you to be.

In our family, identity is something we speak over our children every single day. My wife, Rachel, has a powerful message of identity and purpose she speaks over our youngest children each night. We have eight-plus children—foster care and adoption are beautiful callings God has placed on our lives. And every night, when she speaks that blessing over them, it's a reminder of who they are in God's eyes.

It's not just words—it's truth being planted deep into their hearts. And now they can recite it themselves.

Who you are becoming is the identity God already knows exists inside of you. He speaks it over you. Now would be a great time to listen to what He is saying.

When you align your identity with Him, you live with boldness, with purpose, and with freedom. You stop carrying the crushing weight of false labels. You stop striving to prove your worth. You start walking in the truth of who you already are:

- You are chosen.
- You are loved.
- You are called.
- You are equipped.
- You are unstoppable.

And that identity? It's unshakable.

So, here's the real question you have to face today: Are you ready to fight for the truth of who you are? Because make no mistake—the enemy will attack. He will whisper lies and stir doubt. But he wins only if you let him. It's time to stand firm. It's time to claim your true identity. It's time to rise.

CHAPTER 25

THE SPIRIT OF COMPARISON

God knows if I am chasing after holy behavior or if I'm consistently excusing my love or tolerance for worldly desires and the pride of accomplishments. It all begins with my heart's intentions. Will I chase after purity of heart and mind, resulting in a change of actions? Will I do so even if those who are close to me don't?
—JOHN BEVERE

COMPARISON IS THE silent thief of joy, the unseen enemy of progress, and one of the greatest destroyers of potential. It doesn't announce itself at your door with a warning—it creeps in quietly, slipping in through the back window of your mind, whispering, "You're not good enough." And before you even realize it, you're no longer living your own life—you're living a constant evaluation of how your life measures up to someone else's.

Think about it. You doomscroll through social media and see someone traveling the world, driving a nicer car, or launching a successful business. Immediately, your brain shifts into judgment mode: "Why am I not there yet? Why is my life so ordinary?" And just like that, the energy that should be fueling your own journey is now wasted on self-doubt.

And it doesn't stop there. Often, accusations against others are born from a place of comparison. Sometimes we tear others down simply because we can't stand to see them succeed.

As an ultrarunner, I've learned a crucial truth: My only real competition is myself. If I allow it to, comparison becomes a trap that steals both the joy of running and the joy of living.

COMPARISON IS A GAME OF CHUTES AND LADDERS YOU CAN'T WIN

Here's the truth: Comparison is a game designed to keep you losing. It is the casino of life you need to avoid—you will never hit the jackpot there. There will always be someone who seems ahead of you in some way—richer, stronger, more successful, more attractive, more popular. But the problem is, you're comparing their highlight reel to your behind-the-scenes struggles.

You see their victories, but not their battles. You see their success, but not their sleepless nights. You see their results, but forget about your own process.

What if I told you that your journey was never supposed to look like theirs? What if I told you that you're wasting precious time trying to fit into someone else's story when God has already written a unique, powerful script just for you?

WHERE COMPARISON CONQUERS, IDENTITY IS LOST

The most dangerous part about comparison isn't just the jealousy or insecurity—it's what it does to your identity.

The moment you start measuring yourself against someone else, you stop listening to who God says you are. Instead of walking boldly in your purpose, you start questioning it. Instead of pushing forward, you hesitate. Instead of celebrating progress, you feel like you're falling behind. It is my belief that much of tearing others down and a hypercritical spirit is born out of a lost identity in who we are and who others are. Comparison is never done knowing all the facts. This is why it is dangerous to do so.

So here's the key: Your calling, your gifts, your purpose—they're tailor-made for you. No one else can do what you were created to do, in the way you were created to do it. The enemy knows that. That's why he desperately wants you distracted—looking from side to side at everyone else—rather than fixing your eyes on God. Because the more distracted you are, the more ineffective you become.

THE COST OF COMPARISON

Comparison isn't just frustrating—it's paralyzing. It drains your energy, steals your peace, and blinds you to the blessings in your own life. Instead of moving forward, you stay stuck. Instead of taking action, you analyze. And in that state of hesitation, you lose precious time and momentum.

How many dreams have been delayed because someone spent too much time worrying about whether they were good enough? How many opportunities have been missed because fear of not measuring up kept someone from stepping forward? The enemy doesn't have to destroy you outright—he just needs to keep you distracted long enough for you to give up on yourself.

Religion will always seek to make you compare yourself to other Christians. Legalistic people often, whether they realize it or not, believe you should look, act, and think more like them. But the gospel? It's not about comparison. It's about transformation. It's about becoming who Christ says you are—not a copy of anyone else.

HOW TO BREAK FREE FROM COMPARISON

So how do you stop this cycle? How do you reclaim your energy and confidence? Here are four powerful steps you can take:

1. Focus on your own lane.

The only competition you have is yesterday's version of you. Measure progress, not perfection. If you're growing, learning, and taking steps toward your purpose, you're already winning.

2. Control your inputs.

If social media is fueling comparison, limit it. Stop feeding your mind with images that make you feel like you're not enough. Be intentional about what you consume—choose inspiration over frustration. As my friend Mike Signorelli says, stop doom-scrolling. Become a creator, not a consumer.

3. Celebrate others.

Instead of feeling threatened by someone else's success, let it inspire you. Their victory doesn't mean your defeat. When you shift your mindset from competition to collaboration, you open yourself up to limitless possibilities. One of the best actions you can take when you see someone succeed? Send them a message of genuine congratulations. I promise you—every time I have done this, I've never once regretted it.

4. Anchor your identity in truth.

If you're not constantly reminding yourself of who God says you are, the world will be happy to tell you your identity instead. And their version won't serve you. Replace the lies of comparison with the truth of God's promises:

- You are fearfully and wonderfully made (Ps. 139:14).
- You are chosen (1 Pet. 2:9).
- You are more than a conqueror (Rom. 8:37).

TAKE IT BACK!

It is time to go to the enemy's camp and take back what he stole from you. Stop looking sideways. Start looking forward. Your purpose is too big, and your calling is too important, to waste time measuring yourself against someone else's race.

Own who you are. Step into what God has for you. And never apologize for being you.

CHAPTER 26

FIGHT, FIGHT, FIGHT: THE SPIRIT OF RESILIENCE

The greater the problem, the greater your chance for greatness.
—DONALD J. TRUMP

'LL NEVER FORGET where I was when I heard the news. I was in the middle of a thirty-mile run when I got word about the attempt on Donald Trump's life. It stopped me in my tracks—not just because of the gravity of the moment, but because of what it revealed about the human spirit.

No matter your political affiliation, there's something powerful we all can learn from how President Trump responded that day.

We must remember that in life, challenges are not mere obstacles; they are the crucibles that forge our character, test our mettle, and define our destiny. On July 13, 2024, former president Donald Trump faced a crucible moment during a rally in Butler, Pennsylvania—a moment that not only tested his resilience but also underscored the unyielding spirit that propels individuals to confront adversity head-on.

As Trump addressed a sea of supporters, casting his vision with characteristic fervor, an unforeseen calamity struck. A gunman, perched atop a nearby building, opened fire. Amid the chaos Trump was grazed by a bullet on his right ear. Tragically, the attack claimed the life of Corey Comperatore, a firefighter attending the rally, and critically injured two others.

Secret Service agents reacted immediately, surrounding Trump and rushing him to safety. But what happened next is truly what captured the world's attention: Trump returned to the stage, raised his fist in the air, and declared, "Fight, fight, fight!" Who hasn't seen that now iconic photo—is it not the embodiment of resilience? The "millimeter miracle" was very real that day. Had the bullet struck slightly differently, the outcome would have changed history.[1]

THE POWER OF RESILIENCE IN THE FACE OF ADVERSITY

But let's pull back for a moment—because this isn't just about politics. This is about you. It's about what it means to fight for your life, your destiny, your purpose when everything around you says to give up.

What about you? What challenges are you facing right now? What opposition or hardship is threatening to take you out? Maybe it's a setback in your career. A betrayal from someone you trusted. A health crisis. Or maybe it's an internal battle—fear, doubt, discouragement—that no one else even sees.

Resilience isn't reserved for public figures or history books. It's woven into the DNA of every person who chooses not to give up. Resilience is the fire that keeps you standing when life tries to knock you down. It's the whisper inside your spirit that says, "Get up." It's the decision to fight.

So let me ask you: What bullets are flying at you right now—on the inside and outside? And more importantly, how will you respond?

WHAT DEFINES A FIGHTER?

A fighter isn't someone who never gets knocked down. A fighter is someone who refuses to stay down. Think about it: Some of the greatest victories in history weren't won by those who had it easy—they were won by those who decided to keep fighting when the odds were against them.

And that same resilience—that same fight—is available to you. This is your Rocky Balboa moment. It's time to rise.

HOW TO BUILD RESILIENCE IN YOUR OWN LIFE

So how do you cultivate resilience? How do you develop the kind of inner strength that allows you to stand in the storm instead of being swept away by it?

Shift your mindset.

Resilient people see obstacles as opportunities. They don't ask, "Why is this happening to me?" Instead, they ask, "What can I learn from this? How can this make me stronger?"

Control your narrative.

The story you tell yourself determines the story you live. If you believe you're a victim, you'll live like one. But if you believe you're a fighter, you'll rise to the occasion every time. Choose your narrative wisely. Craft your narrative intentionally. Speak it and shout it to yourself.

Surround yourself with history makers.

You become like the people you spend the most time with. If you surround yourself with people who quit when things get hard, you'll do the same. But if you surround yourself with warriors—people who push forward no matter what—you'll adopt that mindset too.

Take action, even when it's hard.

Resilience is built in motion. You don't wait to feel strong to act—you act, and that's what makes you strong. Take one step forward today, no matter how small. Progress is progress.

IT'S TIME TO TAKE BACK WHAT'S YOURS

Your energy, your confidence, your drive—hardship has stolen enough of it. It's time to take it back.

Stop looking at the obstacles. Start seeing the opportunities. Your purpose is too big, and your calling is too important, to be paralyzed by fear or setbacks. Decide today to fight. Fight for your future. Fight for your faith. Fight for your purpose.

You are stronger than you think, and your story isn't over yet.

Stand up. Take back your power. Walk boldly into the life God has called you to live. And never apologize for being fully, powerfully, authentically *you*.

CHAPTER 27

FROM ORPHAN TO HEIR: WALKING IN YOUR TRUE IDENTITY

I will not be silent, but cry out all the more.
—Philip Anthony Mitchell

MOST PEOPLE GO through life feeling like they don't quite belong—like they're on the outside looking in. There's an ache, a deep longing to know who we are and where we fit in the grand scheme of things. It's the orphan spirit at work, whispering lies that we are alone, unwanted, and unworthy. But here's the truth: You were never meant to live as an orphan. You were created to walk as an heir.

If there is an area of my life that I struggle with the most, it would be this. An orphan spirit. I am not sure if it is because I was adopted. I have often wondered whether this is what has fueled my obsession to do the insane. Regardless, we cannot allow ourselves to live with an orphan spirit.

THE ORPHAN VS. THE HEIR

Think about the difference between an orphan and an heir. An orphan fends for themselves, always striving, always uncertain of their place. They live with a scarcity mindset, afraid that if they don't fight for everything, they'll be left with nothing.

An heir, on the other hand, walks in confidence. They know who they are. They know they have an inheritance. They don't beg for scraps because they understand that what belongs to their Father belongs to them.

The world and the enemy want you to believe you're an orphan—alone, forgotten, rejected. But God's Word tells a different story. Romans 8:15 says, "The Spirit you received does not make you slaves, so that you live in fear again; rather, the Spirit you received brought about your adoption to sonship. And by him we cry, '*Abba*, Father.'"

You are not abandoned. You are not alone. You are an adopted child of God, an heir to His kingdom.

BREAKING THE ORPHAN MINDSET

To fully step into our identity as heirs, we must confront and break free from the orphan mindset. This mindset manifests in many ways:

- **Striving for approval**—Orphans believe they have to earn love, constantly working to be "good enough." Heirs know they are already loved, accepted, and chosen.

From Orphan to Heir: Walking in Your True Identity | 107

- **Fear of rejection**—Orphans live in fear of being abandoned. Heirs rest in the security of their Father's love.

- **Scarcity mentality**—Orphans believe there's never enough—love, resources, opportunity—so they grasp and fight for every bit. Heirs trust that God provides abundantly.

- **Self-reliance**—Orphans feel they must do everything alone. Heirs rely on their Father's strength and guidance.

This orphan spirit creeps in subtly. It whispers lies that make us question our worth, pushing us to strive harder, proving ourselves to people who will never satisfy our need for belonging. But the key to walking in our true identity is renewing our minds to see ourselves as God sees us. He calls us sons and daughters, heirs to a kingdom—seated in heavenly places with Christ (Eph. 2:6).

WALKING AS AN HEIR

Once we recognize the orphan mindset for what it is, we must take intentional steps to live as heirs:

Renew your mind with truth.

Stop feeding yourself the lies of rejection and unworthiness. Meditate on what God says about you:

- You are loved (Jer. 31:3).
- You are chosen (Eph. 1:4–5).
- You have an inheritance (Gal. 4:7).

Fill your mind with His promises rather than the world's opinions.

Stop striving and start receiving.

You don't have to work for God's love. He already gave it freely through Jesus. Stop striving to prove yourself. Start walking in the grace that is already yours. When you fully grasp this, you will experience the rest and peace that come from knowing your worth is secure in Him.

Live with boldness and authority.

An heir doesn't live timidly. You have a purpose, a calling, and a destiny. Walk in it with confidence, knowing that you are backed by the King of kings. You were never meant to live in fear or insecurity. As His child, you carry His authority.

Embrace your kingdom inheritance.

As an heir you have access to the Father's wisdom, peace, provision, and power. Stop living like a beggar and start stepping into what is already yours. If a king's child walked around acting like a servant, it wouldn't change the fact that they were royalty—it would only mean they weren't living in their rightful identity.

RECOGNIZING YOUR TRUE IDENTITY

You may still wonder, "How do I know if I'm truly walking as an heir?" Here are some signs that you are stepping into your true identity:

- You no longer seek validation from people because you know your worth comes from God.
- You make decisions based on faith rather than fear.
- You trust in God's provision instead of living in worry and anxiety.
- You celebrate the success of others rather than feeling threatened or jealous.
- You walk with peace and confidence, knowing that your Father is in control.

These aren't just idealistic goals; they are the natural by-products of a heart that knows its place in God's family. When you live as an heir, you stop striving and start abiding. You stop competing and start trusting. You stop fearing and start walking in freedom.

OVERCOMING THE LIES THAT KEEP YOU STUCK

The enemy wants to keep you trapped in an orphan mentality because as long as you believe you are an orphan, you will live beneath your potential. But today, you have a choice to break free.

Here are some common lies the enemy uses and the truths that will set you free:

Lie	Truth
"You are alone."	"God will never leave you nor forsake you." (See Deuteronomy 31:6.)
"You have to earn your worth."	"You are saved by grace, not by works." (See Ephesians 2:8–9.)
"You'll never be good enough."	"You are fearfully and wonderfully made." (See Psalm 139:14.)
"You don't have a purpose."	"God has good plans for you, plans to prosper you and not to harm you." (See Jeremiah 29:11.)

When these lies try to take root, replace them immediately with God's truth. The more you immerse yourself in His Word, the more unshakable you become. I would highly suggest speaking out loud something like this: "The lie I used to believe is this.

However, the truth is _____ (fill in the blank)." Do this one hundred times as loud as you can, and you won't be the same person. I promise you that.

THE CHOICE IS YOURS

You don't have to live another day believing you are an orphan. The moment you accept who you are in Christ, everything changes. Your past no longer defines you. Your struggles no longer imprison you. You are an heir—and it's time to start walking like one.

It won't always be easy. The enemy will try to pull you back into old ways of thinking, making you question your identity. But stand firm. Refuse to believe anything that contradicts what God has spoken over you.

Imagine the freedom that comes when you no longer live in fear, striving for approval or doubting your worth. Imagine stepping fully into the inheritance that has been yours all along. That's what happens when you embrace your identity as an heir.

So today, make the decision. Reject the orphan mindset. Walk boldly as a son or daughter of the King. The inheritance is already yours—it's time to claim it.

CHAPTER 28

THE ROAR OF THE REDEEMED

Let us not glide through this world and then slip quietly into heaven, without having blown the trumpet loud and long for our Redeemer, Jesus Christ. Let us see to it that the devil will hold a thanksgiving service in hell, when he gets the news of our departure from the field of battle.
—C. T. STUDD

WHEN THE REDEEMED of the Lord rise, it's not with a whisper—it's with a roar! All of hell trembles when a child of God awakens to their true kingdom authority. When a believer refuses to stay silent, the kingdom of darkness shakes. Yet too many Christians have lost their voices in today's age. Many have forfeited their roar for a mere whimper, exchanging their boldness for fear and their authority for man's approval.

But listen up. God did not save you to stay silent. He did not redeem you to blend in. He put His fire within you to speak, to declare, and to shake the nations.

WHY HAVE WE GONE SILENT?

One of the enemy's greatest weapons is intimidation. He knows that if he can keep you quiet, he can keep you powerless. He uses fear, rejection, and accusations to muzzle the church. He has convinced believers that speaking boldly is offensive, that truth must be watered down, and that standing firm is unloving. The spirit of accusation has been at work—strategically attempting to silence voices in the church.

But take a look at the early church. They didn't cower before others. They didn't soften their message to be more appealing. They stood before rulers and religious leaders and declared the name of Jesus with power! When Peter and John were commanded to stop preaching, they answered, "We cannot help but declare what we have seen and heard" (Acts 4:20, MEV).

This is the roar of the redeemed—the bold, unshakable voice of those who have encountered the living God and cannot stay silent.

You weren't created to remain quiet. You were born to sound the alarm—to rise, shine, and carry the blazing light of Christ into a world desperate for hope. But let's be honest. Boldness doesn't come easily. Some of us, like Moses, feel unqualified, unsure, and even unwilling. So where does that kind of courage come from—the kind that speaks up, stands tall, and won't back down? It's not about personality. It's not about hype. And it's definitely not about pretending to be fearless. Real boldness is rooted in something deeper, something eternal. Here are the keys that unlock it.

110

The Holy Spirit—The Ultimate Power Source

Boldness is not just a personality trait; it is a supernatural empowerment. Acts 4:31 says, "And they were all filled with the Holy Spirit and spoke the word of God boldly." If you lack boldness, don't just wish for courage—*ask* for a fresh filling of the Holy Spirit. When God's power surges through you, fear has no choice but to step aside.

Conviction of Truth—The Unshakable Foundation

A person who *knows* the truth cannot be shaken. The world is drowning in confusion, desperate for voices that will stand for something real, something unchanging. Boldness comes when you are convinced that Jesus Christ is the only hope for mankind. You don't have to guess or hesitate. You *know*. And when you know, you can stand firm, no matter what.

Love for God and People—The Driving Force

Boldness is not arrogance; it is love in action. When you love God with everything in you, you simply *cannot* remain silent. When you see people bound in deception, you *cannot* stand by and say nothing. Love is what fuels the fire inside you, and when that love is real, it will push you past your fears and into action.

We live in a time when speaking the truth is costly. You will be mocked. You will be rejected. You will be accused. But hear me: *Silence is not an option*. Jesus said, "Whoever is ashamed of me and my words, the Son of Man will be ashamed of them" (Luke 9:26).

So ask yourself, Are you holding back? Are you waiting for the perfect moment to step up? Is fear causing you to shrink back when you know you should be speaking out? I encourage you: Arise! Shake off the fear that's holding you back, stop apologizing for the gospel, and once and for all, step into God's call with the boldness you were created for.

The world does not need more carbon copies; it needs authentic voices filled with fire. Your voice was given to you by God. *Use it*. Speak life. Speak truth. Speak boldly.

The redeemed do not whisper. *They roar*. Will you?

CHAPTER 29

THE SILENT KILLERS: SARCASM, CYNICISM, AND A CRITICAL SPIRIT

It's your reaction to adversity, not adversity itself, that determines how your life story will develop.
—DIETER F. UCHTDORF

THERE ARE ENEMIES that work in darkness—subtle, insidious forces that erode faith, relationships, and even the very foundation of a hopeful life. Unlike blatant sin or obvious deception, these forces disguise themselves as intelligence, humor, or even discernment. They attack not with fire and fury but with whispers, with smirks, with cutting words that seem harmless at first.

Their names? Sarcasm, cynicism, and a critical spirit.

There have been times in my life when I have fallen into being critical, cynical, and sarcastic—without even realizing the damage I was causing. These enemies are sneaky, disguised as harmless—yet they are anything but.

In the church today, skeptics and critics are being celebrated. Snarky remarks are rewarded with applause, while sincerity is treated with suspicion. We've grown so accustomed to this that many have come to believe that being jaded is the same as being wise. That mockery equates to enlightenment. That trusting others is just naivete.

But these are not marks of strength. They are symptoms of a heart growing cold.

Sarcasm, cynicism, and a critical spirit don't just taint how you see the world—they slowly distort who you are becoming. They harden you. They isolate you. They make you less capable of faith, less open to love, and less willing to see the goodness of God in a broken world.

This is not just an issue of personal character—it is a spiritual battle.

THE POISON OF SARCASM

Sarcasm is often disguised as humor, but it is rarely innocent. It is humor laced with bitterness. It is wit turned into a weapon. The word itself comes from the Greek *sarkazein*, which means "to tear flesh." Think about that—sarcasm, at its root, is verbal tearing.[1]

It cuts. It wounds. And often, it does so under the guise of a joke.

A sarcastic remark may get a laugh, but it comes at a cost. It creates distance. It subtly diminishes others. It communicates that sincerity is something to be mocked—that vulnerability is something to be ridiculed. And over time, it conditions the heart to stop taking anything—especially hope, especially faith—seriously.

The problem with sarcasm is that it doesn't stay on the surface. It seeps into the soul. It turns people into spectators of their own lives, unable to engage without an ironic smirk. It numbs real emotion and replaces it with a mask of indifference. And worst of all, it creates an internal atmosphere where faith cannot flourish.

Because faith *requires* sincerity. Hope *requires* openness. Love *requires* vulnerability. And sarcasm kills all three.

Biblical Warning: "Let your conversation be always full of grace, seasoned with salt, so that you may know how to answer everyone" (Col. 4:6).

THE TRAP OF CYNICISM

Cynicism is a form of self-protection. It tells you, "Don't trust too much. Don't believe too deeply. Don't hope too high, because you will be disappointed."

It is the voice that says, "People always have an agenda. Churches are just about money. Politicians are all corrupt. Nobody really changes."

At first glance, cynicism seems like wisdom. It presents itself as realism, as if seeing the world through jaded eyes is the only way to avoid being deceived. But here's the problem: *Cynicism is not wisdom. It is woundedness parading as insight.*

A cynical heart is often the result of disappointment that was never healed. It is faith that was once alive but got burned and never recovered. It is hope that was once vibrant but was crushed too many times, so instead of hoping again, it chose to build a wall.

But here's the truth: You cannot be cynical and walk in faith at the same time.

Faith *requires* expectation. Cynicism kills expectation. Faith *requires* trust. Cynicism kills trust. Faith *requires* a heart open to seeing God move. Cynicism blinds you to His work because it is always expecting failure, corruption, or disappointment.

Jesus encountered cynicism in His hometown when He tried to perform miracles. The people scoffed, "Isn't this just the carpenter's son?" They had already made up their minds that nothing miraculous could happen through Him. And because of their cynicism Jesus did very few miracles there (Matt. 13:58).

Cynicism will rob you of miracles.

If you are convinced that nothing good will happen, you will be blind to the good that *is* happening. If you are certain people cannot change, you will never see the evidence of transformation. If you assume God will not move, you will not position yourself to receive what He is offering.

Cynicism does not protect you. It imprisons you.

Biblical Warning: "Blessed is the one who trusts in the LORD, whose confidence is in him" (Jer. 17:7).

THE CURSE OF A CRITICAL SPIRIT

A critical spirit is not the same as discernment. Discernment is a gift—it allows you to see clearly, to navigate wisely, and to recognize truth. A critical spirit, however, does not seek truth—it seeks superiority.

114 | Time to Rise

People with a critical spirit are always looking for what's wrong. They analyze, they dissect, they tear down. They are quick to point out flaws, slow to give encouragement. They claim to be standing for truth, but in reality, they are standing above others— using criticism as a way to feel in control. Accusation does not bring accountability just as criticism does not bring contrition.

A critical spirit does not build up—it destroys. It does not correct in love—it condemns in pride. It does not heal—it wounds.

And here's the real danger: *A critical spirit can disguise itself as righteousness.*

It can make you feel like you are "one of the few" who sees what others don't. It can make you feel like your negativity is actually discernment. It can even make you feel spiritually superior, thinking you "see through" what others are too blind to recognize.

But Scripture is clear: *A critical spirit is toxic.*

+ It breeds division (Prov. 6:16–19).
+ It poisons relationships (Eph. 4:29).
+ It turns people into legalists rather than lovers of Christ (Matt. 23:23–24).

A critical spirit is not about truth—it is about control. And nothing suffocates the Spirit of God like a heart that is too proud to receive grace.

Biblical Warning: "Do everything without grumbling or arguing, so that you may become blameless and pure" (Phil. 2:14–15a).

BREAKING FREE: THE CALL TO A RENEWED MIND

If sarcasm, cynicism, and a critical spirit have taken root in your heart, the way out is not easy—but it is necessary. These are deeply ingrained patterns of thought, and breaking them requires intentionality.

Repent and renew your mind.

Ask God to reveal where sarcasm, cynicism, and criticism have shaped your thinking. Repent for the times you have used words to wound rather than heal. Then actively fill your mind with truth. Replace mocking with encouragement, suspicion with trust, and criticism with grace.

Choose sincerity over sarcasm.

Stop using humor as a shield. Speak with authenticity. Say what needs to be said— in truth and love, not in jest.

Challenge your cynicism.

If you catch yourself assuming the worst in someone, pause and ask yourself, "Is this actually true, or is it just what I expect?" It's critical we give people and situations a chance to prove themselves before we write them off entirely.

Shift from criticism to contribution.

Instead of tearing others down, build them up. Instead of exposing flaws, offer solutions. Instead of highlighting what's wrong, why not invest in what is right—by speaking life, showing support, and encouraging growth?

Remember, faith requires that we look unto Jesus. Walking in the fullness of God's power starts with a heart that is willing to believe. Hope requires risk. Trust requires vulnerability. Faith requires openness, because in the end a hard heart never protects you—it only keeps you from experiencing the goodness of God.

Everything changes in your life when you make these shifts. Everything in you and around you will challenge you to not follow through. People who make these shifts are uncommon. You must draw a line in the sand of your life and refuse to let sarcasm, cynicism, or a critical spirit define your story.

CHAPTER 30

TEN PRINCIPLES FOR IDENTITY AND AUTHORITY

No matter how big the failure, no matter how dark the hallway, no matter how great the pressure, no matter how challenging the transition, you've got to believe that God saves the best for now. That's the power of expectation.
—JENTEZEN FRANKLIN

IDENTITY ISN'T SOMETHING you stumble into—it's something you build, brick by brick, through intentional action and clarity. You don't just drift into your God-given authority. You own it. You fight for it. And when life knocks you down—and it will—the ones who rise aren't the ones who never fall. They're the ones who refuse to stay down. They remember who they are, and they reclaim what hell tried to steal.

What I'm about to give you isn't just a list—it's a war map. Ten battle-tested truths that will anchor you when the storm hits, when the enemy whispers lies, and when the pressure's on. Build your life on these, and you won't just get through—you'll rise with fire, clarity, and unshakable purpose. The haters, critics, trolls, and inner voices of depression, anxiety, and overwhelm will not stop you no matter how hard they try.

1. YOU ARE NOT YOUR PAST—BUT YOU MUST RECKON WITH IT

The past is not a prison—though it can feel like it at times—but it *is* a teacher. You are not defined by your failures, nor are you limited by the wounds inflicted on you. But if you do not them, they can govern you in unseen ways. Face your past with courage—drag the chaos into order. Redeem it before it starts whispering lies into your future.

2. THE HERO'S JOURNEY BEGINS WITH A CHOICE

You are called to something greater than mere survival. Some of the greatest stories belong to those who leave comfort behind, confront trials head-on, and emerge transformed. This is your journey. No one else can walk it for you. You can stay in the village, passive and unseen—or you can step into the unknown, face the dragon, and claim your destiny. The choice is yours.

3. TO LIVE UNSHAKEN, YOU MUST ANCHOR YOURSELF IN TRUTH, NOT APPROVAL

The world is full of opinions, most of them fleeting and contradictory. If you define yourself by their applause, you'll be destroyed by their criticism. The antidote is knowing who you are and why you are here. Root yourself in something eternal—truth, conviction, purpose. Then, when the storms come, you will not be moved.

4. YOUR IDENTITY IS THE FIRST BATTLEFIELD—KNOW THAT YOU ARE BEING ATTACKED

Satan's first attack is always on identity. He questioned Eve's understanding of God's word. He questioned Jesus in the wilderness: "If you are the Son of God..." (Matt. 4:3). Why? Because if he can make you doubt who you are, he can manipulate everything else. Guard your identity fiercely. When you know who you are, you become dangerous to the forces that seek to control you.

5. THE SPIRIT OF COMPARISON WILL ROB YOU BLIND—FOCUS ON YOUR OWN PATH

Comparison is a poison. It distorts your perspective and makes you resent blessings that were never meant for you in the first place. The moment you envy another person's journey, you abandon your own. Focus on what *you* are called to build. Let others succeed. Cheer them on. Their success does not diminish your potential—it only proves what's possible.

6. FIGHT, FIGHT, FIGHT—BECAUSE NO ONE WILL FIGHT FOR YOU LIKE YOU CAN

No one else is responsible for your destiny. No one else will fight for your mind, your purpose, your calling, if you will not. Others can encourage you, but they cannot walk the road for you. Take responsibility for your life. Wage war against complacency. Fight apathy. Fight self-doubt. Fight against every voice that tells you to settle for less than what you were made for.

7. FROM ORPHAN TO HEIR—YOU ARE NOT A VICTIM, YOU ARE AN OVERCOMER

An orphan mindset says, "I must fend for myself. I am alone. I am unloved." An heir mindset says, "I have a legacy. I have authority. I am part of something greater." If you live like an orphan, you will always be grasping for scraps. But if you walk in your true identity—as a son or daughter of the King—you will move with confidence, wisdom, and strength.

8. THE ROAR OF THE REDEEMED—YOUR VOICE SHAPES YOUR REALITY

Speak boldly. Declare truth. Stop apologizing for existing. Your words create culture—both internally and externally. If you speak weakness, you will live weak. If you speak defeat, you will walk in it. But if you speak life, if you declare what is true, if you proclaim victory even in the face of defeat, you will shift atmospheres. Speak as one who has authority, because you do.

9. BEWARE THE SILENT KILLERS—SUBTLE COMPROMISES BECOME MAJOR DEFEATS

The greatest threats are rarely the obvious ones. It is not always the blatant betrayal, the open attack—it is the small compromises. The tiny lies you tell yourself. The seemingly harmless distractions. The bitterness that you let take root. The cynicism that goes unchecked. These are the things that weaken your foundation until, one day, it crumbles. Root them out before they take hold.

10. OWN YOUR IDENTITY, OR SOMEONE ELSE WILL DEFINE IT FOR YOU

If you do not consciously claim who you are, the world will decide it for you. Culture will impose its labels. Fear will dictate your limits. Other people's expectations will shape your path. Reject that. Take ownership of your identity. Define your purpose. And then—walk in it with unwavering conviction.

Your identity is your foundation. If it is weak, everything built upon it will shake. But if it is strong—if it is forged in truth, tested by fire, and held with confidence—nothing can take it from you.

Now rise. The world needs the real you.

PART IV

THE WEIGHT OF CHOICES— WALKING IN POWER

NEVER APPROACH JESUS for a miracle as if He's some divine slot machine—where, if we're lucky, we hit the jackpot and get what we never truly believed would happen in the first place. Jesus is miraculous in and of Himself, and knowing Him is the greatest miracle of all.

Let me tell you about a miracle that took place a few years ago in my life and in the life of our church.

It was in September 2018, a Friday night, and we were gathered for a prayer meeting. By that time, we had already transitioned from a Baptist church to a more charismatic one, and we were in the midst of an unbelievable shift in our church life. That night, as we prayed, we believed we heard the Lord say, "Believe Me for a miracle." It was exciting, but we didn't know when or where. We just held on to those words.

Less than twenty-four hours later, we would come to understand exactly what that meant—and just how large of a miracle we would need.

The next morning, as I was going about my usual Saturday routine as a pastor, my phone rang. It was a member of our church, their voice filled with urgency. They told me their ten-year-old son, Xavier, had fallen from a tree house—landing face down onto an eighteen-inch metal meat skewer.

Horrified, I struggled to process what I was hearing. These were the kinds of words you never expect to hear. I didn't know whether he was alive or dead. All I knew was that we needed to believe God for a miracle.

It happened like this: It was an ordinary summer day in Harrisonville, Missouri, when Xavier Cunningham had been climbing into a treehouse with his friends. A swarm of yellow jackets attacked, sending Xavier scrambling for safety. In his frantic escape, he fell—landing face-first onto a foot-long metal meat skewer that had been left standing upright in the ground.

The skewer pierced his face, entering just under his left eye and exiting the back of his skull. The impact severed his jugular vein but miraculously missed his carotid artery by one millimeter and his brain and spine by just a few millimeters. Xavier remained conscious and able to speak as his horrified mother rushed him to the hospital with the skewer still lodged in his face.

The situation was dire. As he drifted in and out of consciousness at the hospital, he would softly sing the song "Reckless Love" by Cory Asbury before fading out again.

By that time, we had mobilized everyone we could to pray. Our entire church. People online. Friends and believers across the nation—and beyond. We cried out for an absolute miracle.

The doctors were solemn. Their faces carried the weight of how critical Xavier's condition was. All night long, they worked to develop a strategy to save his life. By morning they were ready to begin a seven-hour surgery.

I was there in that waiting room, praying, believing, and standing in faith. Hours later, the doctors finally emerged. Their words stunned us all.

"This is a one-in-a-million miracle. There's no damage. Xavier is going to be just fine."

A team of surgeons at the University of Kansas Health System had carefully removed the skewer in a delicate, high-risk procedure. Against all odds, Xavier survived without permanent damage—a true medical miracle. His incredible story of survival left doctors and his family in awe, calling it nothing short of divine intervention.

How could a young boy fall from a tree house, land face-first onto a metal skewer, sever a jugular vein—yet suffer no damage? It was beyond medical explanation. It was incredible.

But that wasn't the end of the story.

A few days later, as I visited Xavier in the hospital, I asked him, "How did you know you were going to be okay?"

Without hesitation he said, "Because before they took me into surgery, I saw Jesus come into my room. His eyes lit up the entire place, and I knew I was going to be okay."

People often ask me, "Do you really believe he saw Jesus?"

My answer is the same every time: Absolutely.

Miracles are for today. It is time to rise.

bit.ly/3UQ0Cde

CHAPTER 31

LIVING WITHOUT OFFENSE

Many are unable to function properly in their calling because of the wounds and hurts that offenses have caused in their lives. They are handicapped and hindered from fulfilling their full potential. Most often it is a fellow believer who has hurt them.
—JOHN BEVERE

OFFENSE IS A prison—and honestly, far too many of us are living behind its walls without even realizing it. In a world where disagreements seem to flare up daily and outrage spreads like wildfire on social media, learning to live without offense feels almost revolutionary. But here's the truth: Offense is a choice. Every day, you and I are faced with the option—will we pick it up and carry it like a heavy weight on our souls, or will we lay it down and walk free? Jesus showed us how to live without offense, and He invites us to do the same. It's not always easy, but it's always worth it. We should do everything we can to live without offense—because freedom is found on the other side.

WHY DO WE GET OFFENDED?

If we're honest, offense usually sneaks in when our expectations aren't met—when someone's words cut deeper than we expected, or when an action (or lack of action) feels like a betrayal. At the core, offense often comes as pride and self-protection. We feel disrespected. Undervalued. Misunderstood. We want justice. We want people to see things the way we see them. And when they don't, offense creeps in quietly, whispering lies like "They don't care about you. They don't respect you. You should be angry."

And if we're not careful, that offense doesn't just stay tucked away. It grows. It festers. It turns into resentment, bitterness, and even hatred if left unchecked. It blinds us to the truth, poisons our relationships, and builds walls around our hearts that were never meant to be there.

That's why we have to fight against it intentionally. Because the reality is, we weren't created to be prisoners to our own pain. Jesus didn't just set us free from sin—He set us free from the weight of offense too.

THE HIGH COST OF OFFENSE

Offense isn't just an emotional reaction we brush off—it's actually one of the enemy's favorite strategies to keep us bound. It poisons relationships. It severs friendships. It divides families and even entire churches.

122 | TIME TO RISE

Have you ever noticed how quickly offense can creep in and isolate people? One hurtful comment, one misunderstood action—and suddenly, years of connection can start to unravel. The truth is, the enemy doesn't always need to destroy us outright; if he can divide us, that's enough. He knows what Jesus said is true: A divided house can't stand (Mark 3:25).

But offense costs us even more than broken relationships. It puts distance between us and God. Jesus was clear when He said, "If you do not forgive others their sins, your Father will not forgive your sins" (Matt. 6:15). Unforgiveness builds a wall between our hearts and God's presence—and that's a price far too high to pay.

And here's the hard truth: As long as we stay offended, it will always feel like it's someone else's fault. It's only when we choose forgiveness that we break free.

HOW TO LIVE WITHOUT OFFENSE

Living without offense doesn't just happen by accident—it's a choice you have to make with intention. It's a decision to guard your heart before the hurt has a chance to settle in. The truth is, offense will always have an opportunity to knock at your door. But you get to decide whether you let it in.

Walking in true freedom begins with learning how to keep your heart soft and unoffended—especially in a world that seems to thrive in division. Here's how you can start building a life free from offense today:

Decide that you will not be offended.

Living without offense begins with a decision. Proverbs 19:11 says, "A person's wisdom yields patience; it is to one's glory to overlook an offense." Decide now that you will be unoffendable. When an opportunity for offense comes, remind yourself: "I refuse to let this take root in my heart." The enemy is looking for a foothold. Don't give it to him. Let it go before it grabs hold of you.

Examine your heart for pride.

Many times, offense is fueled by our own pride. We want to be right. We want to be seen. We want to be understood. And when we aren't, it stings. But look at Jesus—the King of kings—who humbled Himself and didn't lash out when He was insulted. If anyone had the right to defend Himself, it was Him. Yet He chose surrender over retaliation.

When you feel offense creeping in, take a moment and ask yourself, "Is my pride keeping me from letting this go?" If the answer is yes, surrender it. Pride demands that we defend ourselves, but humility trusts God to be our defender.

Practice quick forgiveness.

Forgiveness isn't about excusing wrong behavior—it's about freeing your own heart. Jesus said in Matthew 6:14, "If you forgive other people when they sin against you, your heavenly Father will also forgive you." Forgiveness must become a lifestyle. Don't wait to feel like forgiving—choose it, daily. The longer you hold on to an offense, the deeper its roots grow. Uproot it before it hardens your heart.

Stop taking things personally.

People's words and actions are often more about their own pain than about you. Hurt people hurt people. Instead of internalizing their behavior, ask, "What is going on in their heart that makes them act this way?" Shifting your perspective will help you respond with compassion instead of offense. Remember Jesus, hanging on the cross— mocked, rejected—and yet He said, "Father, forgive them, for they do not know what they are doing" (Luke 23:34). If He could forgive, so can we.

Refuse to replay the offense.

The more you replay an offense in your mind, the more power it gains over you. Stop rehearsing what happened. Stop revisiting the pain. The enemy loves to keep you stuck in a cycle of hurt—but you don't have to stay there. Philippians 4:8 reminds us to fix our thoughts on what is true, noble, and praiseworthy. Instead of replaying the offense, replay God's promises.

Keep your eyes on eternity.

In light of eternity, most offenses are incredibly small. Ask yourself, "Will this matter in five years? In eternity?" What matters most is your relationship with God and the people He's placed in your life. Don't let temporary hurts rob you of eternal rewards. Satan wants you consumed with small grievances. God calls you to lift your eyes and live with bigger purpose.

Speak life, not strife.

When you're tempted to speak negatively about someone who has hurt you, stop. Your words have power. Proverbs 18:21 says, "The tongue has the power of life and death." Choose to speak life. Bless those who curse you. Pray for those who hurt you (Matt. 5:44). This isn't weakness—it's one of the most powerful acts of spiritual warfare you can engage in. When you refuse to curse those who offend you, you break the enemy's cycle.

THE RESULT? A LIFE OF FREEDOM

Living without offense doesn't mean you pretend injustice isn't real—it simply means you refuse to let bitterness take root in your heart. You were called to live free. Unshaken. Full of grace. And every time you choose to let go of offense, you're stepping into a supernatural peace that no one—not even the enemy—can steal from you.

Think about Jesus. He walked among sinners. He was rejected by His own people. Betrayed by His closest friends. Crucified by those He came to save. Yet somehow, He carried no offense. He lived in perfect freedom—and that same freedom is available to you right now.

IT'S TIME TO BREAK FREE

The enemy wants to keep you offended because an offended Christian is an ineffective Christian. But today, you have a choice. You can stay bound by offense, or you can step into the life of peace, power, and freedom that Jesus died to give you.

Make the decision right now: "I will not live offended. I will not carry bitterness. I will walk in love. I will walk in forgiveness. I will walk in freedom."

This is what it looks like to live as an overcomer. This is the power of the redeemed. When we refuse to be bound by anything but the love of God, we shake the gates of hell.

So today—rise up. Live free. And never let offense steal another moment of your life!

CHAPTER 32

LIMITING BELIEFS AND THE LIMITLESS LIFE

The rare people who do become truly exceptional at something do so not because they believe they're exceptional. On the contrary, they become amazing because they're obsessed with improvement. And that obsession with improvement stems from an unerring belief that they are, in fact, not that great at all.
—CAMERON R. HANES

WILL NEVER FORGET the moment I first did the famous Tony Robbins "Fire Walk" and officially became a "firewalker." This is where you walk across fifteen feet of blazing hot coals barefoot.[1] What seems to many as impossible becomes very possible when you step up with absolute certainty to any situation you face. Including but not limited to blazing hot coals. Once you do something you once thought impossible, you begin to think, "What actually is there that limits me?" Most of our limitations are in our minds—and that is where the real battle resides.

The battle for your life is not fought in your circumstances—it's fought in your mind. Read that again if you need to. Your mind is where the real war happens. The beliefs you carry about yourself are either the chains that keep you bound or the keys that set you free.

Limiting beliefs aren't just stray negative thoughts. They're deeply ingrained stories we tell ourselves. Stories that shape how we see the world. How we see others. And most importantly—how we see ourselves.

But here's the good news: Those stories aren't set in stone. They can change. You don't have to live held hostage by the lies that shaped your past. You have the power to rewrite your narrative. To take back control. To step into the person you were created to be.

WHERE DO LIMITING BELIEFS COME FROM?

Most of our limiting beliefs don't actually start with us. They come from moments and voices outside of us—childhood experiences that whispered, "You're not good enough." Painful failures that screamed, "You'll always be a disappointment!" Harsh words spoken over us that lingered: "People like you never succeed." Even the culture around us reinforces it: "Stay in your lane. Be realistic."

And over time, something dangerous happens: We start to internalize these voices without even realizing it. What began as someone else's opinion quietly becomes the script we live by. We don't just hear the words anymore—we start believing them. Acting out of them. Building our lives around them.

But here's the truth you need to hear: Just because a belief has been with you for years doesn't mean it's true. And just because someone said it about you doesn't mean you have to carry it another day.

THE POWER OF AWARENESS: CONFRONTING THE INNER VOICE

Freedom begins with recognizing that the voice in your head isn't always telling the truth. The next time a limiting thought rises up, pause and ask yourself, "Is this belief serving me or stopping me? Where did I learn this—and why did I accept it? What if this belief isn't true?"

Awareness is powerful because it creates distance between you and the lie. The moment you recognize a false belief for what it is, its grip on you begins to weaken. Your job is not to passively listen to every thought—but to challenge anything that keeps you stuck, small, or silent. If a thought is not empowering you, it does not belong in your mind. Period.

REPLACING LIES WITH TRUTH

You don't overcome a lie by trying harder—you overcome it by renewing your mind. It's not about forcing yourself to "be better" or pretending you don't struggle. It's about learning to hear the old worn-out lies for what they are—and choosing to replace them with truth. If you catch yourself thinking, "I'm not good enough," pause and say, "No, I am created with purpose, and I already have everything I need." When the thought "I always fail," creeps in, answer with "Every challenge I face is shaping me into someone stronger." And when you hear, "I'll never change," remind yourself, "Transformation is happening within me—even if I can't see it yet."

The truth is, the words you speak to yourself matter more than you realize. Your inner dialogue shapes your destiny. Change the dialogue—and you'll change your life. The world doesn't get to define who you are. Your past doesn't get the final say. Your mistakes don't have the last word. You get to define you. And when you choose to align your thoughts with what God says about you—everything begins to shift.

LIVING BEYOND LIMITS: THE POWER OF A NEW IDENTITY

True change doesn't come from trying harder or forcing yourself to act differently. Real change happens when you become someone new—from the inside out. If you believe you're a failure, eventually, you'll act like one. If you believe you're powerless, you'll live like a victim. But the moment you start seeing yourself through the lens of truth—who God says you are—those limiting beliefs begin to lose their grip.

So let's strip away the lies. You are not your past. You are not your mistakes. You are more than enough. You are strong. You are capable. You are created to live a life of impact, not a life of intimidation.

Limiting Beliefs and the Limitless Life | 127

The truth is, most people never step into that reality. They stay stuck, living inside a box someone else built for them—boxed in by fear, failure, or someone else's opinion. They keep rehearsing all the reasons they *can't* instead of stepping out and discovering what's possible.

But that's not your story.

You're here because you're ready. You're here because deep down, you know there's more for your life—and you refuse to settle for less. And you know what? You're absolutely right. There *is* more. And it's waiting for you to rise and claim it.

A LIMITLESS LIFE BEGINS WITHIN

So where do you go from here? How do you start breaking free from the beliefs that have been holding you back? It begins right here—on the inside.

1. **Identify the lie.** What's the belief that's been chaining you down? Be honest about it. Write it down. Get it out of your head and onto paper where you can see it for what it is—a lie, not the truth.

2. **Challenge it.** Ask yourself, "Is this actually true? Where did this belief even come from? Is it helping me or hurting me?" Most of the time, when you pull a lie into the light, it loses its power.

3. **Replace it with truth.** Find a new life-giving statement that counters the lie—and don't just think it; speak it out loud. Over and over again. Repetition matters. The more you affirm the truth, the deeper it will take root in you.

4. **Take action.** Don't just sit there believing differently—*live differently*. Do the thing you thought you couldn't do. Speak up. Step out. Show up as the person you are becoming, not the person you were.

You don't need a perfect set of circumstances to live free—you need a better belief system that matches who God created you to be. That's where the battle is won—in your mind and in your spirit.

Refuse to accept a version of reality that keeps you small. Think bigger. Believe deeper. Step boldly into the life you were created for. Because the truth is—you were never meant to live held back by your limits. You were meant to rise, to build, to impact, to create. And the only thing standing in your way is a belief system that no longer deserves to be part of your story.

So what's it going to be?

You already have the power to change. The only question now is—will you use it?

WHAT IF ALL YOU NEED IS IN YOU NOW?

If the limitless God is inside you right now, then what's really holding you back? The truth is, the only thing that can stop us is our own unwillingness to surrender to His leadership. That's it.

What if all the love you need…all the joy, all the peace, all the strength, all the forgiveness, all the resources, all the faith, all the endurance—you name it—is in you now? Again, I say to you that it is.

My challenge to you is to do what I learned from Tony Robbins. Go on a run or walk and begin to say (or shout!) with absolute certainty, "All I need is in me now!"

It is in you because of Jesus.

All I need is in me now.

All I need is in me now.

All I need is in me now.

All I need is in me now.

CHAPTER 33

COMMITTED TO A LOCAL CHURCH

The church is not a theological classroom. It is a conversion, confession, repentance, reconciliation, forgiveness and sanctification center, where flawed people place their faith in Christ, gather to know and love him better, and learn to love others as he designed.
—PAUL DAVID TRIPP

JESUS DIED FOR the church. He loves His bride—the church. You and I? We need the church too. Not just once in a while, not just when it's convenient—we need it woven into the fabric of our everyday lives.

Let's be real—life was never meant to be lived alone. From the very beginning, God made it clear: "It is not good for…man to be alone" (Gen. 2:18). And this wasn't just about marriage—it was about *life itself.* You were wired for connection. Built for belonging. Designed to thrive inside a spiritual family.

The church isn't just a building we go to on Sundays. It's the lifeline God gave us so we could grow, be encouraged, and step into the fullness of what He's called us to do.

But today? More and more people are walking away from the very thing God designed to sustain them. They say things like "I can do church at home" or "I don't need organized religion. I have YouTube. I have the Spirit. I don't need anyone else."

Listen, I get it—yes, you can absolutely watch sermons online. You can pray in your room. But you cannot replace the power of true face-to-face community. You can't substitute real-life relationships with pixels on a screen.

Jesus didn't call us to an isolated faith. He didn't die and rise again so we could live disconnected. He built His church—a living, breathing family of believers, coming together to worship, to grow, and to serve side by side.

When we unplug from that, even if we don't feel it right away, we can start to drift. We cut ourselves off from the very environment designed to sharpen and strengthen us for the battles we were never meant to fight alone.

ISOLATION IS THE ENEMY'S STRATEGY

One of the most dangerous places you can be in your spiritual journey is alone. And make no mistake—the enemy knows it. That's why he works overtime to isolate you. Because when you're alone, you're vulnerable. When you're isolated, the lies get louder. Lies like these:

- "You don't belong."
- "No one really cares about you."

130 | Time to Rise

+ "You're better off figuring things out on your own."

And here's the hard truth: Those lies don't just stay small. They take root. They grow. They shape how you see yourself, others, and even God.

While lies may flourish in isolation, truth grows in community. When you stay connected to a local church, you're surrounded by people who see you. They fight for you. And they remind you of who you really are when you forget.

Now, I get it. Maybe you've been burned by church before. Maybe you trusted leaders who let you down. Maybe you've seen hypocrisy up close and personal—and it hurt. If that's you, hear this: I'm so sorry. That pain is real.

The church isn't perfect—because it's made up of imperfect people chasing after a perfect Savior. But it's still God's idea. And it's still His plan to help you heal, grow, and walk into your calling.

If you've been hurt, don't stay stuck in that place. Let God heal you. Let Him plant you somewhere healthy, somewhere life-giving. You were made for community—and community was made for you.

THE LOCAL CHURCH IS WHERE YOU GROW

Spiritual growth doesn't happen in a vacuum. You can't level up in isolation. Growth happens in relationships—in real conversations, real accountability, and real service to others. And that's exactly what the local church is meant to be: an environment where you are strengthened, stretched, and supported.

It's a place where

+ your faith gets anchored through sound teaching and biblical truth;
+ you're challenged to step beyond your comfort zone and trust God more deeply;
+ you build deep, meaningful friendships that hold you up when life gets heavy; and
+ you get the chance to serve and make a real difference in the lives of others.

Think about it for a second—the biggest breakthroughs in your life didn't happen when you were locked away in your own thoughts. They happened when the right people showed up at the right time and spoke truth into you. They happened when you let others walk the journey with you. That's the beauty of the local church—it's a place where iron sharpens iron, where wisdom is passed down, and where encouragement fuels your faith to keep moving forward.

Now, let's be honest. I hear it all the time: "I'm just not getting anything out of church." And I get it—sometimes it feels that way. But let me ask you: Are you just attending, or are you engaging? Growth doesn't happen by osmosis. It doesn't happen just because you show up and sit through a service. Growth requires investment. It requires showing up with your heart open, your hands ready, and your mind engaged.

If you come on Sundays but never build relationships, never serve, never truly lean in—you're going to feel disconnected. It's not because the church is broken. It's because connection and growth were never meant to be passive.

Stop waiting for church to feed you—start taking responsibility for your own growth. Step in. Get planted. Serve. Build. Invest. And watch what God does in and through you when you do.

YOU ARE A PART OF SOMETHING BIGGER

The local church isn't just about what you can receive—it's about what you can give. There are people right now who are waiting for what only you can bring: your encouragement, your wisdom, your strength, your heart. You carry something unique that the body of Christ desperately needs. And when you pull back, when you withdraw, the whole body feels it—even if you don't realize it.

Think about it: If the hand decided it didn't want to function, or the eye refused to see, the entire body would suffer. In the same way, when you stay on the sidelines, it doesn't just affect you—it affects the whole family God is building. You were never designed to spectate. You were created to be an active, vibrant part of what God is doing in His church.

And let's be honest: Serving isn't always glamorous. Sometimes it means stacking chairs. Sometimes it's holding babies in the nursery. Sometimes it's showing up early when you're tired or staying late when no one else notices. But Jesus—the King of kings—got on His knees and washed feet. He modeled servanthood, not spotlight. And He's calling us to do the same.

The church isn't meant to be a place where we consume—it's meant to be a place where we contribute. The more you give of yourself, the more you grow. The deeper your roots go, the stronger your faith becomes.

IT'S TIME TO GET PLANTED

A tree that is constantly uprooted never grows strong. And the same is true for your faith. If you're jumping from church to church, or if you're just floating through life without spiritual roots, you're stunting the very growth God wants to bring into your life.

It's time to stop making excuses. Stop waiting for the perfect church (spoiler alert: it doesn't exist). Stop treating church like an optional extra to your spiritual life. Find a local church. Get planted. Build relationships. Serve with passion. Lean in and watch what happens when you commit to something bigger than yourself.

Let me share with you something I recently shared with our church. Every person needs a pastor. To have authority, you must be under authority. You are not your own pastor. Somewhere along the way people began to view pastors as chaplains and not the spiritual covering God has placed in your life for spiritual growth and spiritual health. You really need a local church to belong to.

132 | TIME TO RISE

This is where transformation happens. This is where faith comes alive. This is where you step into the fullness of who God created you to be. The church isn't just a place you attend—it's a family you belong to. And when you find your place in it, everything changes.

Now, I need to say something that might sting a little—but it's said with love:

Many people leave churches in the wrong way. They hop from place to place, chasing an experience, chasing a feeling, but never planting roots. If you can't be satisfied anywhere, the problem isn't the church—it's likely something deeper God wants to heal in you.

Here's the key: Find a church that hosts the presence of Jesus. A church that truly believes Jesus is everything. A local church—not just an online livestream. A church that treasures the Word of God and honors the Lord's Supper. And once you find it? Go all in.

Attend every service.

Give generously—above and beyond.

Show up to prayer meetings.

Let yourself be pastored.

Not all churches are equal. And let's be honest—the church in America largely failed the COVID-19 test. Many churches shut their doors out of fear. Many feared man more than they feared God. And today, too many are still afraid to speak boldly about the issues that matter.

Now hear me: Politics isn't the mission of the church. But avoiding truth altogether is a mistake. The church must step up. We need bold pulpits again. We need pastors and leaders who are more concerned about pleasing God than pleasing crowds. And yes, pastors and churches should be involved in politics.

The church is still God's plan. So get planted. Get involved. And watch what God does when you give yourself fully to the family He's building. I am convinced even now that many discouraged pastors would not quit the ministry if they knew they had just a few valiant men and women around them who would fight for and with them. I can't tell you how many times I have been crushed and betrayed in ministry. Yet every time God has surrounded me with a few good men and women who leaned in and said, "I am with you, pastor."

CHAPTER 34

HOW TO PURSUE UNITY AND NOT DESTROY RELATIONSHIPS

I despaired at the thought that my life might slip by without seeing God show himself mightily on our behalf.
—JIM CYMBALA, FRESH WIND

LIFE IS BUILT on relationships—some that feel rock-solid, some that feel fragile, and some that, if we're honest, have ended in ashes. Hurt, misunderstanding, pride...they've led a lot of people to live surrounded by the ruins of burned bridges, holding on to grudges they never meant to keep. But what if was a better way? What if, instead of setting fire to relationships, we chose to become bridge builders—people who fight for unity, healing, and a second chance?

THE COST OF BURNING BRIDGES

Every time we walk away from a relationship in anger, we lose more than just a connection—we lose an opportunity for growth, healing, and maybe even redemption. Whether it's a friendship, a family bond, or someone at church, when a bridge burns, part of us feels it. Offense builds walls around our hearts. It tells us we're justified in being bitter, that we're safer alone. But isolation was never the plan. It's never the answer.

Burning a bridge can feel empowering in the moment—like we're taking control back. But the truth? It's often a sign of woundedness, not strength. It's far easier to walk away than to stay, work through the mess, and heal. But Jesus calls us to something better. He calls us to be the kind of people who don't give up when it gets hard. Who don't trade connection for convenience. The real question is, will we say yes to that call?

JESUS, THE ULTIMATE BRIDGE BUILDER

If you think about it, the entire message of the gospel is a story about building a bridge. When sin separated us from God, Jesus didn't become bitter. He didn't cut us off. He didn't walk away. He came closer. He forgave. He made a way where there was none.

If Jesus was willing to build a bridge back to us, after everything, how can we justify burning bridges with people in our lives?

In Matthew 5:9, Jesus said, "Blessed are the peacemakers, for they will be called children of God." Notice He didn't say blessed are the ones who are always right, or blessed are the ones who win at every argument. No—blessed are the peacemakers. A sign of true maturity isn't how loudly we defend ourselves; it's how fiercely we fight for peace.

133

134 | Time to Rise

HOW TO BUILD BRIDGES INSTEAD OF BURNING THEM

Everyone talks about unity. But let's be real—it's not easy. It's messy. It's emotional. It's inconvenient. When tensions rise and misunderstandings hit, most people check out or blow things up. There is a rare group of people who have risen and realize something much greater: Unity isn't about agreeing on everything—it's about choosing to build bridges when burning them would be easier. It's a daily decision. It reflects choosing to do very hard things. Not being bound by emotional sabotage. Rather, looking unto Jesus and choosing to do what He would do and did. It is a bold choice to lead with humility, forgiveness, and relentless courage. And on the other side of that choice? Relationships that infuse life into your purpose. Real connection. Real growth. So how do you actually live this out? Let's get into it:

Choose understanding over judgment.

Most conflicts don't happen because someone was out to hurt us—they happen because something got misunderstood. Before you assume the worst, slow down. Ask questions. Really listen. James 1:19 says it like this: "Everyone should be quick to listen, slow to speak and slow to become angry." When you lead with curiosity instead of conclusions, you'll be amazed how many bridges you can build instead of burn.

Refuse to let offense take root.

Offense is sneaky. It doesn't explode—it simmers, slowly burning under the surface until one day it has scorched something that matters to you. When you feel that sting of offense, stop and ask yourself, "Is this really worth losing a relationship over?" Most of the time, it's not. Proverbs 19:11 says, "It is to one's glory to overlook an offense." Letting things go isn't weakness—it's wisdom. It's strength. And it's one of the greatest gifts you can give yourself. The number one reason people leave a church is they were offended and did not know how to deal with it. Then, to excuse it away, they reframed the story into something it was not. Tell me I am wrong.

Extend grace, even when it's undeserved.

Let's be honest—none of us deserve the grace we've been given. And yet God extends it freely, time and time again. Colossians 3:13 reminds us, "Forgive as the Lord forgave you." Grace doesn't excuse bad behavior, but it frees you from carrying the weight of bitterness. The longer you hold on to offense, the heavier your heart becomes. Forgiveness sets *you* free.

Have hard conversations in love.

Avoiding conflict doesn't make it disappear—it only deepens the divide. Sometimes the most loving thing you can do is have a hard conversation. But it matters how you approach it. Don't come to win. Come to heal. Ephesians 4:15 says we are to "[speak] the truth in love." Love leads the way. Truth walks hand in hand with humility. When handled right, conflict doesn't have to end relationships—it can actually make them stronger.

If I could be honest again for a moment, I must admit that for the longest time

How to Pursue Unity and Not Destroy Relationships | 135

I have avoided hard conversations out of a desire to be liked. Call it what you like, avoiding difficult conversations never ends well for me. Many people avoid conflict. This is an area, even now, I am growing in.

Value relationships over being right.

Here's the reality: You can win the argument and lose the person. Pride demands to be right. But love is willing to lay down its right to win in order to fight for reconciliation. Philippians 2:3 challenges us: "Do nothing out of selfish ambition or vain conceit. Rather, in humility value others above yourselves." Relationships are too important to sacrifice at the altar of pride. And at the end of the day, choosing unity over ego doesn't make you weak—it makes you wise.

THE POWER OF REBUILDING BRIDGES

Maybe you've burned some bridges in the past. Maybe there are relationships you look at now and wonder whether they're just too broken to ever be repaired. If that's you, hear this today: God is a God of restoration. He specializes in rebuilding what feels lost and breathing life into what looks dead. If you're willing to take even the first step toward reconciliation, He'll meet you there with the grace you need to finish what you can't do on your own.

Rebuilding a bridge takes humility. It takes patience. It takes choosing love over pride, even when it feels uncomfortable. Sometimes, it means being the first one to apologize, even if you weren't the only one who was wrong. Other times, it means choosing to see the best in someone, even when your emotions are pulling toward judgment. But every time—it means choosing restoration over resentment.

Second Corinthians 5:18 says, "All this is from God, who reconciled us to himself through Christ and gave us the ministry of reconciliation." Reconciliation isn't just something we receive—it's something we are called to live out.

The truth is, the world has enough scorched bridges. What it needs is more people willing to build them. More people willing to reach out instead of pull away. More people willing to say, "Let's find a way forward" instead of "Forget it—I'm done."

If you've burned a bridge, it's not too late. Maybe the first step toward rebuilding is small—a simple message, a phone call, a quiet prayer asking God for the words to say. And if you find yourself tempted right now to burn a bridge, I encourage you to pause. Ask yourself, "Is there a better way forward? Could God be inviting me to be a bridge builder instead of a bridge burner?"

Sometimes God even uses us to help build bridges between others who are at odds. And that's a gift. I've seen it firsthand. Having spent time among different denominations and theological circles, I've learned that just getting people in a room, having a real conversation, can change everything. It's often in those simple, humble moments of connection that bridges are built.

You might be surprised what God can do through you—if you're willing to be a bridge builder.

CHAPTER 35

THE DOMINO EFFECT: HOW ONE CHOICE CHANGES EVERYTHING

One person in pursuit of excellence raises the standards of everyone around them. And as they strive for greatness, they bring out the greatness in others.
— JON GORDON

IN HIS FILM *Domino Revival*, my friend Mike Signorelli revealed how one simple step of obedience, followed by another, and another, can lead to things we never thought or dreamed possible.[1] It's like this: Every action, every decision, every single choice you make sets something in motion. Like dominoes lined up in perfect formation, one small push—one decision—can create a chain reaction that changes everything. The real question is this: Are your choices pushing you toward power, purpose, and destiny—or setting you up for regret, fear, and stagnation?

THE POWER OF A SINGLE CHOICE

You are never stuck. You are never trapped. You are never powerless. One of the greatest lies the enemy will ever tell you is that your choices don't matter—that you're a victim of circumstances, that your past defines your future, that change isn't possible for you. But here's the truth: Your life right now is the sum of your choices. And the best news? One new decision can break every negative cycle. One choice can rewrite your entire future.

Every success story begins with a choice. Someone decided to get back up when staying down felt easier. Someone decided to believe truth instead of lies. Someone chose to step into faith instead of giving in to fear. Every hero you admire, every person who made a lasting impact, had a moment when they made one defining choice that changed the game. What's stopping you from making yours? For me, this is why I love interviewing those who have done very hard things. I want to learn from those who did not stop and did not quit. The psychology of resilience is fascinating to me. Those who allowed their worst days to become their best days. This is why I am drawn to the Tony Robbinses, David Gogginses, Garrett Whites, and Cameron Haneses of this world. This is why I love reading autobiographies of men and women of God of a previous generation. The Leonard Ravenhills, Hudson Taylors, and Rees Howellses inspire me to aspire to greater. Let every person become your teacher. We can learn if we are teachable. These lessons can never be learned in a classroom. Perhaps this is another reason I choose to run ultramarathons. I want to discover the limit of what is possible and go further.

SMALL CHOICES, MASSIVE IMPACT

You don't have to make ten changes today—you just have to make one. Because that one change, like a domino, will hit the next and the next, and soon enough, your entire life will look different.

One choice to forgive can break years of bitterness.

One choice to speak life instead of death can transform your relationships.

One choice to discipline your mind can pull you out of anxiety and fear.

One choice to trust God can shift your entire destiny.

And the opposite is just as true. One compromise leads to another. One small excuse justifies the next. One moment of settling leads to a life of regret. Your life isn't shaped by a few huge, dramatic moments—it's shaped by hundreds of small, daily choices that build on one another. Success and failure are the result of compounded decisions over time. What you choose today is setting the stage for the life you'll live tomorrow.

WALKING IN POWER: NO MORE PASSIVE LIVING

If you want to live in power, you have to own your choices. Weakness and defeat aren't random—they're the natural result of passivity, of letting life happen to you instead of taking authority over the life God has given you. Scripture is clear: "I have set before you life and death, blessing and cursing; therefore choose life" (Deut. 30:19, NKJV).

That's it. You get to choose. You are not at the mercy of your past. You are not bound by your mistakes. You are not trapped by the words others have spoken over you. The enemy will try to convince you that you're powerless—that you're stuck—but God says you have the authority to change your direction *right now*.

So stop waiting. Stop procrastinating. Stop believing the lie that you need perfect timing, the perfect plan, or the perfect conditions to move forward. If there's one thing I've learned in my faith journey, it's this: There's never a "perfect time" to obey what God is asking of me. There's only the here and the now—His voice calling me forward today. It's about trusting Him completely, even when everything inside me wants to wait for the stars to align. The perfect time to change your life isn't someday. It's *right now*.

THE ENEMY OF DECISION: FEAR AND INDECISION

If the power of one choice is so life-changing, why don't more people make it? One word: fear. Fear of failing. Fear of rejection. Fear of the unknown. Fear of what others might think. Fear has kept too many people standing still when they were born to move.

Indecision is one of the enemy's sharpest weapons. The more you hesitate, the more you overanalyze, the more you delay, the more momentum you lose. The longer you stay stuck "thinking about it," the harder it becomes to act.

But here's something you need to grab hold of: *God moves when you move.* When Peter stepped out of the boat and onto the water, he didn't wait for the waves to calm down. He didn't wait for a sign that the timing was perfect. He simply stepped—and in that moment, God sustained him.

You don't have to have every answer figured out. You just have to take the first step.

DECIDE TODAY: SET THE RIGHT DOMINO IN MOTION

So here's the choice before you: Are you going to let life happen to you, or are you going to set the first domino in motion toward your God-given future?

Choose boldly.

Take action.

Speak life.

Step out in faith.

Change your story.

One decision today—right now—can create a domino effect that shifts your entire future.

So what's it going to be?

CHAPTER 36

WHEN THE WRONG SOCIAL MEDIA POST FEELS RIGHT

The biggest thing that you need to realize is they don't know you. People criticize me all the time but they have no idea who I am or what I do. They read one quote or look at one clip, out of context, and they think they know me. I'm not too big on constructive criticism when it comes from people who have no idea what they're talking about. Judge the judger who's judging you.
—GARYVEE

YOU'VE BEEN THERE. The anger bubbles up inside. Someone posts something ignorant, offensive, or just plain wrong. Your fingers hover over the keyboard, your heart is pounding, you're ready to fire off a response that will set the record straight. You type it out, read it over, and for a moment—it feels good. Really good. Like justice. Like truth. Like you're standing up for what's right.

But are you?

The digital world has made it dangerously easy to act on impulse. The wrong social media post feels right because, in that moment, it gives us a false sense of power. It feels like control. It satisfies an immediate craving—to be heard, to be right, to prove a point. But what happens next? The dopamine rush fades. The backlash begins. And suddenly we're stuck defending, deleting, or regretting what we thought was a "righteous" post.

THE ILLUSION OF POWER

Social media gives everyone a platform, but it doesn't give everyone wisdom. It hands us a microphone before we've taken time to measure our words. It rewards reaction over reflection. Noise over nuance. And the moment we hit "post," we set something in motion—something we might not be able to take back.

James 1:19 says it so clearly: "Be quick to listen, slow to speak and slow to become angry." But let's be honest—social media flips that completely upside down. It pushes us to be quick to react, slow to listen, and eager to argue.

We convince ourselves, "They need to hear this." "I'm just speaking truth." "I'm just calling things out." But deep down we have to ask, "Is it really truth spoken in love? Is it conviction or just frustration?" Are we building people up—or just tearing them down?

139

THE COST OF REACTING INSTEAD OF RESPONDING

Every time you post something online, you're building something—your reputation, your influence, your credibility. Whether you realize it or not, people are watching. And one emotional, reactionary post can undo years of trust in an instant.

The wrong post can fracture relationships. Even if you don't mean to, you can push away friends, family members, or people who might have been open to listening before.

The wrong post can distort your witness. It doesn't matter how right you are if your words are laced with sarcasm, hostility, or arrogance. People won't remember how clever you sounded—they'll remember how your words made them feel.

The wrong post can trap you in a cycle of negativity. Online battles can be addictive. The more you argue, the more you crave the next fight. It feeds something toxic inside.

But what if, before reacting, you simply paused? What if you gave yourself a moment to step back and breathe?

THE POWER OF RESTRAINT

Here's the truth: You don't have to clap back. You don't have to respond to every ignorant comment. You don't have to prove yourself to strangers on the internet.

Before posting, ask yourself these questions:

- Does this reflect who I really want to be?
- Is this drawing people toward truth—or just stirring up more division?
- Will I still be proud of this post a year from now?

Social media is just a tool. It's not your enemy—and it's not your source of validation. Use it wisely. Use it to speak life, not just to air opinions. Build up, not tear down. Because sometimes the greatest power isn't found in what you say—it's found in what you choose to leave unsaid.

THE ROI OF ONLINE WISDOM

Let's get real—your energy is a currency. Every comment you drop, every argument you engage in, every minute you spend fuming over someone else's ignorance is a withdrawal from your personal energy bank. And if we're being honest? Most of the time, there's zero return on investment.

Think about it. Would you invest money into a company that was guaranteed to fail? Of course not. So why would you keep investing your time and energy into digital battles that will never change anyone's mind?

If your goal is influence—if your goal is to actually make an impact—then every post, every comment, every method of engagement needs to be strategic. And by strategic, I don't mean fake or manipulative—I mean *intentional*.

What are you building with your voice? What are you reinforcing every time you post? Are you depositing wisdom—or just contributing to the noise?

Every time you show up online, you're reinforcing a brand. Not some curated, polished, fake brand—but the real "this is who I am" brand. Are you showing up as someone who's reactive, emotional, and easily triggered? Or someone who speaks truth with grace, picks battles wisely, and doesn't need to win every argument to know they've already won in Christ?

WHEN SILENCE SPEAKS LOUDER THAN WORDS

Sometimes the most powerful thing you can do is nothing at all. Not because you're weak. Not because you're scared. But because you understand that silence can actually say more than a thousand arguments ever could.

Silence says, "I'm not giving my energy here."

Silence says, "I know what matters most, and this isn't it."

Silence says, "I'm not called to fight every battle—I'm called to stay on mission."

Jesus didn't waste time debating every critic who misunderstood Him. He didn't chase after every Pharisee who slandered His name. He stayed focused. He stayed locked in on His purpose. And if we're serious about following Him, we should do the same. I can't remember where this quote originated from, but don't listen to criticism from someone you would never take advice from.

USE YOUR PLATFORM FOR PURPOSE

Social media isn't evil. It's a tool. It's a megaphone. It's a way to reach the world. But like any tool, it can be used to either build something beautiful or tear something down.

So, before you post, take a gut check:

- **Check your motive.** Are you posting to add value—or just to vent?
- **Check your tone.** Would you say this to someone's face, not just behind the screen?
- **Check your timing.** Are you reacting out of emotion—or responding after prayerful reflection?
- **Check your impact.** Will this build a bridge—or burn one down?

If it doesn't pass the test, don't post it. It's that simple.

Social media will always tempt you to react. The world will always reward the loudest voice in the room. But real power? Real influence? It's found in the wisdom to know when to speak, when to stay silent, and when to simply walk away.

So, before you hit "post," pause. Think. Reflect. Because the wrong post might feel good in the moment—but wisdom will feel good for the rest of your life.

CHAPTER 37
YOU ARE NOT A VICTIM

When you believe things are your fault, you feel like you're in control and you have the ability to fix it. I feel like when you point fingers, it's an incredibly sad place to be. Because you feel helpless, which leads to a lot of levels of anxiety, depression, and unhappiness.
—GaryVee

THE HAPPIEST PEOPLE I've ever met aren't the ones who dwell on everything that's gone wrong. They're the ones who have a compelling vision of what could be. They aren't chained by their past. They're fueled by their future. But if you believe the situations in your life are the reason you're not who or where you want to be, you're trapped in one of the most destructive mindsets there is: victimhood.

Now hear me clearly—I am not for one second saying that what has happened to you was excusable. I'm not saying you deserved the pain you've been through. What I am saying is this: You have to take ownership of right here and right now. Because if you don't, you'll keep living in chains that Jesus already unlocked.

The spirit of accusation thrives where blame is present. It loves when people point fingers, shift responsibility, and excuse away the places where real accountability belongs.

Let me say this loud and clear: *You are not a victim.*

Victimhood isn't a life sentence—it's a mindset. It's an identity people slip into because it feels easier than fighting for something better. It gives permission to stay stuck, to keep living in the past, and to avoid taking ownership of the future.

But here's the hard truth you can't afford to miss: Your life is the sum of your choices. And the moment you shift from victim to victor, you take back your power.

Am I saying bad things won't happen to you? Absolutely not. They will. You'll be mistreated. You'll face unfair situations. You'll get knocked down by things you never asked for. But here's what I am saying: *Those things don't get to define you—unless you let them.*

It amazes me how easily people rewrite their memories to match their bitterness. Moments that were once beautiful—once full of life and joy—get twisted into something negative. What was once a great memory or meaningful experience becomes tainted by victimhood.

You need to hear this: It's not your parents' fault. It's not your spouse's fault. It's not the government's fault. It's not the economy's fault. It's not even God's fault. The moment you start blaming everyone else, you hand over the keys to your future. You're basically saying, "Someone else gets to determine how my story ends." But that's not who you are. That's not the life you were created for. The story God wants to write through your life is way too good, way too powerful, and way too important to be held hostage by blame, bitterness, and excuses.

OWN YOUR SIN AND MISTAKES—FULLY

Taking ownership isn't just about shaping what's ahead—it's about owning what's behind you too. You can't move forward if you're still dragging around a pile of excuses, justifications, and blame. Growth doesn't happen by pretending things didn't happen or convincing yourself it's always someone else's fault. Growth happens when you get real.

Winners aren't perfect—but they're honest. They own their failures, learn from them, and rise stronger because of it. Losers? They keep making excuses, shifting blame, and wondering why they're still stuck.

If you messed up, admit it. If you hurt someone, apologize. If you've been running from responsibility, stop. The most powerful thing you can do isn't pretending you've got it all together—it's facing the truth head-on, owning it fully, and then moving forward with humility and strength.

Growth begins where excuses end. Stop waiting for the perfect conditions. Stop hoping someone will come along and fix everything for you. Rise up. Take responsibility. Step into the future God has for you.

And let's be honest—how many of us, deep down, believe we've done no real wrong? And if we *have* messed up, we quickly find a way to blame it on someone else. It's pride that whispers, "It's not your fault." But freedom comes when we stop listening to that voice—and start owning our part, fully.

OWN YOUR LIFE—FULLY

Because of Jesus—because of what He has already done for us—we live from a place of victory. That means we don't sit around waiting for life to be fair. We don't wait for apologies, reparations, or a perfect set of circumstances to move forward. We take radical ownership of our lives, right here and right now.

You have one life. No one is coming to hand you your dreams on a silver platter. You want something different? Then do something different.

The only way forward is to stop making excuses and start making changes. Decide right now that you're done blaming, complaining, or waiting for someone else to fix your situation. Your mindset is everything. The way you feel today is a direct result of what you focus on. Change your focus, and you'll change your future.

THE POWER OF A DECISION

As we've discussed, every transformation starts with one decision. One moment when you say, "Enough. I refuse to live like this." That's the moment everything shifts—from passive to powerful, from stuck to unstoppable.

Your emotions will try to pull you back. Your old habits will whisper lies. But you are stronger than your excuses. The most successful people you admire? They didn't have an easy path—they simply refused to quit.

144 | Time to Rise

If you want to change your life, it starts by changing your story. Tell yourself the truth:

- ◆ "I am not powerless."
- ◆ "I am not a victim."
- ◆ "I am in control of my future."
- ◆ "I will not waste another day blaming, complaining, or doubting."

To break free from a victim mindset, here's where you start:

- ◆ **Stop talking about what you don't have.** The more you focus on lack, the more powerless you feel. Shift your focus to what you *can* do, not what you can't.
- ◆ **Rewrite your narrative.** What story are you telling yourself? If it's full of blame and excuses, rewrite it. Speak life, not limitation.
- ◆ **Get around people who refuse to play small.** Whom you surround yourself with will determine your mindset. Get around people who challenge you, not people who reinforce your excuses.
- ◆ **Take immediate action.** You don't have to have it all figured out. Just take one step. Action kills fear. Action builds momentum. Action changes everything.

Here's what I know: There's greatness inside you. There is the power of a thousand blazing suns inside you. The greatest battle will always be you vs. you and learning to hear the voice that speaks so much more over you. There is a purpose for your life. But you will never step into it as long as you keep playing small, making excuses, or waiting for the world to be fair.

Life isn't fair. But that doesn't mean you can't win.

So here's the question: Are you ready to step up? Are you ready to take back your power and walk boldly into the future God has for you? Because if you are, then this is your moment.

Right here, right now, decide: No more blaming. No more excuses. No more waiting. Your future starts today. Make it count.

CHAPTER 38

REVIVAL STARTS WITH ONE DECISION—YOURS

As long as God is on His throne, revival is as possible as the sun rising tomorrow morning.
—DEL FEHSENFELD JR.

IT HAS ALWAYS been my belief that those who need revival the most live like they need it the least, and those who need revival the least live like they need it the most.

The very word *revival* has come to mean many things to many people. But when I speak of revival, I speak of something that is the heritage of the church since the Book of Acts and not the Christian lottery. Revival looks like Jesus. It is an upgrade in the Christian experience that marks us. It creates intense love for Jesus.

How can we have personal revival? How can we have an encounter with Jesus that changes the ethos and essence of who we are? A decision.

The spirit of accusation comes against the idea of revival and labels it emotionalism or fanaticism. Please remember this for as long as you walk the earth: No fire has more damage to the church than strange fire.

A genuine authentic move of God in revival isn't an event. It's not a church service. It's not a movement that swoops in from nowhere. Revival starts with one decision. Your decision. What exactly is that decision? Buckle up. Keep reading.

We love the idea of revival—crowds crying out to God, lives being transformed, cities shaking with His presence. But too often, we're waiting for someone else to spark it. We act like revival is something "out there" that just happens when the conditions are right. But the truth is, revival begins the moment one person refuses to stay the same.

REVIVAL STARTS IN YOU

Before revival ever sweeps through a church, a city, or a nation, it first has to ignite in one heart—one heart that says, "I'm done settling." If you're sitting around waiting for a preacher to light your fire, for a conference to shake you awake, or for the perfect moment to finally surrender—you're waiting too long.

Revival begins the moment you say, "Enough. I will not live half alive anymore. I won't compromise. I refuse to be a lukewarm believer."

Desperation fuels hunger—and hunger is what accelerates revival.

You don't need a packed stadium. You don't need the perfect worship set or the

146 | Time to Rise

perfect atmosphere. You don't have to wait for some "move of God" to happen. You *are* the move of God.

Revival isn't about a place. It's not about a stage, a service, or a special event. It's about a posture of your heart. God isn't waiting for better conditions, bigger crowds, or louder voices. He's simply waiting for one person—just one—to say, "Here I am, Lord. Use me." Are you willing to be that person?

THE COST OF REVIVAL

The cost of revival is one thing. The price to maintain it? That's something else altogether. There's a spirit of accusation against revival that tries to dismiss the idea of revival today. It whispers, "Second Chronicles 7:14 isn't for America. That was just for the Old Testament Israel." But make no mistake—revival is still for us. Right here. Right now. And yes, it's costly.

Revival demands death to self. It means tearing down every idol—comfort, apathy, sin, pride. It means choosing holiness when no one is watching, deciding again and again that God's presence matters more than your preferences. Revival isn't just a feeling—it's a fight. A fight against the lies that tell you nothing will change. A fight against compromise. A fight against every excuse that says, "Maybe later." Later is the enemy of revival.

True revival isn't about emotion; it's about transformation. It's not about one powerful service—it's about lasting surrender. It's waking up every morning and choosing Jesus over everything else, even when it's hard, even when it's unpopular, even when no one around you seems to care. Are you willing to pay that price?

ONE DECISION CHANGES EVERYTHING

It all starts with one decision to seek God with your whole heart. One decision to stop playing games. One decision to let go of what's holding you back. This is why you must win the inner war every day. You must not retreat. I have regretted the time I have wasted not letting go of what was holding me back.

Every great move of God in history started the same way: someone who got desperate enough to say, "God, use me. Start with me." Moses had to say yes before he could lead a nation out of Egypt. David had to say yes before he could take down Goliath. Esther had to say yes before she could save her people. The disciples had to say yes before they could turn the world upside down.

What if you stopped waiting for a better time? What if today was your day? What if right now you stepped into the fire instead of standing on the sidelines? Revival isn't just for pastors. It's not just for evangelists or worship leaders. It's for you. Right now. Right where you are. The only question is this: Will you say yes?

Where are the repenters? Where are the ones willing to lay it all down? Where are the ones willing to burn for Him?

THE TIME IS NOW

Revival isn't coming. Revival is here. The question is, will you step into it? The greatest tragedy isn't that revival tarries—it's that so many people choose not to embrace it when it comes. God is moving. He's awakening hearts. He's stirring His people. But He's not going to force you to respond. The decision has always been—and will always be—yours.

Will you let distractions drown out His voice? Will you let fear keep you stuck where you are? Will you let comfort convince you that "good enough" is good enough? Or will you rise? Will you say yes to everything He's been waiting to release through your life? It doesn't start with a crowd. It doesn't even start with a movement. It starts with one decision. Make it. Light the fire. Refuse to settle for anything less than the life you were made for.

The world doesn't need more spectators. It needs warriors. It needs men and women who are done with casual Christianity—believers who burn so brightly that others can't help but be drawn to the flame. You don't need more information. You don't need another sermon. You don't need permission from anyone else. You just need to decide.

Revival isn't waiting on God. God is waiting on you.

So what will you do?

The answer is simple.

Decide.

CHAPTER 39

INTERNAL IDENTITY AND THE POWER OF CHOICE

A clear conscience laughs at a false accusation.
—PUBLILIUS SYRUS

YOUR INTERNAL IDENTITY is not just something you inherit—it's something you choose. Every emotion you feel, every belief you hold, every perspective you live by at its core comes down to choices you've made. The choice to hold on to past wounds or let them refine you. The choice to define yourself by achievements or by something deeper. The choice to believe truth over emotion.

Identity is not fixed. It's not something you're stuck with. It's a series of small decisions, stacked one on top of the other, forming the foundation of how you see yourself and how you show up in the world.

I think of my close friend and fellow pastor, Chris Williams. I have watched him model this so beautifully as he's led the church he serves. Years ago his church made a choice to declare their identity: They would be a church with the motto Live to Bless. And they didn't just say it—they became it. When that truth got down deep into who they were, I watched God breathe on it. Their church exploded with growth and favor. What Jesus is doing in and through them is nothing short of miraculous. Identity matters.

At the amazing church I serve, there's something similar. We have an addiction—to the presence of Jesus. It's who we are. Eventually, our church will be renamed Presence Church because hosting His presence is not just what we do—it's our very identity. Again, identity matters.

At some point every one of us comes to a crossroads. One path leads to a life dictated by emotions—always up, down, tossed around by every disappointment, every success, every heartbreak. The other path leads to a life anchored in truth. A life where emotions are still real but no longer in control. Where feelings are indicators, not dictators.

And every day, you and I make choices that either strengthen or weaken our internal identity:

- Will I choose to see myself as a victim of my past or an overcomer?
- Will I choose to seek validation through achievement or live from a place of security?
- Will I choose to let my emotions define me, or will I define them?

Identity isn't just about what you say—it's about what you decide. Choose wisely.

Internal Identity and the Power of Choice | 149

CHOICE #1: THE WOUNDED VS. THE HEALED

Identity Question: Will I let my pain define me, or will I rise above it?

We've all been hurt. We've all faced betrayal, rejection, failure. But too many people get stuck there—trapped in their wounds, replaying the same moments over and over, letting pain shape who they are. Here's the truth: Pain is inevitable, but suffering is a choice. The difference between someone who stays wounded and someone who heals comes down to how they choose to see their story. The Overcomer chooses to see hardship as a refining fire, not a prison. The Rooted chooses to trust in a greater purpose instead of settling into bitterness. Healing happens when you decide your past doesn't get the final say. You move from "I am broken" to "I am being restored." From "This is who I am" to "This is what I've been through—but it does not define me."

CHOICE #2: THE PERFORMER VS. THE ROOTED

Identity Question: Am I chasing approval, or am I standing in confidence?

The Performer identity thrives on external validation. It whispers, "If I achieve enough, I will be enough." But this is a trap—because there is always another level, another goal, another person's approval to chase. The alternative? The choice to be *rooted*—to know your worth apart from accomplishments. The Rooted person doesn't need applause to confirm their identity. They don't need a platform to validate their worth. They wake up every morning grounded in the truth—the unshakable truth that they are already enough. Every morning, you make a choice. Will you let the opinions of others determine your value? Or will you stand in confidence of who you already are in Christ?

Will you run yourself ragged on the treadmill of achievement—always hustling, always proving—or will you step off, take a breath, and embrace the simple yet radical truth that you are already fully loved, fully accepted, fully enough?

CHOICE #3: REACTING VS. RESPONDING TO EMOTIONS

Identity Question: Do my emotions control me, or do I control them?

Emotions are powerful. They're real, and they're meant to be felt—but they don't always tell the whole truth. If you let anger, fear, or anxiety call the shots, you'll end up living in constant instability—always reacting, always tossed by the latest wave of feeling. The Wounded react to emotions without question. The Overcomer feels the emotion but still chooses their response. The Rooted stay steady—they filter emotions through truth before they act.

The choice here is simple, but it will shape your life: Will you let emotions dictate your identity—or will you take ownership? Will you live by feelings—or will you live by wisdom? You can feel deeply without being led blindly. You get to choose whether emotions drive your life or simply inform it.

CHOICE #4: SCARCITY VS. ABUNDANCE MINDSET

Identity Question: Do I see life through the lens of fear or faith?

How you see the world shapes how you see yourself. Some people live stuck in a scarcity mindset, always believing there's not enough—never enough time, never enough opportunity, never enough love to go around. Scarcity fuels insecurity, it stirs up competition, and it convinces you that you're always one step behind. But those who are Rooted live with an abundance mindset. They choose to believe that they are not lacking, that opportunity isn't running out, and that they are exactly where they're meant to be—even when the path doesn't look like they expected.

Scarcity says, "I will never be enough." Abundance says, "I am already enough." Scarcity says, "There's not enough for me." Abundance says, "What is meant for me will always find me." Every single day, you get to choose: Will you live from fear—or will you live from faith? One will drain the life out of you. The other will set you free.

CHOICE #5: COMPARISON VS. CALLING

Identity Question: Will I live by comparison or embrace my unique path?

Comparison is a silent thief. It creeps in when you're not even looking, whispering that you're falling behind, that someone else is doing it better, faster, bigger. And if you're not careful, it starts to diminish your confidence and distract you from the race you were already created to run. But here's the truth: Your identity isn't found in someone else's story. You were never called to copy their life. You have a unique path, a specific assignment, and a purpose that is yours alone.

The Wounded compare and shrink back. The Performer compares and hustles for worth. The Overcomer learns from others but stays true to their own lane. And the Rooted? They walk forward without wavering, eyes locked on their own calling, not someone else's applause. Every time you compare, you have a choice: Will you let it steal your identity—or will you refocus on what God uniquely placed inside you?

YOUR IDENTITY IS THE SUM OF YOUR CHOICES

You are not your past. You are not your emotions. You are not your achievements. You are the sum of the choices you make—day after day, moment by moment. The choice to heal instead of staying wounded. The choice to stand in confidence instead of seeking validation. The choice to control emotions instead of being controlled by them. The choice to live with an abundance mindset instead of believing in scarcity. The choice to embrace your calling instead of comparing yourself to others.

No one else can make these choices for you. But once you start making them, everything changes.

At the end of the day, identity isn't something you stumble across. It's something you build by the choices you make over and over again.

Internal Identity and the Power of Choice | 151

So ask yourself, "Who am I choosing to be today? What belief about myself do I need to let go of? What truth do I need to step into?"

The moment you take ownership of your internal identity is the moment you stop being tossed by circumstances, emotions, and other people's opinions. You don't have to stay wounded. You don't have to live on the treadmill of proving yourself. You don't have to be pulled under by every emotional storm. You can be rooted. You can be confident. You can walk with authority. You were made for more—and the choice is yours.

> Here's to the crazy ones. The misfits. The rebels. The troublemakers. The round pegs in the square holes. The ones who see things differently. They're not fond of rules. And they have no respect for the status quo. You can quote them, disagree with them, glorify or vilify them. About the only thing you can't do is ignore them. Because they change things. They push the human race forward. And while some may see them as the crazy ones, we see genius. Because the people who are crazy enough to think they can change the world are the ones who do.
>
> —STEVE JOBS

CHAPTER 40

TEN PRINCIPLES FOR WALKING IN POWER

To give anything less than your best is to sacrifice the gift.
—STEVE PREFONTAINE

THERE'S A WAR going on inside you every single day. One voice says, "Believe the lies about yourself and others and go along with the crowd." The other says, "Now is the time to rise." And let's be clear: The anointing of God comes through desperation and hunger. It's how transformation comes—choice by choice, truth by truth, fire by fire. Life will test you. It will try to crush you. But those moments? That's where strength is forged. Over the years, I've uncovered ten principles that aren't just motivational fluff—they're battle-tested foundations. If you're tired of shrinking back and ready to live unshakable, this is where it starts:

PRINCIPLE 1: THE STRENGTH TO BE UNOFFENDED IS THE STRENGTH TO LEAD

Being easily offended is not a sign of moral high ground—it's a sign of fragility. If every disagreement leaves you wounded, you're giving others control over your peace. True strength is learning to listen, discern, and stay unshaken when offense comes. The ability to stay calm, clear-headed, and focused when others try to provoke you is a superpower few ever master.

PRINCIPLE 2: YOUR MIND IS EITHER A PRISON OR A GATEWAY—BREAK FREE FROM LIMITING BELIEFS

Most people aren't limited by reality—they're limited by the stories they tell themselves. If you believe you're incapable, you won't even try. If you think success is only for "someone else," you'll never reach for it yourself. Your beliefs set the parameters of your world. Shatter the ceilings you've inherited or built for yourself. True freedom starts in your mind.

PRINCIPLE 3: STOP LOOKING FOR THE PERFECT CHURCH—FIND ONE AND COMMIT

We live in an age of church hopping, where people chase the perfect fit, the perfect sermon, the perfect worship set. An ideal that doesn't exist. But the church isn't supposed to cater to your preferences—it's supposed to help shape your life. Real transformation happens in commitment, not convenience. Stop shopping for community. Plant yourself in one. Grow roots. Become part of something bigger than you. The church is meant to become your family—plant yourself.

PRINCIPLE 4: BURN THE BRIDGES THAT KEEP YOU IN CHAINS; CROSS THE BRIDGES THAT LEAD TO YOUR GROWTH

Not everything or everyone deserves a permanent place in your life. Some relationships, habits, and environments are chains disguised as comforts. Burn the bridges that tether you to your old identity. Cross the bridges that demand courage. Seek mentorship, accountability, discipline, and faith. Freedom and growth require wisdom: knowing what to leave and what to lean into.

PRINCIPLE 5: EVERY DECISION IS A SEED—PLANT WISELY

You don't just make choices—your choices make you. Each decision you plant today will grow into something tomorrow. Compromise in small things leads to weakness in big things. One bad habit tolerated becomes a life dominated. But the opposite is also true—one act of courage today can change your entire trajectory. Plant wisely. Your future depends on it.

PRINCIPLE 6: THE INTERNET IS NOT YOUR DIARY—THINK BEFORE YOU POST

In a world addicted to venting online, wisdom looks like restraint. Social media is flooded with impulsive outrage, unfiltered emotions, and careless accusations. Every post matters. Every word carries weight. Your digital footprint is building your real-world credibility—or tearing it down. Think before you type. Silence, sometimes, is the loudest form of wisdom.

PRINCIPLE 7: OWN YOUR MISTAKES OR BE OWNED BY THEM

Weak people blame everyone else for their failures—the system, their leaders, their past. Strong people look in the mirror and say, "This is my responsibility, and I will make it right." Ownership isn't weakness. It's a doorway to freedom. You can't change what you're not willing to own.

PRINCIPLE 8: REVIVAL IS NOT AN EVENT—IT'S A DECISION

People talk about revival as if it's something that happens to them—a wave of emotion, a collective spiritual high. But real revival starts in the private moments of decision. It happens when one person chooses to live fully alive, fully committed, and fully surrendered to their purpose. If you want revival, don't wait for it—be it.

PRINCIPLE 9: YOU ARE ALWAYS AT A CROSSROADS—MAKE THE RIGHT CHOICE

Every moment of your life presents a choice. You can choose the easy path or the right path. You can choose comfort or growth. You can choose safety or significance. The most dangerous mistake is assuming that *not choosing* is an option—because inaction is a choice, and it almost always leads to regret.

PRINCIPLE 10: NO ONE IS COMING TO SAVE YOU—RISE UP AND WALK IN POWER

There is a brutal but liberating truth: No one is responsible for your future except you. Yes, God is with you. Yes, people can help. But the weight of your life will always rest on your own shoulders. Own it. Carry it well. And watch how powerful you become when you stop waiting and start rising.

These principles aren't just ideas—they're battle-tested foundations. Your life will rise or fall on the choices you make day after day. Choose power. Choose growth. Choose to live fully alive and fully awake in Christ.

PART V

THE RIGHT QUESTIONS— UNLOCKING WISDOM AND PURPOSE

In December 2024, I attended a life-changing event with Tony Robbins called Date with Destiny. Over the course of six days and six nights, I was overwhelmed with the truth of who I had become and was becoming. For the first time in a long time, I was able to uncover what was truly driving me and how it was destroying my life. Then, in a place of absolute gratitude and certainty, I was given a gift. The gift to change everything, and I did. New vision. New values. New life.

When I was at Date with Destiny, I realized that when honest, I considered my life a failure. Not that it actually was a failure, but my rules to have success and happiness made it impossible not to feel that way. My belief is that you might be there as well.

I can say without a doubt—attending this event was one of the greatest decisions I've ever made.

In this final section of the book, I want to unpack several key takeaways from that event. It changed everything. It rewired everything. For the first time, I began to understand certain things—why I had certain patterns, habits, and responses. I firmly believe that those who truly want to grow will grow. Those who want to change will change. But it requires a deep desire, a relentless pursuit, and an openness to let God divinely guide us into the moments that transform everything.

I want you to discover for yourself that the only way to overcome the external and internal accusations is to rise—to rise and become the person you have been called to become. Accusation seeks to steal identity. But when you ask the right questions about who you are and who you are to become, you soon realize that you don't have time to let accusations live rent-free in your mind.

bit.ly/451EWRy

CHAPTER 41

WHO AM I BECOMING? ASKING THE RIGHT QUESTIONS

You've probably noticed life presents many opportunities to test our limits: But the main limit to greatness is saying to yourself, "I can't."
—JAMES LAWRENCE

SOMETIMES YOU WAKE up feeling empty with no purpose or passion in your life because deep down, you don't have a clear, compelling vision of the person you're called to be. Every single day, with every single choice—no matter how big or small—you are designing your future. The real question isn't just "What am I doing?" It's "Who am I becoming?"

Most people never stop to ask the real question. They drift through life, reacting to circumstances, getting stuck in routines, doing what's expected. Then one day they wake up, staring at a reality they never intentionally created, asking themselves, "How did I get here?" The truth is—they never took control. They never made intentional decisions about who they were becoming.

But you can.

If you spent the next eighteen months completely, fiercely focused on becoming the version of yourself that doesn't yet exist, what would that person look like? What thoughts would they have every day? What emotions would define their life? What kind of faith would they walk in? What would their family look like? Their fitness? Their finances?

Until you have a clear, compelling vision of who you're becoming in every area of life, you'll keep bouncing through the pinball machine of life—ricocheting from one sad and overwhelming day to the next, wondering why nothing changes.

If you want a better life, start by asking better questions. Your internal world—and eventually your external world—is shaped by the questions you dare to ask yourself. Weak questions produce weak answers. Strong, intentional questions force you to take ownership of your life and your future.

Ask yourself:

- "Am I becoming the person I want to be?"
- "Do I have a clear vision of who that person is?"
- "What is getting in the way of becoming that person?"
- "How would I feel if I actually became them?"
- "Am I living with passion and purpose—or just surviving the days?"

157

158 | TIME TO RISE

- "Who is influencing me—and are they pushing me closer to growth or pulling me into distraction?"

If you don't like the answers, it's not the end of the story. It's the beginning of a new one. Because the moment you ask better questions is the moment you can start living a better future.

When would *now* be a good time to pause and answer these questions for real? Maybe take a moment—before you read any further—to prayerfully write your answers down. Grab a notebook. Open your phone. Whatever it takes. Just remember: Clarity isn't found by chance. It's fought for.

YOU ARE NOT TRAPPED

One of the greatest lies people believe is that their lives are set in stone—that their habits, emotions, and identity are fixed. But nothing could be further from the truth. You are not stuck. You are becoming someone every single day—whether you realize it or not. Whether by intention or by default, you are shaping who you will become.

The difference between a life of success and a life of regret comes down to two simple things: awareness and action. The moment you wake up and recognize that you have the power to shape your identity, everything shifts. You stop blaming circumstances. You stop waiting for motivation. You stop making excuses. Instead, you take full responsibility for your future—and start making choices that align with the person you were born to be.

WHAT WORDS DO YOU SPEAK MOST OFTEN?

Your words aren't just sound waves floating in the air—they are seeds planted deep into the soil of your heart and mind. What you speak consistently, you will begin to believe. And what you believe will eventually shape the reality you live in.

Proverbs 18:21 says, "The tongue has the power of life and death, and those who love it will eat its fruit."

Either you are speaking life over yourself—or you are speaking death. You are either declaring possibility or reinforcing limitation.

If you constantly say, "I'm not good enough," you'll live as though it's true. If you declare, "I always fail," your mind will find ways to prove that right. If you whisper, "I'm not strong enough to change," you will remain exactly where you are.

But what if you changed the script? What if you started speaking words of power, purpose, and identity over your life?

- "I am growing into the person God created me to be."
- "I have the wisdom, strength, and discipline to make the right choices."
- "God's plan for my life is bigger than my fears."

The words you repeat to yourself are building the framework of your identity—brick by brick, belief by belief. If you want to change your life, start by changing your words.

YOUR THOUGHTS BECOME YOUR REALITY

Just like your words, your thoughts have power. The way you think shapes the way you feel, and the way you feel determines how you act. If fear, insecurity, and doubt are allowed to dominate your thoughts, your life will start to shrink around them. You'll live smaller than you were ever meant to live.

Romans 12:2 challenges us, "Do not conform to the pattern of this world, but be transformed by the renewing of your mind." Your mind is not a fixed system. It's not stuck. It can be rewired. Reprogrammed. Renewed. But it starts with awareness.

Ask yourself:

+ "What thoughts are ruling my life? Are they empowering me—or limiting me?"
+ "Am I thinking about possibilities—or problems?"
+ "Am I focused on what's missing—or on what's still possible?"

When you change your thinking, you change your life. The key is to stop letting negative thoughts run on autopilot—and start intentionally shaping the way you think. Your mind was never meant to be a battlefield you simply endure. It's meant to be territory you reclaim—through Christ, with confidence and authority.

TAKE CONTROL OF YOUR LIFE

Transformation doesn't happen by accident—it happens on purpose. And it starts when you refuse to become domesticated and sedated and when you take 100 percent responsibility for who you are becoming. Here's where we begin:

1. Get honest about where you are right now. You can't change what you won't acknowledge. Where are you coasting? Where are you compromising? Where are you making excuses? Get real with yourself—because the moment you own it, the sooner you can change it.

2. Clarify who you want to become. Write it down. Speak it out loud. Be specific. Do you want to be a bold leader? A person of deep faith? Someone who walks with unshakable confidence and purpose? If you don't define it, you won't become it.

3. Audit your daily decisions. Your identity isn't formed by one big, heroic moment—it's built by the small, ordinary choices you make every single day. Are your habits actually leading people toward the person you say you want to be? If not, it's time to change them.

4. Guard your words and thoughts. Start speaking words that build you up. Start rejecting the thoughts that tear you down. Write down declarations of truth. Speak

160 | Time to Rise

them over yourself every day. The more you reinforce who you're called to become, the faster you'll get there.

5. Surround yourself with the right people. You will either rise or fall based on the voices you allow closest to you. Choose relationships that challenge you, sharpen you, and call you higher. Get around people who make you want to be better—people who won't let you settle for easy when greatness is within you.

Decide right now: Who must I become to live the life God has called me to live?

And remember, this question isn't just for today. It's for every day of your life. Transformation isn't something you experience once and then move on from. It's a daily commitment. If you want to be a person of integrity, start by acting with integrity today. If you want to be physically strong, make strong choices today. If you want deeper faith, seek God today. If you want to encounter Him, let gratitude for His grace and mercy move you right now.

Who you become tomorrow is determined by the choices you make today. And if we're being honest—you have to stop. We all have to stop looking around at everyone else. Your future doesn't depend on anyone else. It begins with you, with the choices you make right here, right now.

THE DECISION IS YOURS

Either you are moving toward the person God created you to be—or you are drifting further away. There is no standing still. Every thought, every word, every action are shaping your future whether you realize it or not.

So ask yourself these questions:

- "Am I becoming stronger—or weaker?"
- "Am I growing in faith—or slipping into complacency?"
- "Am I stepping into my calling—or making excuses?"

The choice is yours.

No more waiting. No more excuses. No more playing small.

Who are you becoming?

Because the answer isn't somewhere out there—it's right here, in your hands.

CHAPTER 42

TOWARD VALUES: THE PATH TO A LIFE OF PASSION AND PURPOSE

Your life will never be the same again.
—OG MANDINO

EVERY DECISION YOU make is either moving you toward your values or pulling you further away from them. The problem? Most people have no idea what their true values actually are. They chase after what seems important in the moment—money, approval, comfort—without ever stopping to ask, "Is this really taking me where I want to go?"

When I was at Date with Destiny, I realized something that changed everything: All of us are moving toward something we want more of. More love. More joy. More happiness. More success. More health. But if we don't get clear on *why* we want those things—and what must happen for us to experience them—we almost never reach them.

This is why understanding the spirit of accusation is so critical. Satan does come to steal, kill, and destroy. And he's not subtle about it. I've seen him use the trials and storms of life. I've seen him use the careless words and hurtful actions of others to derail the destinies of so many—including yours, and mine too.

Here's the thing most people don't realize: A belief is just a rule you've decided to live by. It's a story you tell yourself about how life *has* to work—or how it never will. So let me ask you: What must happen in your life to have more joy, more happiness, more success, more love, more fulfillment?

For me I discovered that everything was external and in the future. For me to have more success and more joy, everyone had to be pleased with me, I had to keep everyone happy, everyone had to stay in the church I serve, and none of my digital media clients could end working with me.

Do you see a major problem in this? I hope you do. It was impossible.

The truth is, your values shape your destiny. If you don't choose them intentionally, the world will choose them for you. And if you let the world decide, you'll always end up feeling empty. Because the world will tell you that success is measured by wealth, that happiness comes from approval, and that security is found in comfort. But deep down, you already know none of these things will ever be enough.

So what will? A life where every choice you make points back to something bigger than you. A life where you wake up every morning knowing you're not chasing anything—you're exactly where you're meant to be.

WHAT DO YOU REALLY VALUE?

Let's get brutally honest for a second. Most people think they know what they value—but their actions tell a very different story. You might say you value health, but do your daily habits actually prove it? You might say you value faith, but are you prioritizing time with God? You might say you value family, but are you truly present with them—or just physically in the same room?

Your values are not simply what you *say* they are. Your values are what you *consistently choose*. Every decision you make is revealing what truly matters to you—whether you realize it or not.

If you want a powerful life—a life of deep meaning, unshakable confidence, and unstoppable momentum—you have to get crystal clear on what truly matters. And then you have to start aligning every decision you make with those values.

THE BATTLE BETWEEN COMFORT AND CALLING

Here's another hard truth to consider: Living by your values will always require sacrifice. It will always demand that you choose between comfort and calling.

- If you value growth, you have to be willing to step into discomfort.
- If you value integrity, you have to reject the easy shortcuts.
- If you value faith, you have to trust God even when nothing makes sense.

Most people shrink back when these choices show up. They let fear dictate their next steps. They tell themselves, "I'll start later" or "It's not that big of a deal." But deep down they know they're betraying themselves. And nothing shatters your confidence faster than living out of alignment with your own values.

But when you consistently choose *toward* your values—when you choose your calling over comfort—something shifts inside you. You start trusting yourself. You start walking taller. You stop second-guessing your decision, because you know your life is being built on something real. Something that will last.

THE POWER OF IDENTITY-BASED DECISIONS

If you want real, lasting transformation, you have to stop making decisions based on how you feel in the moment. Feelings can be fickle. They change with the weather. One minute you're motivated, the next you're discouraged. If your emotions lead your path, you'll spend your life swerving off course.

Instead, start making decisions based on *the person you're determined to become.* Ask yourself, "Would the future me—the one I'm building—say yes to this? Does this decision line up with what matters most to me? Will this move me closer to who I'm called to be or keep me stuck where I am?"

When you consistently choose based on your identity and values instead of your emotions, everything changes. You stop feeling lost. You stop wondering whether you're on the right path. You *know* you are. Because you've already decided who you're becoming—and now, every action you take is simply a step closer to that person.

HOW TO ALIGN YOUR LIFE WITH YOUR VALUES

Knowing your values is step one. Living them? That's the real game. You can't just hope your life drifts into purpose and impact—you must do the hard work. Most people talk about passion, but passion without alignment is just noise. If you want to live on fire with clarity, conviction, and impact, it starts by locking in your values like nonnegotiables. This isn't theory. It's your foundation. So let's break it down:

1. Define your core values.

Sit down and write out what truly matters to you—not what sounds good, but what you *must* live by to feel fully alive. Think beyond surface-level desires. Go deeper. What principles do you want guiding your life? If it's faith, then God must come first. If it's health, then your daily choices have to show it. If it's family, then your time and attention need to prove it. Your values shouldn't just sound inspiring—they should be clear, nonnegotiable, and strong enough to guide every decision you make.

2. Audit your life.

Take an honest look at your daily actions. Are they aligned with your values, or are you simply going through the motions? What about your schedule? Does it reflect what you say is important? Do your financial decisions back up your values? Are your relationships helping you grow—or pulling you away from who you want to be? Awareness is the first step toward realignment. If something is off, don't beat yourself up—just decide to change it.

3. Make value-based decisions.

Every time you face a choice, ask yourself, "Does this align with who I am becoming?" If not, walk away. If you value discipline, you won't hit snooze. If you value honesty, you won't cut corners. If you value personal growth, you won't waste hours on distractions. Small choices add up faster than you think. Over time they define you.

4. Eliminate what's out of alignment.

You cannot move forward while you're still holding on to things that keep pulling you back. If something isn't serving your values, it doesn't deserve a place in your life. Cut out toxic relationships that drain your energy. Stop giving your time and attention to things that don't align with your purpose. Break free from habits that keep you stuck playing small.

Your environment shapes your decisions more than you realize. Make sure it's pushing you toward who you're called to become—not keeping you tethered to who

164 | TIME TO RISE

you used to be. And if it's not? Then it's time to make some changes. The right community won't just support you—it will launch you further and faster than you ever imagined.

5. Take action—*now*.

Stop waiting. Stop overthinking. Stop telling yourself you need more time. The person you are becoming isn't shaped someday—it's shaped today. Want to be healthy? Make one healthy choice right now. Want to be successful? Take one bold step right now. Want to live by faith? Trust God right *now*. There is no perfect moment. There is only *this* moment. So choose toward your values *now*.

Your values are the blueprint for your best life. They will guide you when the path isn't clear. They will keep you strong when challenges come. They will shape you into the person you were created to be. But values don't mean anything if you don't choose them. So choose them. Live them. And watch everything change.

MY NEW TOWARD VALUES

Allow me to share with you by example my new values. I chose them based on deciding who I wanted to become. These now drive me. I repeat them often.

1. Healthy fire. Anytime I feel the manifest presence of Jesus, see a challenge as an opportunity, run, do anything that makes me strong, drink water, fast, get in shape and make my move, or think about Jesus, or make the smallest of healthy choices.

2. Love and devotion. Anytime I tell Jesus I love Him, am kind and encouraging to others, tell Rachel I love her, tell my kids I love them, remember the love I always have inside me, choose to be kind, am present with others, or run.

3. Brightness. Anytime I show up with a smile or laugh; make others laugh; am upbeat, playful, or outgoing; spark life in others; don't take myself or circumstances too seriously; wear my red jacket; or run. *(I have a bright red jacket that people know me for, FYI.)*

4. Intelligence and curiosity. Anytime I learn from anything or anybody, simply notice what is going on around me, ask better questions, ask God for wisdom, seek feedback, learn one thing from what I used to consider failure, or remember God is in me.

5. Authentic vulnerability. Anytime I am honest about myself and others, stand for others publicly or privately, share from my soul, or run.

6. Serve and encourage. Anytime I send an encouraging text, tell my wife how beautiful she is or simply praise her, speak life and identity over my kids, praise others, encourage others on social media, create content, or help others win.

7. Fun and happiness. Anytime I wake up, run, do crazy things, smile, laugh, dance, stop work early just because, read a book, or make others realize how amazing they are.

CHAPTER 43

AWAY VALUES: WHAT YOU MUST LEAVE TO STEP INTO GOD'S BEST

It may be satisfactory, but that's another word for mediocrity.
—DAVID GOGGINS

IN THE RECENT past, I had to get brutally honest about the things in my life I wanted to avoid. I had to face the patterns and mindsets that were quietly running the show underneath all my good intentions. We can call these "away values." And if you're serious about stepping into your best life, you're going to have to face yours too.

Most of us fixate on what we want—more success, more confidence, more faith, more impact. But few of us recognize that getting there isn't just about adding more to your life. It's just as much about what you subtract.

The life you want is waiting for you—but it's on the other side of letting go of everything that's been holding you back. These obstacles—your away values—aren't just bad habits or random struggles. They're the toxic patterns, the limiting beliefs, and the old mindsets that drain your energy, sabotage your momentum, and trap you in cycles you promised yourself you'd break.

Here's the truth: Freedom doesn't just happen. You don't stumble into greatness. You don't accidentally drift into purpose. You break free the moment you make a conscious, ruthless decision about what you refuse to carry anymore. Because if you don't actively reject your away values, they will rule your life by default—and over time, they'll quietly steal the future you were created to live.

WHAT ARE AWAY VALUES?

Away values are the things you need less of in your life. They're the patterns that keep you stuck, small, and struggling—and half the time, you don't even realize they're there. The problem is, most of us end up living on autopilot, wondering why we feel unfulfilled, without ever tracing it back to what we've been tolerating for too long.

If you want a life of power and purpose, you must identify and eliminate these away values:

- **Fear-based decision-making**—living your life based on what could go wrong instead of what could go right
- **Excuses and justifications**—blaming circumstances instead of owning your choices

- **Procrastination**—waiting for the "perfect" moment to act (spoiler: it never comes)
- **Toxic comparison**—measuring your worth against other people's highlight reels instead of your own calling
- **People-pleasing**—living for approval instead of living for your purpose
- **Negative self-talk**—rehearsing limiting beliefs that reinforce failure and doubt
- **Settling for comfort**—choosing the easy path when you were made for the meaningful one
- **Victim mentality**—believing life happens *to* you rather than *for* you

THE IMPACT OF AWAY VALUES ON YOUR LIFE

Here's a brutal truth: You will never rise higher than the worst habit you're still willing to tolerate.

You can set the best goals, read all the right books, and listen to the most inspiring messages—but if your away values are still controlling your decisions, you will stay stuck exactly where you are.

Think about it:

- If you constantly compare yourself to others, how will you ever feel confident?
- If you keep making excuses, how will you ever achieve your goals?
- If you let fear dictate your choices, how will you ever take bold action?

What you allow will always determine who you become.

ELIMINATING AWAY VALUES FROM YOUR LIFE

If you're ready for real transformation, you must deliberately reject your away values. Here's how:

1. Identify the away values controlling your life. Be brutally honest. What toxic emotions, thoughts, or behaviors are running your daily decisions? Write them down. Don't sugarcoat. If you don't name them, you can't change them.

2. Associate massive pain with these values. You will never change what you're still comfortable tolerating. You must make these away values unbearable. Ask yourself:

- "What has fear cost me?"
- "What has procrastination stolen from my life?"
- "What will happen if I don't change?"

168 | TIME TO RISE

Pain is a powerful motivator. Use it. Let it drive you away from what's keeping you stuck.

3. Replace away values with empowering values. You don't just eliminate away values—you replace them with something stronger. Fear has to be replaced with courage. Excuses have to be replaced with action. Comparison has to be replaced with self-belief. Choose the values you want your life to stand for.

4. Take immediate action. Stop waiting. Stop thinking about it. Stop planning to change "someday." The shift happens when you decide—right now—that enough is enough. Cut the habits. End the cycles. Walk away from the thoughts and behaviors that reinforce away values.

You are either moving toward your destiny or drifting away from it.

The choice is yours. Choose wisely.

MY AWAY VALUES

Allow me to share with you my away values and the rules I now associate with them. I have discovered that everywhere I go and speak about values, sharing my own helps people.

1. Consistently draining negativity and worry. Only if I were to consistently be upset about things before they happen or fearful about things that might happen if I miss calls or texts. Instead of remembering that whatever comes into my life, I can create an effective plan. I am Dr. Run.

2. Consistent destructive feelings of overwhelm. Only if I were to consistently believe the illusion that I get it all done. Instead of realizing that nothing will be as important a hundred years from now as it feels now. Instead of determining how I feel. I remember that abundance and beauty are all around me.

3. Consistent dark feelings of rejection/criticism. Only if I were to consistently believe the illusion that people who don't know me have an opinion more important than what Jesus knows, feels, and thinks about me. Instead of realizing that I am the only person who determines and creates who I am.

4. Consistent dark illusions of failure and shame. Only if I were to consistently focus on the false belief that I can fail. Instead of realizing that I have succeeded anytime I learned something. Instead of remembering that I am forgiven by the One who knows me better than I know myself.

5. Consistent debilitating imposter syndrome. Only if I were to focus on the false belief that I will be exposed as a failure. Instead of realizing that every day in every way I am getting better and better. Instead of remembering I am Dr. Run. I ran 153 marathons.

6. Consistent destructive anger and irritation. Only if I were to consistently treat people harshly. Instead of realizing that everyone has bad days, moments, rules, and beliefs. They are doing the best they can with the resources they have. It's not about me. I reject "assume" culture.

CHAPTER 44

THE QUESTION THAT CONTROLS YOUR LIFE

The sooner we become less impressed with our life, our accomplishments, our career, our relationships, the prospects in front of us—the sooner we become less impressed and more involved with these things—the sooner we get better at them. We must be more than just happy to be here.
—MATTHEW MCCONAUGHEY

WHAT IF I told you there's a question shaping your life right now—and you might not even realize it? A single question that's quietly steering every choice you make, every emotion you feel, and every action you take. It's called your primary question, and until you name it, it will keep calling the shots behind the scenes.[1]

Most people never stop to figure out what this is. They just live with it—like background noise they've gotten used to. But it's there, shaping everything. Maybe your primary question sounds like "Why does this always happen to me? What if I fail? How can I make sure people like me? Am I good enough?" And without realizing it, you start filtering everything—every opportunity, every relationship, every setback—through that single hidden question.

If your primary question is rooted in fear or insecurity, it's not just a thought. It becomes a lens. A lens that keeps you stuck. A lens that tells you who you are and what's possible—and most of the time, it lies. The truth is, until you recognize the question you're living by, you'll keep living small without even knowing why.

WHY YOUR PRIMARY QUESTION MATTERS

Your brain is designed to seek answers. It can't help it. Whatever question you feed it—good or bad—your mind will work overtime to find an answer. Even if the question is destructive.

If your primary question is "Why am I always struggling?" your brain will find reasons to confirm that belief. You'll see obstacles instead of opportunities. You'll notice everything that's wrong while ignoring what's right. Without realizing it, your life will become a reflection of that question.

But what if you changed the question? What if your primary question became "How can I use this challenge to grow?" Suddenly your brain would shift to find solutions. You'd start looking for strength instead of weakness, resilience instead of discouragement, and action instead of hesitation. The quality of your life is determined by the quality of the questions you dare to ask.

The Question That Controls Your Life | 171

IDENTIFYING YOUR CURRENT PRIMARY QUESTION

Take a step back. Get honest. What's the question that comes up most often when you face a challenge, make a decision, or evaluate yourself?

Do you find yourself asking one of these:

+ "What will people think of me?"
+ "Am I doing enough?"
+ "Why do things never work out for me?"

Be real with yourself. Write it down. Don't just think it—put it on paper. Because the question you ask yourself most often is shaping your destiny, whether you realize it or not.

Some primary questions lead you to confidence, growth, and action. Others trap you in cycles of insecurity, fear, and hesitation. Your job is simple—and if it's not serving you, it's time to change it.

CHOOSING A NEW AND EMPOWERING PRIMARY QUESTION

If you've been living by a question that limits you, it's time to trade it in with one that calls you higher.

Here are some examples of powerful primary questions you could start asking:

+ "How can I grow through this?"
+ "How can I glorify God in this situation?"
+ "What can I do right now to create momentum?"
+ "How can I bring more love and impact to the people around me?"
+ "How can I live today with passion and purpose?"

The right question doesn't just change what you think—it changes what you see. It opens doors where you used to see walls. It moves you forward when everything around you says to stay stuck.

Think about it. A person whose primary question is "How can I live with excellence today?" will show up very differently than someone who's constantly asking, "What if I mess up?" One builds confidence, growth, and bold faith. The other builds fear, hesitation, and regret.

So, let me ask you this: What's your new question going to be?

MY NEW PRIMARY QUESTION

For a long time, without realizing it, the question I was living by was this: "How long until everything falls apart?"

It wasn't obvious at first. It hid under busyness and good intentions. But it was there—whispering, tightening my chest, making me live in constant fear of losing

172 | Time to Rise

everything I was working so hard to hold together. And it wasn't just fear speaking. It was the planted accusation of the enemy, weaving lies into my heart about who I was and what I could expect from life.

Everything changed the day I decided to ask a better question. Just recently, I chose this: "How can I appreciate even more of God's beauty and perfection in this moment?"

Do you see the difference?

Now, instead of bracing for impact, I start by trusting that there's beauty already here—right now. I start from faith, not fear. And the more I ask that question, the more God shows up to answer it.

Maybe, just maybe, this question isn't just for me. Maybe it's for you too. Maybe this is the reason God led you to pick up this book in the first place.

If you feel it stirring in you, borrow it. Make it yours. Say it out loud. Say it with fire. Say it until it sinks into your bones. Move your body when you say it. Shout it if you need to. Get it so deep inside you that when fear tries to whisper again, all it hears back is faith.

Because if I've learned anything, it's this: When you dare to ask better questions, God is faithful to show you better answers. That's just who He is.

IMPLEMENTING YOUR NEW PRIMARY QUESTION

Choosing a better question is a powerful first step. But it's not enough to just choose it—you have to live it. You have to wire it into the way you think, speak, and act until it becomes part of who you are. Here's how to start:

1. Write it down. Your brain needs reminders. Write your new primary question somewhere you'll see it often—on your bathroom mirror, in your journal, on your phone's lock screen. Let it be a constant reinforcement of the mindset you are choosing.

2. Speak it over your life. Your words shape your reality. When you declare your new primary question out loud, you rewire your brain to search for answers you actually want to find. Say it daily: "How can I grow through this?" "How can I glorify God today?" I highly suggest going for a run and shouting this question fifty times at the top of your lungs. (Yes, people might look at you funny. No, you won't care.)

3. Use it in every situation. When challenges arise, consciously filter your response through your new question. If your old habit was asking, "Why do I always fail?" replace it in the moment with "What can I learn from this?" The shift might feel small at first, but over time, it will completely change your perspective.

4. Refuse to entertain negative questions. Your old questions will try to creep back in when you're tired, stressed, or stretched thin. When you catch yourself slipping into negative thinking—"What if I fail?" or "What's the point?"—stop immediately. Don't let those questions run the show for even a second. Replace them with the new truth you're choosing to live by.

THE QUESTION THAT DETERMINES YOUR FUTURE

Your life is shaped by the questions you ask yourself the most. Choose the right question—and everything can change.

Instead of asking, "What if I fail?" ask, "What if this works out better than I ever dreamed?"

Instead of asking, "Why do things always go wrong for me?" ask, "How can I make the most of this opportunity?"

Instead of asking, "Am I good enough?" ask, "How can I show up today as the person God created me to be?"

Your mind is always working in the background, searching for answers. It never stops. The only question now is this: Are you sending it in the direction you want your life to go?

CHAPTER 45

WHAT IS REAL FORGIVENESS?

A person who cannot forgive has forgotten how great a debt God has forgiven them.
—John Bevere

I N 2024, THERE was an event at the National Mall in Washington, D.C.,—a gathering of thousands of women standing together in worship and prayer, crying out for our nation.[1] It was led by Lou Engle and others, and I remember watching online, feeling deeply provoked by the Spirit of God as it unfolded.

At one point, they led the crowd into a moment of forgiveness. People began forgiving those who had wronged them, hurt them, and even abused them. It was raw, real, and powerful.

It didn't take long for clips from that moment to start circulating on social media—and it didn't take long for the Failure Porn Cartel to lose their minds. I started to see comments accusing the event of promoting "toxic forgiveness." I was shocked to read that statement. Forgiveness is powerful, not toxic.

Let's be clear—the only so-called "toxic forgiveness" was what Jesus offered on the cross. The ultimate act of forgiveness was bloody, brutal, and costly. It wasn't cheap grace. It was everything.

This is why I believe the spirit of accusation—whether it comes from the outside or rises up inside you—isn't just a personal struggle. It's an attack on the gospel itself. It's an attack on the cross and the crucified Lamb of God. Anything that tries to pull us away from mercy, grace, love, and forgiveness isn't born of heaven—it's forged in hell.

So let's get one thing straight: Forgiveness isn't weakness. It's strength. It's not rolling over and letting people walk all over you. It's not about excusing what happened or pretending it was okay. Forgiveness is about you taking your life back. It's about choosing to take control of your mind, your emotions, and your future. Because the truth is, as long as you're holding on to bitterness, you're not punishing them—you're only punishing yourself.

You ever hear the saying, "Holding on to resentment is like drinking poison and expecting the other person to die"? That's exactly what happens when you refuse to forgive. The anger, the pain, the betrayal—it eats away at you. Meanwhile, the person who hurt you? They're out there living their life, completely unaffected. The only person suffering…is you.

WE ALL CAN FORGIVE LIKE THIS

In his book *7 Women*, Eric Metaxas shares an incredible story of forgiveness from the life of Corrie ten Boom, a Dutch woman imprisoned in the Nazi concentration camp

Ravensbrück with her sister Betsie. "Healing was linked to forgiveness," Corrie wrote.[2] Each woman at Ravensbrück had something to forgive, whether it was a neighbor who had turned her in to the Nazi authorities or a vicious camp guard or a brutal soldier.

In mid-May 1945, the Allies marched into Holland, to the unspeakable joy of the Dutch people. Despite the distractions of her work, Corrie was still restless, and she desperately missed her beloved Betsie, who had died at Ravensbrück. But now she remembered Betsie's words: that they had to tell others what they had learned.

Thus began more than three decades of travel around the world as a "tramp for the Lord," as Corrie described herself. She told people of her story, of God's forgiveness of sins, and of the need for people to forgive those who had harmed them.

Corrie herself was put to the test in 1947 while speaking in a Munich church. At the close of the service, a balding man in a gray overcoat stepped forward to greet her. Corrie froze. She knew this man well; he'd been one of the most vicious guards at Ravensbrück, one who had mocked the women prisoners as they showered.

> It came back with a rush: the huge room with its harsh overhead lights, the pathetic pile of dresses and shoes in the center of the floor, the shame of walking naked past this man.
>
> ...Now he was in front of me, hand thrust out: "A fine message, *fräulein*! How good it is to know that, as you say, all our sins are at the bottom of the sea!"
>
> And I, who had spoken so glibly of forgiveness, fumbled in my pocket-book rather than take that hand. He would not remember me, of course—how could he remember one prisoner among those thousands of women?
>
> But I remembered him and the leather crop swinging from his belt. It was the first time since my release that I had been face to face with one of my captors and my blood seemed to freeze.
>
> "You mentioned Ravensbrück in your talk," he was saying. "I was a guard in there." No, he did not remember me.
>
> "But since that time," he went on, "I have become a Christian. I know that God has forgiven me for the cruel things I did there, but I would like to hear it from your lips as well. *Fräulein*"—again the hand came out—"will you forgive me?"
>
> And I stood there—I whose sins had every day to be forgiven—and could not. Betsie had died in that place—could he erase her slow terrible death simply for the asking?[3]

The soldier stood there expectantly, waiting for Corrie to shake his hand. She wrestled, knowing that God commanded her to forgive him but not having the strength to do it. Then she remembered that forgiveness is an act of the will—not an emotion. "Jesus, help me!" she prayed. "I can lift my hand. I can do that much. You supply the feeling."[4]

Corrie thrust out her hand.

176 | Time to Rise

And as I did, an incredible thing took place. The current started in my shoulder, raced down my arm, sprang into our joined hands. And then this healing warmth seemed to flood my whole being, bringing tears to my eyes.

"I forgive you, brother!" I cried. "With all my heart."

For a long moment we grasped each other's hands, the former guard and the former prisoner. I had never known God's love so intensely as I did then. But even so, I realized it was not my love. I had tried, and did not have the power. It was the power of the Holy Spirit.[5]

FORGIVENESS IS NOT FORGETTING—IT'S FREEDOM

Let's get one thing straight: forgiving doesn't mean forgetting. Some wounds cut deep. Some betrayals shake you to your core. Pretending it didn't happen won't heal you. Stuffing the pain down won't make it go away. But forgiveness? That's your way out. That's your key to freedom.

Forgiveness isn't about erasing the past—it's about refusing to let the past have the final say over your future. The moment you say, "I forgive," you start breaking the chains that have been tying you down. You stop carrying around the weight of what someone else did. And here's what most people miss: Forgiveness isn't about them at all. It's about *you*. It's about reclaiming your emotional energy, your mental clarity, your peace of mind. No person, no betrayal, no memory should get to decide how you feel anymore. That right belongs to you—and to God.

FORGIVENESS IS A CHOICE, NOT A FEELING

If you're waiting for forgiveness to *feel easy*, you'll be waiting a long time. Forgiveness doesn't happen because the pain suddenly disappears. It happens because you decide you're done letting it control you. It's a conscious, sometimes gut-wrenching, no-going-back choice to stop letting anger and resentment have the steering wheel.

Look at Jesus. Betrayed. Abandoned. Mocked. Murdered. And what did He say? "Father, forgive them, for they do not know what they are doing" (Luke 23:34). That's real power. That's real freedom. He didn't wait for an apology. He didn't wait until the pain was gone. He forgave right in the middle of it.

And that's exactly what you're called to do too.

You don't need an apology. You don't need validation. You don't need them to admit they were wrong. You just need to decide that your peace is worth more than your pain. Because when you choose forgiveness, you take back what bitterness tried to steal—you take back yourself.

THE FIVE-STEP FORGIVENESS STRATEGY

Forgiveness isn't just an idea—it's an action. It's something you *do*, not just something you think about. But before you take these five steps, hear me: Go to the cross first.

What Is Real Forgiveness? | 177

See Jesus there, hanging in your place, arms stretched wide. Let that revelation be your fuel. It's the only source strong enough to empower real forgiveness.

Here's how you walk it out:

1. Face it head-on. Stop pretending you're not bothered. Acknowledge the hurt. Name it. If you don't, it will keep controlling you from the shadows. Healing begins the moment you drag the pain into the light.

2. Decide that forgiveness isn't a feeling—it's a choice. Right now, decide you're done letting this situation own you. Even if the emotions don't line up yet, the choice is the first step toward freedom.

3. Kill the story. The more you replay the betrayal, the deeper it roots itself. Every time you rehearse the pain, you reinforce its power. Stop feeding the fire. The past is over. The only thing keeping it alive is how much attention you give it.

4. Rewrite the meaning. What happened to you doesn't get to define you. It's part of your story, sure—but it's not your whole story. Take the lesson and ditch the weight. Ask yourself, "How can this make me stronger? What can I learn from this? How can I turn this pain into purpose?"

5. Take back your power. Forgiveness isn't about letting someone off the hook— it's about refusing to let them control your life for one more second. When you forgive, you're saying, "This moment doesn't get to own me anymore." That's what real freedom looks like.

BREAKING FREE FROM THE CHAINS OF UNFORGIVENESS

Here's the truth: Bitterness is a prison. It keeps you locked inside your past. It makes you cynical, angry, and emotionally exhausted. And worse? It spills over into other areas of your life.

Unforgiveness doesn't stay isolated. It spreads. It changes the way you see yourself, the way you trust others, and the way you show up for your future. It builds walls where there should be bridges. It keeps you replaying old conversations and reliving old pain when you should be building new memories.

But when you forgive? You step out of that prison. You choose healing over hurt. You choose love over resentment. And most importantly, you choose your future over your past.

FORGIVING YOURSELF

And let's not forget—sometimes the hardest person to forgive is the one staring back at you in the mirror. Maybe you've messed up. Maybe you've said or done some things you wish you could undo. Maybe you feel like you've let yourself down.

But hear me clearly: You are not your worst moment. Holding on to shame won't make you better. Beating yourself up won't fix what's already done. You can't rewrite the past—but you *can* choose what happens next.

Forgiving yourself means refusing to let guilt define you. It means accepting that

THE REAL WIN

And at the end of the day, forgiveness is never about them. It's about you. It's about taking back your joy. Taking your peace back. Taking *you* back. It's about refusing to let pain have any influence over your destiny any longer. It's about waking up lighter, freer, unchained—without carrying around the weight of something you were never meant to hold forever. It's about choosing freedom over bitterness. Healing over hurting. Life over survival.

So ask yourself, "Who or what are you still giving that kind of power to?" And when you find the answer—make the decision. Let it go.

Because the second you do?

You're free.

CHAPTER 46

WHO WOULD JESUS LOVE?

God's definition of what matters is pretty straightfor-
ward. He measures our lives by how we love.
—FRANCIS CHAN

ACCUSATION DOES NOT want to talk about the love of Jesus. It would rather focus on judgment, guilt, and shame. But if you really want to understand who Jesus is, look at who He loved—not just with words, but with action.

Jesus didn't love based on status, reputation, or whether someone "deserved" it. His love wasn't reserved for the powerful, the religious, or the people who had their act together. His love was radical. Relentless. Completely upside down compared to everything else the world expected. He loved the outcast, the broken, the sinner—even the self-righteous. His love shattered expectations. It flipped social norms upside down. It challenged the deepest parts of human judgment and pride.

JESUS LOVED THE ONES THE WORLD REJECTED

The religious elite of His day were looking for a Messiah who would align Himself with the respected, the righteous, the influential. Someone who would validate the powerful. But Jesus had an entirely different mission. Instead of chasing the approval of the religious, He ran straight toward the ones the world had given up on. Those society had cast aside.

Whom did Jesus spend time with?

- The tax collectors—the corrupt and despised, seen as traitors to their own people
- The prostitutes—those living with shame, judged and thrown away by society
- The lepers—the untouchables, forced to live outside the city, avoided and feared by all
- The demon-possessed—those completely broken, abandoned, and written off as beyond saving

And here's the thing: Jesus didn't just tolerate these people. He pursued them. He sat with them. He ate with them. He called them friends.

When the religious leaders saw Him reclining at a table with tax collectors and sinners, they scoffed, "Why does your teacher eat with such scum?" (Matt. 9:11, NLT). But Jesus didn't flinch. He looked them straight in the eye and said something that still shakes the

179

180 | Time to Rise

world today: "It is not the healthy who need a doctor, but the sick. I have not come to call the righteous, but sinners" (Mark 2:17).

Jesus wasn't looking for people who had it all together. He came for those who knew they were lost.

JESUS LOVED HIS ENEMIES

It's one thing to love the broken. It's another thing entirely to love those who hurt you. Yet Jesus did both.

When Judas betrayed Him for thirty pieces of silver, Jesus still called him *friend*. When Peter denied Him three times, Jesus didn't push him away. He restored him.

When the soldiers nailed Him to the cross, He didn't curse them. He prayed for them—"Father, forgive them, for they do not know what they are doing" (Luke 23:34).

Jesus didn't just teach about love. He lived it. He breathed it. He became it. "Love your enemies and pray for those who persecute you," He said (Matt. 5:44).

That kind of love isn't natural. It's supernatural. It's the kind of love only a Savior could offer—a love that refuses to give up on people, even when they turn their backs on Him.

JESUS LOVES YOU—RIGHT NOW

Here's the truth: Jesus loves you right here, right now. Not some future version of you. Not the polished-up, perfect version you think you need to be. Just you—as you are. With all the mistakes, all the regrets, all the struggles you're carrying today.

His love isn't based on performance. You don't earn it. You can't lose it. It's a gift—straight from His heart to yours.

Maybe you feel like you've messed up too much. Maybe you've been told you're unworthy. Maybe you've believed the lie that God could never truly love someone like you. I know what that feels like, as I shared at the start of chapter 27 of this book. Believe me, you are never beyond God's love.

WILL YOU LOVE LIKE JESUS?

Jesus didn't just come to love us—He called us to love like Him. That means loving the difficult people in our lives. It means choosing love over bitterness, over offense, over judgment.

Will you love those who have hurt you? Will you love the ones the world has rejected? Will you love without conditions, just as Jesus loved you?

Because the world doesn't need more judgment. It needs more Jesus.

The real question isn't just whom Jesus loved—it's whom will you love.

CHAPTER 47

ARE YOU GOING TO RISE OR KEEP MAKING EXCUSES?

When God is the supreme hunger of your heart, he will be supreme in every-thing. And when you are most satisfied in him, he will be most glorified in you.
—JOHN PIPER

RIGHT NOW, THIS is your moment of truth. No distractions. No justifications. No dodging the question. Are you going to *rise* and become the person God is calling you to be—or are you going to lie to yourself for another day and keep making excuses?

Answer with complete honesty. No half-truths. No sugarcoating.

I'm convinced that many are on spiritual hospice care—and they don't even know it.

I have the unique privilege to be an entrepreneur called by God to help others strategize on how to reach millions of people online. And let me tell you, it's amazing to see people use social media to tell a better story and impact people. Right now, I can verify that the viral content in my feed and those I serve is content that provokes people to be hungry for more of God. Millions upon millions are responding to it. Hunger is rising. Is it rising in you?

Are you hungry for more of God—or have you become satisfied with just enough to get by?

Consider the reality that the older we get, the more we have to cultivate and create spiritual hunger in our lives. Passion and zeal fade in the midst of disappointments and disillusionment of life. One day we wake up complacent and critical, no longer in awe but in accusation of others.

I believe this is why the apostle Paul said in Galatians 5:7, "You were running well. Who hindered you from obeying the truth?" (ESV).

THE WAR FOR YOUR SPIRITUAL HUNGER

One of the greatest strategies of the enemy is to starve you of hunger for God. He'll use accusation. Distraction. Pain. Pride. The enemy will use anything—even your own reputation, even your own disappointment—to make you stop pursuing Jesus. And too often, we let him.

We have a generation that can post about hunger but not provoke it.

We have an older generation that justifies its lukewarmness with a plea for "balance."

182 | Time to Rise

But the last thing the church needs in this hour is balance. We don't need moderation. We need a hunger for Jesus that burns hotter than anything the world has ever seen.

You can become spiritually satisfied and not even know or justify it. How does this happen? It happens slowly. What are the effects or signs that it has happened? Just take a look:

- You notice the sins of others more than your own.
- You feel justified in your complacency.
- Your fire has been replaced with critique.

Listen to me: *Hunger for God is rare. Passion for Jesus is costly.*

Don't let the enemy steal it. Don't let life numb it. Don't let the opinions of others tame it. Hold on to it like your life depends on it—because it does.

I've discovered that nothing restores spiritual hunger like fasting. As I mentioned earlier, a forty-day fast changed my life in a supernatural way. In 2020, Matt Brown and I, with some friends, started what is called the Roaring Twenties Fast—a movement of the next generation picking up the mantle of foodless days and sleepless nights.[1] I can't begin to tell you how amazing it is to hear and read stories of how fasting has changed lives. Every January, we issue a call to twenty-one days of prayer and fasting, and every year, we see the power of fasting as a tool to create hunger and change lives.

It's incredible to watch the next generation pick up the mantle of fasting. It's amazing to see what God is doing right now on college campuses across America through a ministry called Unite Us.[2] It was amazing to witness what God did at Asbury University in revival just a few years ago. Every time my friend Zach Meerkreebs tells me more about what led to Asbury, it provokes me to want to go lower and experience more of Jesus.

I was there at Asbury on the final night of the revival and can attest to the glory of God filling the room. The hunger of the next generation was fueling it. Not emotionalism, not publicity, just pure and holy hunger.

I truly believe holiness and hunger for God are returning to His church.

A MARTYR'S PRAYER

One of the most provoking declarations I have ever read is this prayer from an unknown martyr:

I am part of the fellowship of the unashamed. I have Holy Spirit power.

The die has been cast. I have stepped over the line. The decision has been made: I am a disciple of His. I won't look back, let up, slow down, back away or be still. My past is redeemed. My present makes sense. My future is secure. I'm finished with low living, sight walking, small planning, smooth knees, colorless dreams, tamed visions, worldly talking, cheap giving, and dwarfed goals.

I no longer need preeminence, prosperity, position, promotions, [plaudits], or popularity. I don't have to be right, first, tops, recognized, praised, regarded or rewarded. I now live by faith, lean on His presence, walk by patience, am uplifted by prayer and labor by power.

My pace is set. My gait is fast. My goal is heaven. My road is narrow. My way rough. My companions few. My guide is reliable and my mission is clear.

I cannot be bought, compromised, detoured, lured away, turned back, deluded or delayed. I will not flinch in the face of sacrifice, hesitate in the presence of the adversary, negotiate at the table of the enemy, pander at the pool of popularity or meander in the maze of mediocrity.

I won't give up, shut up, let up, until I've stayed up, stored up, prayed up, paid up, preached up for the cause of Christ.

I am a disciple of Jesus. I must go till He comes, give 'til I drop, preach till all know, and work till He stops me. And when He comes for His own, He'll have no problem recognizing me. My banner will be clear![3]

WHAT ABOUT YOU?

You've just read the words of someone who refused to live a tame life. Someone who didn't make excuses. Someone who burned for Jesus with everything they had. So here's the question: Are you going to rise or keep making excuses? Because at the end of the day, it's not about what you say. It's about what you do.

Are you hungry for God? Are you desperate for revival? Are you willing to sacrifice comfort for calling?

A FINAL CLARION CALL

If you're tired of complacency—prove it. Get on your knees. Cry out to God for hunger. Fast. Kill your flesh and stir your spirit. Turn off distractions. Refuse to settle for a lukewarm life. Go all in. Right now. No more excuses.

This is your moment of decision. No more waiting. No more putting it off. Either you rise, or you don't.

Choose wisely.

CHAPTER 48

WILL I STOP REVIVAL?

The fame of revival spreads the flame of revival.
—DR. MALACHI A. O'BRIEN

SEVERAL YEARS AGO, while I was finishing my doctorate, I had a conversation that left a mark on me—one I still can't shake. Dr. Alvin Reid, my professor and dissertation chair, said something during one of our discussions on revival that I didn't fully grasp at the time. But as the years passed, its truth only became more piercing. He looked at me and said, "I may not be young enough to start a revival, but I may be old enough to stop one."

I nodded, but I didn't get it—not yet. He knew I didn't get it.

History tells the same story over and over. The greatest moves of God are almost always sparked by the next generation. Even now, revival is sweeping college campuses—thousands of students saved, baptized, and surrendering fully to Jesus. It's raw. It's messy. And it's undeniably real.

When I post about it online, the response is explosive. One video alone—over a million views. Because people aren't just interested. They're starving for revival.

But here's the heartbreaking pattern: The older we get, the easier it becomes to critique the very things we once cried out for. Skepticism creeps in. Cynicism takes the place of hunger. And the very ones who should be the loudest voices cheering revival on—the spiritual fathers and mothers—become spectators instead. Arms crossed. Analyzing. Dissecting. And sadly, sometimes even tearing down the move of God right in front of them.

I've seen it. Respected voices in the church—people with influence and platforms—publicly criticizing healings, miracles, and the fresh wind of the Spirit. But do you know who's not doing that? The ones actually in revival. The college students laid out on the floor before God. The young people pressing in with reckless abandon. They're not online debating moves of God—they're too consumed by His presence to care.

So who would criticize a move of God?

The accuser would.

Satan's strategy hasn't changed. He doesn't just resist revival—he manipulates believers into stopping it. He fuels pride. He whispers skepticism. He stirs a religious spirit that says, "This isn't real. This isn't biblical. This isn't how God moves."

And the moment we give our voice to accusation, we are no longer on the side of heaven.

GRIEVING THE HOLY SPIRIT

Here's what grieves the Holy Spirit: when believers tear down leaders they've never even met, ministries they've never been part of, and expressions of Christianity they don't understand. We become modern-day Pharisees—standing on the sidelines, policing a move of God instead of participating in it. To do this lacks honor and authority.

Let me ask you—when revival breaks out, are you the one running to the altar? Or are you the one critiquing from the pews?

Because here's the truth: God doesn't move according to your preferences. He moves according to His presence. He's not asking for our permission. He's not waiting for our approval. He's looking for hungry hearts—those that will say yes even when it's uncomfortable, even when it's unconventional, even when it's unfamiliar, even when it doesn't fit inside our safe religious boxes.

Revival is costly. It will demand that you surrender control, lay down pride, and burn for Jesus in a way that makes the religious spirit uncomfortable. This religious spirit is demonic.

And if you won't step into what God is doing—you might just become the obstacle standing in the way.

This is not discernment. This is division.

The Holy Spirit does not anoint the hypercritical.

He anoints those who are consumed with Jesus.

So the question isn't just "Will I be part of revival?" It's "Will I be the one who stops it?"

Don't criticize. Contribute.

Don't tear down. Build up.

Don't stop revival. Fan the flames.

Revival isn't coming—it's already here. The only question is, will you be in it?

CHAPTER 49

ORDER OF THE FLAME: A CALL TO BURN

*I think whenever you are given the opportunity to do something challenging
and difficult, you should. Today was very, very difficult, but worth it.*
—ULTRAMARATHONER COURTNEY DAUWALTER AFTER
WINNING THE ULTRA-TRAIL DU MONT-BLANC

LET'S GET BRUTALLY honest for a moment. There are two kinds of people in the world—those who watch the fire and those who *are* the fire. Some stand at a distance, fascinated but hesitant, warming their hands by the flame but never daring to step any closer. They want the light but not the heat. They admire the passion, but they're afraid to be consumed by it. Others try to contain the fire, to control it, to dictate where it burns and how far it spreads—playing it safe, keeping revival manageable and predictable.

But then there are those rare ones—the ones who don't fear the fire. They walk straight into it. They let it consume them. They don't just carry the flame. They become the flame.

Somewhere along this journey, I realized there needed to be a name for it—for the way of life God was calling me (and others) into. I started calling it the Order of the Flame. A place for those who do very hard things. Those called to be part of a dangerous obsessed society. Not just a name but a calling. A way of life. A sacred commission for those who refuse to live in the shadows of mediocrity. It's for those who won't settle for lukewarm living. It's for those who won't trade their calling for comfort, who would rather burn brightly for a season than blend in forever. But before you claim this fire, you have to answer the real question: Are you truly ready to burn?

THE FIRE WILL COST YOU

Fire is dangerous. It consumes. It refines. It burns away anything that can't survive its heat. And if you want to be part of the Order of the Flame, you have to be willing to let it transform you—no matter the cost. It means stepping into the fire and letting it burn away everything that's weak, everything that's false, everything that doesn't align with the life God is calling you to live.

And that's where many hesitate. Because to burn means to *change*. It means nothing can stay the same.

Ask yourself honestly, "What in my life is resisting the fire? Where am I choosing security over transformation? Am I willing to let the flame consume everything that is not aligned with my true calling?" Because here is the truth—you cannot be lukewarm and be in the fire at the same time.

Many want the power of the fire without the cost. They want the boldness, the passion, the clarity—but they are unwilling to endure the refining process. They want to keep their old ways, their old fears, their old excuses. But the fire demands everything.

If you're not willing to let go of what's holding you back, you're not ready to burn.

THE FLAME IS A COMMISSION, NOT A COMFORT

The Order of the Flame is not about status. It's not about being admired for your passion or building a platform. *You do not join the fire. The fire joins you.*

It refines you until you stop fearing the heat. It calls you to carry the flame into the darkest places—to stand when others fall, to speak when others are silent, to act when others hesitate. It means you refuse the lesser path, even when taking it would be so much easier.

And the fire will ask hard questions:

- Are you willing to stand alone if you have to?
- Will you keep burning when the world tries to extinguish you?
- Can you carry the weight of responsibility that comes with carrying the fire?

Because fire does not exist for itself. It spreads. It ignites. It calls others into the blaze. And if you are unwilling to spread the fire, you will eventually lose it.

THE TRIALS OF THE FLAME

There is a price for burning. The fire will test you. It will strip away your ego, your pride, your illusions of control. It will expose weaknesses you didn't even know you had and force you to face them head-on. And here's the truth that most won't tell you: Many will shrink back when the fire gets too hot. Some will walk away when the cost becomes clear. Some will try to smother their own flame because they fear what it might demand of them. Some will reject the fire altogether, choosing comfort over calling, silence over boldness, neutrality over truth.

But not you.

If you are called to the Order of the Flame, you will endure the heat. You will face the trials. And you will come out stronger, purer, unstoppable.

The question is this: Will you stay in the fire when it gets uncomfortable? Or will you run from the very thing meant to refine you?

Because the truth is—many will talk about the fire. Few will actually burn. What I also know is this: There is someone reading this right now who knows they were made to go through the fire and not avoid it. You are rare, and you are needed now more than ever.

THE MARK OF THE FLAME

To burn with true fire is to live differently:

- **You refuse to be ruled by fear.** Fear has no authority over those who burn.
- **You carry truth, no matter the cost.** The world is full of deception, but the ones who burn are unshakable.
- **You are relentless in your purpose.** The fire doesn't stop when it's tired—it keeps going until everything it touches is changed.
- **You call others into the flame.** You don't burn just for yourself—you ignite those around you.
- **You live with intensity and conviction.** Half-hearted living isn't an option for those who carry fire.

But here's the reality—*fire attracts opposition.*

Some will fear you. Some will misunderstand you. Some will try to put out your fire because they do not understand it. They will call you too extreme, too radical, too much.

But the fire does not apologize for being fire. It simply burns.

And so must you.

I have friends who are marked by holy fire—and every one of them has faced the price. Attacks from without. Accusation from within. I think of Pastor Greg Locke. One of the greatest honors of my life was speaking at the National Deliverance Conference he hosted—thousands gathered under a tent, signs and wonders breaking out, miracles unfolding in front of our eyes. But along with the miracles came the criticism, the mockery, the attack. God is using Greg in a God-sized way—and the cost has been real opposition. I have seen thousands come against Greg and yet not be able to stop him.

I think of my friend Pastor Paula White. She leads the White House Faith Office. I've had the privilege of watching firsthand how God has used her—and my friend Jenny Korn—to open doors for pastors and faith leaders to have a voice inside the White House. Pastor Paula is the president's pastor and is the reason there are faith leaders around him.

I was in the Oval Office on February 7, 2025, when President Trump signed the executive order establishing an Office of Faith. An office located in the West Wing of the White House for people of faith everywhere. It was a moment I will never forget, praying over the president and even experiencing the time of worship in the Roosevelt Room afterward. Just as the psalmist said, this is the Lord's doing, and it is marvelous in our eyes.

And please hear me when I say—even the White House shall be called a house of prayer.

But as amazing as this moment was, it didn't come without opposition. When Paula got named by President Trump, I witnessed the spirit of accusation rise against her. Critics from every side. And yet—Paula remained unmoved. Resolute in the call God had placed on her life.

I think of others too—Pastor Travis Johnson, Landon Schott, Joseph Z, Matt Brown, Mike Signorelli—all men of God who have discovered firsthand that the price of the anointing is relentless accusation. Their fire—the one they carry, the one they refuse to let go out—challenges and encourages me daily. I am honored to run with them.

I remember being with Mike Signorelli in Times Square in New York City in late 2023 when, against all odds, they got miraculous permission to hold a "Domino Revival" event there in the heart of NYC. What I know with all of my friends, and others not mentioned, is that every one of them has faced attacks from without and from within. Because they kept pressing on, God anointed them even more.

Why do I share these stories? Because if you are going to be used by God in a great way, you will face opposition that seeks to put out your fire. That's the mark of the flame: They cannot stop what Jesus began. It is His holy fire—not theirs. Most critics read about fire. Few actually carry it.

RUNNING INTO THE FIRE

The Order of the Flame is not something you choose—it chooses you. It calls you in moments of deep frustration—when you know there is more to life than what you've been settling for. It stirs in your spirit when you see injustice, when you recognize deception, when you feel the weight of a world that desperately needs something real.

It's not just a passion—it's a burden.

It's not just a feeling—it's a commission.

And here's the thing about the fire: It will never stop calling your name until you answer. So, here it is—the final question: *Will you?* Will you step into the fire, knowing it will cost you everything safe and comfortable? Will you allow it to consume what is weak, so what's unshakable can finally rise? Will you carry the flame into the darkest places, even if it would be easier to play it safe? If the answer is yes—then welcome. Welcome to the fire. Welcome to the weight. Welcome to the Order of the Flame.

CHAPTER 50

LEGACY IN THE FIRE: THE FINAL CHOICE

I was made for the storm, and a calm does not suit me.
—ANDREW JACKSON

THIS IS NOT the end; this is only the beginning. The journey of transformation is one that never ends. Refuse to be those who settle. You have been called to be part of a dangerous obsessed society. Truly the Order of the Flame and those who do very hard things. Those who refuse to let the accusations from without and within stop them. Those who choose to realize that the limitless God has commissioned us to do limitless things.

I want to leave you with two stories—two deeply personal, life-changing parables that have marked me and stayed with me for years. They speak to legacy, integrity, and the unseen spiritual choices that define the lives we live—and the ones we leave behind.

THE HOUSE YOU BUILD

Many years ago, there was a master contractor—highly skilled, wildly successful, and deeply respected. His work was exceptional, his wealth substantial, and his name well known in the industry.

One day, a young man approached him with admiration in his eyes and hope in his heart. "Would you mentor me?" he asked. Though the old contractor had declined many such requests in the past, something stirred in him this time. For reasons he couldn't explain, he said yes.

Over the next few years, he poured everything he knew into the young man—skills, secrets, blueprints, wisdom. The young apprentice learned quickly, rising to success, influence, and wealth in his own right.

Meanwhile, the older contractor's life took a painful turn. He began compromising. Cutting corners. Choosing cheap materials. Making poor decisions. His business collapsed. His relationships shattered. He ended up homeless, broken, and ashamed.

Years later the two contractors' paths crossed again. The young contractor was stunned to see his former mentor in such a state.

Moved by compassion, he asked, "Can you still build?"

With quiet resolve the older man replied, "Yes. I still can."

"Then I want to honor you," the younger man said. "I have a project—an incredible one. I want you to oversee the entire thing. Use whatever materials you need. Take your time. I trust you completely. Just check in every few weeks. When it's done, I'll meet you there."

Grateful for the chance, the older contractor began building. But as construction

Legacy in the Fire: The Final Choice | 191

progressed, old habits returned. Though given a blank check, he once again cut corners—choosing the cheapest wood, the flimsiest nails, the lowest-grade materials. He pocketed the excess money, telling himself it didn't matter. From the outside, though, the house looked stunning—an architectural masterpiece.

When the home was completed, he called the young contractor. "It's done. You have to see it—it's beautiful."

They met at the house. The young man walked through the halls in awe. "You still have it," he said, eyes wide with admiration.

And then came the moment that changed everything.

"I didn't have you build this house for me," he said. "I had you build it for you. This house is yours."

The older contractor froze. Then tears fell—not of joy but of sorrow.

"What's wrong?" the young man asked.

Through sobs the older man confessed: "I used the worst materials. The weakest lumber. The cheapest nails. It won't last. It looks beautiful, but it's hollow. I built it wrong. I failed again. Please...forgive me."

The younger contractor looked him in the eyes and said something that still echoes in my heart:

"You are forgiven. *But you will have to live in the house that you built.*"

Friend, let that settle in your spirit.

Yes—through Jesus you are fully forgiven. But you still live in the house that your choices build.

Every day, your words, your beliefs, your actions—they are framing the structure you will dwell in.

If you choose bitterness, shame, accusation, or fear, you are building with rot. But if you choose truth, love, mercy, and courage—you are constructing something that will endure.

Build wisely. Because one day you will realize this truth: *You will live in the house that you build.*

THE STANDARD BEARER

Now, let me leave you with one final story.

In ancient times, during brutal battlefield clashes, armies would face off in deadly combat. But not all soldiers carried swords. One of the most vital positions in any army was the standard bearer—the one who held the flag high.

The flag wasn't just a symbol. It meant direction. It meant courage. It meant hope. As long as the standard flew above the chaos, the army knew the message: *We fight on.* If the flag dropped, it was a sign to retreat.

One day the two armies collided. Early in the fight, the standard bearer was seriously injured, and the flag fell. A soldier picked it up, only to be struck down moments later. Then a third soldier—a young man, terrified, trembling—reached for the flag.

Fear gripped him. Death was everywhere. But somewhere deep inside, resolve burned hotter.

He gripped the flag, fixed his eyes forward, and began to march.

He remembered why he was there. He thought about his family. His calling. His purpose. With every step his fear broke. Strength surged.

Arrows flew. Swords clashed around him. But he marched—faster, stronger, bolder.

His courage lit a fire in the men behind him. Where fear once ruled, hope took over. The army surged forward.

From behind the lines, the general shouted, "Standard bearer! Bring the standard back to the men!"

But the soldier didn't flinch. He didn't turn around. Instead, his voice rang across the battlefield:

"No, General—bring the men up to the standard."

That's what *Time to Rise* is about.

Not lowering the standard. Not retreating in fear. Not compromising truth. It's about raising it higher. It's about calling people *up*—to Jesus, to boldness, to freedom, to purpose.

So I leave you with this: Raise the standard. Build your life with integrity. Reject the lies of the accuser. Speak life. Live boldly. And when the time comes—because it will—don't wait for permission. This is what *Time to Rise* is all about.

Rise.

It's time to rise.

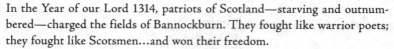

In the Year of our Lord 1314, patriots of Scotland—starving and outnumbered—charged the fields of Bannockburn. They fought like warrior poets; they fought like Scotsmen...and won their freedom.
—Braveheart

TIME TO RISE CREED

I am *not* here by chance.
I was forged with divine purpose, to live with passion.

I refuse to be silent.
I refuse to shrink back.
I refuse to let the spirit of accusation, doubt, or fear define me.

The enemy has tried to distract me, discourage me, and disqualify me.
But he failed. *I am still standing.*

I will not partner with the accuser.

Legacy in the Fire: The Final Choice | 193

I will not tear down what God is building.
I will not be the one who stops revival.

I am called. I am chosen. I am anointed.
I do not wait for revival. *I carry revival.*
I do not fear darkness. *I am light.*

I choose honor over compromise.
I choose worship over worry.
I choose *warfare over passivity.*

I do not settle.
I do not back down.
I do not let offense recruit me.

I will not be caught on the sidelines while God moves.
I will not be found with arms crossed when He calls my name.
I will run to the front lines. I will burn with holy fire.
I speak life.
I build up.
I fan the flames.

I was born for this hour. This is my time.
I am not waiting for permission—*I am taking territory.*

This is my declaration. This is my creed.
It is time to rise.

APPENDIX

I HAVE PUT TOGETHER some bonus content just for you. These are practical tools drawing deeper insights and a few conversations we didn't have room for in the book. Think of it like a field guide for your next steps. Here's what to expect:

When to Respond—and When to Stay Silent: Learn how to discern when to speak up, when to stay silent, and how to stay anchored in truth no matter what's flying around you.

Living the Kaizen-Jesus Way: Discover how daily, small steps of growth—not giant leaps—are the real way Jesus transforms lives. It's not about perfection; it's about showing up every single day.

Is Personal Growth Biblical? Here's why pursuing growth, discipline, and stewardship isn't self-help nonsense—it's actually deeply spiritual when done through the power of Christ.

The Right Kind of Accountability: You'll learn how to surround yourself with people who sharpen you, not shame you.

Using Social Media for Good: Learn how to use your platforms to build, encourage, and carry the fire, without getting sucked into the noise.

Emotional Health and Spiritual Maturity: Learn how healing fuels your ability to reflect Jesus authentically.

Do Very Hard Things: Push past what's comfortable to discover strength you didn't know you had.

Each of these is designed to help you take everything you've read—and live it even louder, even bolder, even deeper.

Scan the QR code and dive in.

bit.ly/4mj7LPK

A PERSONAL INVITATION
FROM THE AUTHOR

GOD LOVES YOU deeply. His Word is filled with promises that reveal His desire to bring healing, hope, and abundant life to every area of your being—body, mind, and spirit. More than anything, He wants a personal relationship with you through His Son, Jesus Christ.

If you've never invited Jesus into your life, you can do so right now. It's not about religion—it's about a relationship with the One who knows you completely and loves you unconditionally. If you're ready to take that step, simply pray this prayer with a sincere heart:

> *Lord Jesus, I want to know You as my Savior and Lord. I confess and believe that You are the Son of God and that You died for my sins. I believe You rose from the dead and are alive today. Please forgive me for my sins. I invite You into my heart and my life. Make me new. Help me to walk with You, grow in Your love, and live for You every day. In Jesus' name, amen.*

If you just prayed that prayer, you've made the most important decision of your life. All of heaven rejoices with you, and so do I! You are now a child of God, and your journey with Him has just begun. Please contact my publisher at pray4me@charisma-media.com so that we can send you some materials that will help you become established in your relationship with the Lord. We look forward to hearing from you.

NOTES

PREFACE

1. Bible Hub, "ruach," accessed April 29, 2025, https://biblehub.com/hebrew/7307.htm.
2. Carolyn Gramling, "The 2004 Tsunami Killed Hundreds of Thousands. Are We Better Prepared Now?" Science News, December 11, 2024, https://www.sciencenews.org/article/2004-tsunami-killed-better-prepared-now.
3. Camp Victory Chorus, "I Came Here to Stay," traditional Christian camp song, author unknown.

INTRODUCTION

1. Jason Drumm, "Paul Washer | Shepherds Conference 2016 | Christ Outweighs Them All," March 18, 2016, YouTube video, 0:41, https://www.youtube.com/watch?v=ID9XVm6Kvl8.

CHAPTER 1

1. Richard Sibbes, *The Bruised Reed*, Monergism, accessed online, https://www.monergism.com/thethreshold/sdg/bruisedreed.html.
2. Jon Acuff, *Soundtracks: The Surprising Solution to Overthinking* (Baker Books, 2021), 22.
3. John Bevere, *The Bait of Satan: Living Free from the Deadly Trap of Offense* (Charisma House, 2004), 166–67.

CHAPTER 2

1. Napoleon Hill, *Outwitting the Devil: The Secret to Freedom and Success*, annotated by Sharon Lechter (Sterling Publishing, 2011).
2. Russell Brunson, "Are You Driven?," *Marketing Secrets* (blog), accessed July 10, 2025, https://marketingsecrets.com/blog/are-you-driven.

CHAPTER 3

1. Garrett J. White (@garrettjwhite), "Declaring truth is a declaration of war in a world filled with lies, making persecution a non-negotiable reality," Instagram photo, December 16, 2024, https://www.instagram.com/garrettjwhite/p/DDmUVwlpDFN/.

CHAPTER 8

1. Basilea Schlink, *Repentance: The Joy-Filled Life* (Evangelical Sisterhood of Mary, 1997).

PART II

1. Ronnie Floyd, *Our Last Great Hope: Awakening the Great Commission* (Thomas Nelson, 2011).

CHAPTER 11

1. Tony Robbins, "How to Change Your Life with Just One Simple Story," Tony Robbins, accessed July 14, 2025, https://www.tonyrobbins.com/blog/how-to-change-your-life-with-just-one-simple-story.

CHAPTER 12

1. Elizabeth Mohn, "Negativity Bias," EBSCO, 2024, https://www.ebsco.com/research-starters/social-sciences-and-humanities/negativity-bias.
2. University Hospitals, "Doomscrolling: Breaking the Habit," The Science of Health, July 9, 2024, https://www.uhhospitals.org/blog/articles/2024/07/doomscrolling-breaking-the-habit.
3. Jon Gordon, "The Power of Positivity," The Jon Gordon Companies, October 16, 2017, https://www.jongordon.com/positivetip/power-of-positivity.html.

CHAPTER 13

1. Tony Robbins, "Discover the 6 Human Needs," Tony Robbins, accessed July 14, 2025, https://www.tonyrobbins.com/blog/do-you-need-to-feel-significant.
2. Robbins, "Discover the 6 Human Needs."
3. Jonathan Haidt, *The Righteous Mind: Why Good People Are Divided by Politics and Religion* (Pantheon Books, 2012).

CHAPTER 14

1. "Illusory Truth Effect," *Psychology Today*, accessed July 14, 2025, https://www.psychologytoday.com/us/basics/illusory-truth-effect.

CHAPTER 20

1. Margaret Rouse, "Kaizen (Continuous Improvement)," TechTarget, May 13, 2021, https://www.techtarget.com/searcherp/definition/kaizen-or-continuous-improvement.

2. Blue Letter Bible, "metamorphoō," accessed July 14, 2025, https://www.blueletterbible.org/lexicon/g3339/kjv/tr/0-1/.

CHAPTER 22

1. Donald Miller, *Hero on a Mission: A Path to a Meaningful Life* (HarperCollins Leadership, 2022).

CHAPTER 26

1. Fox News, "Former President Trump Survives Assassination Attempt, FBI IDs Shooter as Thomas Matthew Crooks," Fox News, July 14, 2024, https://www.foxnews.com/live-news/trump-rally-assassination-attempt-july-14.

CHAPTER 29

1. *Merriam-Webster*, "Word of the Day: Sarcasm," May 4, 2010, https://www.merriam-webster.com/word-of-the-day/sarcasm-2010-05-04.

CHAPTER 32

1. Tony Robbins Firewalker, "What Is the Tony Robbins Firewalk?," November 19, 2017, https://tonyrobbinsfirewalk.com/what-is-the-tony-robbins-firewalk/.

CHAPTER 35

1. Leah MarieAnn Klett, "Mike Signorelli Offers Message of Revival, Healing and Deliverance in New Film," *The Christian Post*, July 17, 2023, https://www.christianpost.com/news/mike-signorelli-brings-message-of-deliverance-in-new-documentary.html.

CHAPTER 44

1. Tony Robbins, "Are You Living Your Primary Question?," accessed July 15, 2025, https://www.tonyrobbins.com/living-primary-question.

CHAPTER 45

1. Mike Hixenbaugh, "Christians Flock to Washington to Pray for America to Turn to God—By Electing Trump," NBC News, October 12, 2024, https://www.nbcnews.com/politics/2024-election/christians-swarm-washington-pray-america-turn-god-electing-trump-rcna175162.
2. Eric Metaxas, *7 Women: And the Secret of Their Greatness* (Thomas Nelson, 2015).

TIME TO RISE

3. Corrie ten Boom, "Guideposts Classics: Corrie ten Boom on Forgiveness," *Guideposts*, accessed July 16, 2025, https://guideposts.org/positive-living/guideposts-classics-corrie-ten-boom-forgiveness/.
4. Corrie ten Boom, *Tramp for the Lord* (Bethany House, 1974).
5. Ten Boom, *Tramp for the Lord*.

CHAPTER 47

1. Think Eternity, "Roaring Twenties Fast 2025," accessed July 16, 2025, https://thinke.org/roaring-twenties-fast.
2. UniteUS, accessed July 16, 2025, https://www.uniteusmovement.com/.
3. Clayton Kraby, "Fellowship of the Unashamed: A Martyr's Prayer," Reasonable Theology, accessed July 16, 2025, https://reasonabletheology.org/fellowship-of-the-unashamed-a-martyrs-prayer/.